What Have They Built You to Do?

What Have They Built You to Do?

The Manchurian Candidate and Cold War America

Matthew Frye Jacobson and
Gaspar González

University of Minnesota Press
Minneapolis
London

Published by the University of Minnesota Press
111 Third Avenue South, Suite 290
Minneapolis, MN 55401-2520
http://www.upress.umn.edu

Library of Congress Cataloging-in-Publication Data

Jacobson, Matthew Frye, 1958–
    What have they built you to do? : *The Manchurian Candidate* and Cold War America / Matthew Frye Jacobson and Gaspar González.
        p.   cm.
    Includes bibliographical references and index.
    ISBN-13: 978-0-8166-4124-6 (hc : alk. paper)
    ISBN-10: 0-8166-4124-2 (hc : alk. paper)
    ISBN-13: 978-0-8166-4125-3 (pb : alk. paper)
    ISBN-10: 0-8166-4125-0 (pb : alk. paper)
    1. Manchurian candidate (Motion picture).   2. Condon, Richard. Manchurian candidate.   3. Cold War.   I. González, Gaspar, 1968–   II. Title.
    PN1997.M2578J33   2006
    791.43'72—dc22   2006021196

Printed in the United States of America on acid-free paper

The University of Minnesota is an equal-opportunity educator and employer.

18 17 16 15 14 13   10 9 8 7 6 5 4 3

To my TAs, who have taught me more than they know;
and to the memory of Shafali Lal

—M. J.

For my mother and father

—G. G.

Contents

Introduction   ix

1. Backstory: Frank Sinatra and the Politics of
   Cold War Cultural Production   1

2. A Culture of Contradiction: Affluence and Anxiety   30

3. Five from the Fifties: Threat, Containment, and
   the Rise of the Security State in Postwar Film   52

4. Bullwhip and Smear: Reading McCarthy   82

5. Like Fu Manchu: Mapping Manchuria   100

6. The Red Queen: Sexuality, Subversion, and
   the American Family   130

7. Strangers on a Train: The Perils of Cold War Courtship   150

8. Cold War Redux: From Kennedy to Reagan's America
   and Beyond   168

Postscript   185

Acknowledgments   195

Notes   201

Index   219

Introduction

Near the conclusion of *The Manchurian Candidate*, as Bennett Marco begins to peel away layers of false memory and dimly to make out the communist plot whose method has included his own brainwashing, he urgently presses Raymond Shaw, another pawn in this monstrous game, "What have they built you to do?" This is of course *the* question within the cosmos of the film: Marco's mind has been tampered with and his memory of events rewritten; Shaw's will has been occupied, as it were, by a foreign power, his very agency made the instrument of another's intention, but to what end? The answer will be revealed only in the tautly paced final scenes.

But the question "What have they built you to do?" resonates well beyond the film itself. Within the context of the Cold War, the question eloquently expresses the fears and anxieties of a political culture in which some nearly omnipotent "they" are presumed to be both encircling from without and gnawing from within. The "they" who have designs on us, the "we" who have been rendered partly or wholly untrustworthy, and the nation's overarching inability to compose its own destiny—this is the very stuff of the Cold War's Manichaean plotlines, from Hollywood B movies to President Harry Truman's foreign-policy speeches to Joseph McCarthy's hectoring accusations from the Senate floor. "What have they built you to do?" is also a particularly poignant version of the question that has long guided the inquiry into "culture" and its workings by theorists such as Antonio Gramsci, Edward Said, Joan Scott, and Stuart Hall. Although in this instance "they" are perhaps invested with less intentionality or motivation than Marco's fantastic Manchurian plotters, still, as Hall writes, social subjects "are unable to speak, to act in one way or another, until they have been positioned by the work that culture does."[1] One has first to be "built," in other words; and there is no fully comprehending the political universe of power relations, hierarchy, domination, contest, and resistance without first understanding how a culture has "built" a particular populace to behave and respond.

What Have They Built You to Do? is an extended meditation on these layers of meaning and the mutual engagements among them—a close reading of *The Manchurian Candidate* (both Richard Condon's 1959 novel and John Frankenheimer's 1962 film), to be sure, but also an analysis of the ways in which this text opens out onto larger questions and themes of American politics and culture in the Cold War years. In its design, the book is intended not only to capture the multiple and contending meanings at work in the film, but to look outward to the wider concerns and tendencies of Cold War America, and from there to the broadest questions of culture and power in general.

The book is composed of eight chapters, each adopting a slightly different angle of vision on *The Manchurian Candidate* as both comment on and expression of common American ideas and ideologies at the height of the Cold War. Some chapters begin with the text and work outward to off-camera concerns, coaxing the film's details and devices to cast some light on the culture and the historical moment that produced them; others tend in the opposite direction, establishing a cultural or political cartography of the era as a way of situating this or that element of the film for interpretation. But taken together these inquiries are meant to converge and to undertake three interlacing projects: to explicate the film; to elucidate the era; and, in carrying out these tasks, to suggest some basic principles in the more general approach to "culture" as a historically and politically significant object of study.

Chapters 1 through 3 are largely contextual, situating both the narrative and the details of *The Manchurian Candidate*'s production against the historical backdrop of the first decade and a half of the Cold War. Chapter 1 excavates the "backstory" of the film's production—not only its source material, Richard Condon's novel, but the off-camera dealings among Frank Sinatra (star), John Frankenheimer (director), and George Axelrod (screenwriter) in getting this property to the screen. Sinatra looms largest here: he was—and remains—the most significant cultural figure associated with the film, linked so strongly to the Kennedy White House and at the time embroiled in a controversy over his having hired a blacklisted screenwriter for a previous project. Specifically, we examine how the Hollywood blacklist, the election of 1960, and Sinatra's own political past prevented him from pursuing another film (an adaptation of William Bradford Huie's 1954 best seller, *The Execution of Private Slovik*) and led him, indirectly, to *The Manchurian Candidate*. The story of how Sinatra came to the project embodies many of the cultural and political currents that produced the fevered vision of the narrative itself.

Chapter 2 expands the frame, reading the film against some of the era's broader cultural contradictions. This was a political moment when individualism was deemed both the hallmark and the chief virtue of American-style "liberty," for example, and yet when nothing was prized quite so highly or enforced quite as sternly as unwavering conformity. Hence America's ever-chafing "organization men," Ben Marco included. It was also a time when McCarthyite repressions were fairly peaceably accepted, in some quarters, as the price to be paid for a society without repression—a slightly disfigured version, perhaps, of the "vigilance" that Thomas Jefferson had spoken of generations earlier. At such a moment of contradiction and paradox, a plotline involving a communist conspiracy spearheaded from the McCarthyite right at once expressed and commented on some of the society's most deeply resonant anxieties.

Chapter 3 continues this investigation of context, examining the relationship of Frankenheimer's masterpiece to five films that, we argue, were crucial in constructing the Cold War cinematic vocabulary that *The Manchurian Candidate* would both borrow from and explode. Our choice of films here is necessarily selective and therefore subjective (this is not a survey); but, as antecedents, they highlight important aspects of the cultural conversation that Frankenheimer was joining. The five films sampled here are forceful meditations on the growing power of the state apparatus (*Panic in the Streets*); on the anxiety surrounding the perceived influence of women—particularly mothers—in the culture (*My Son John*); on the centrality of the nuclear family to Cold War ideology (*Suddenly*); on the growing complexity of geopolitics in the atomic age (*Kiss Me Deadly*); and on the peculiar dualities and contradictions of Cold War culture, including the dangerously unreliable epistemology by which one might know "us" from "them" (*Invasion of the Body Snatchers*). In its method, sensibility, and aesthetic Frankenheimer's film may seem a bolt from the blue; but its most arresting themes engaged and advanced a discussion that had been taking shape in Hollywood for some time.

Chapters 4, 5, and 6 turn toward the text of *The Manchurian Candidate* itself, shuttling between on-screen representations and off-screen social and political realities in an effort to allow each to illuminate the other. Chapter 4 examines the film's portrayal of McCarthy and McCarthyism, as embodied in the figure of Johnny Iselin. The film is among the first sustained and unsparing parodies of McCarthy, and yet so does the conspiracy at the center of this thriller seem to ratify all the claims that McCarthy had written across the firmament in his meteoric rise. This is not an instance of Hollywood trying to have it both ways in cool calculation of the metrics of the market, but rather a sign of just how deeply the epistemology of McCarthyism had taken root in American culture. Appearing at a time when McCarthyism had been repudiated but when the communist threat had yet to be vanquished, the film conveys perhaps more than Frankenheimer knew of the traces that McCarthyism had left on American conceptions of conspiracy, danger, and security. That the film is both McCarthyite and anti-McCarthyite is largely why its detractors can be found on both the left *and* the right.

Chapter 5 examines the "Manchuria" of Frankenheimer's vision, setting the villains Yen Lo and Chunjin within a much longer tradition of anti-Asian imagery from song, story, and screen. Sax Rohmer's Fu Manchu (in both pulp and celluloid) is the most famous exemplar, but Rohmer's "catlike" and "cruelly cunning" monster traces his own lineage back through nearly a century of social commentary and reformist writing (Jacob Riis on Chinatown); the "curiosities" of the Orient (as put on zoological display by P. T. Barnum and others); and scholarly theorizing about the peoples and lands of "the Orient" (Lord Cromer's ruminations on the Orient as the *opposite* of the West). These longer-term ideas about Asia and Asianness assumed heightened significance between the 1940s and the 1960s—the era of U.S. engagement in the Pacific, Korea, and Vietnam—as both hot wars and cold caused American political culture singularly to seize upon interpretations of the Orient as a key to the nation's own destiny. *The Manchurian Candidate* may raise vernacular Orientalism to ridicule, but it replicates its cherished images and its overriding logics just the same.

Chapter 6 similarly reads the themes of gender and sexuality in the film, analyzing the cultural logic by which the *sub*version plotted by Eleanor and Johnny Iselin in the political sphere is finally inseparable from the *per*version of their private lives—the perversion of Eleanor's "unnatural" usurpation of her husband's rightful authority, and the perversion of her relationship with her son, treacherous, smothering, and incestuous all at once. The linkages here were not unusual. As the civic imperatives of the Cold War era collapsed distinctions between the public and the private—as defense of "the American way of life" urged both the definition and the policing of particular patterns that could be *called* "the American way of life"— public figures like McCarthy and J. Edgar Hoover quite openly expressed the political importance of "normal" gender and sexual arrangements, especially patriarchal authority and heterosexual coupling. If communists were "made and not born," as most supposed, then the "normal" family would be among the nation's most important and jealously guarded assets, just as gender or sexual "deviance" would be a fairly reliable symptom of political trouble.

Chapter 7 offers a second angle on the theme of gender, examining what remains one of the film's most celebrated and misunderstood scenes: the moment when Marco (Sinatra) first meets Rosie (Janet Leigh) aboard a New York–bound train. The scene arouses unease not because (as so many critics have argued) Rosie is somehow mixed up in the communist conspiracy, but for the manner in which it exploits

Cold War cultural anxieties regarding gender roles. Comparing the scene to two similar, near-contemporary scenes from Alfred Hitchcock's canon, we argue that the train scene in *The Manchurian Candidate* is not only narratively disruptive but ideologically so because it subverts one of the era's dominant paradigms, the linkage between normative masculinity, female submissiveness, and citizenship. The Marco–Rosie coupling, in other words, offers a variation on the theme more conspicuously treated in the representation of the Iselin family.

Finally, chapter 8 turns outward once again to consider how the film was received during its different releases or iterations: in Kennedy's America upon original release in 1962, and again in Reagan's America during the "second" Cold War in the mid-1980s, when the film, long dormant, was rereleased and discovered anew. As the text traveled, we argue, *The Manchurian Candidate* became a kind of "found" commentary on the Reagan presidency, just as it had been a richly signifying document of the Kennedy era. Finally, we examine the ways in which Jonathan Demme's 2004 remake further extended the original film's function as cultural metaphor. As much an homage as a "remake" per se, Demme's film reweaves the original fabric of cultural anxiety in a way better suited to the descendants of the "organization man," who have seen Americans' earlier, tacit fears of the Organization itself come true. Here the gravest threat of takeover is posed not by a national rival like the old Soviet Union, or even by an extranational one like Al Qaeda, but by multinational "friends" like Halliburton.

For some readers, the question might remain, why would two reasonably intelligent people devote untold months and years to producing an entire book about a single movie? We have done so because, for one thing, our experience with the text tells us that *The Manchurian Candidate* will repay nearly any amount of critical attention that one is willing to pour into it. We don't mind letting our admiration show. But, more important, we have done so because the circuitry of ideas and ideologies from the cultural realm to the political and back again *matters*—it mattered in 1962, in the wake of Korea and at the dawn of Vietnam; and it matters still, as the Cold War's end has come merely to mark the beginning of a new and seemingly perpetual "war on terror." Our government once again makes extraordinary claims upon our allegiance, and it once again tests our settled assumptions about where the line is drawn between the public and the private; about the difference between prudent vigilance and proto-totalitarian surveillance; about the relationship between liberty and danger, and the dangers that "homeland security" itself might pose; and about how to distinguish "us" from "them." And once again along with the government, the culture, too, seems to have gone on high alert—one thinks of TV shows like 24 and the new sword-and-sandal spectaculars like *Troy, Alexander,* and *Kingdom of Heaven*. This project has seemed worth the effort, then—like the enterprise of cultural analysis in general—because in a sprawling democracy whose most important exchanges in the public sphere are necessarily mass-mediated, the preconditions for genuine liberty and meaningful citizenship must include a clear-eyed, conscious reckoning with whatever it is we have been "built" to do.

1

Backstory

Frank Sinatra and the Politics of Cold War Cultural Production

I don't think it's good public relations to talk that way to a
United States senator, even if he is an idiot.

*—Bennett Marco (Frank Sinatra) to
the secretary of defense (Barry Kelley)*

Backstory is the screenwriting term for the portion of the plot that
unfolds before the opening scene of a film. In the case of *The Manchurian Candidate*—the project itself—the backstory has largely been
overlooked. In the most sustained critique of the film, cultural historian Greil Marcus treats *The Manchurian Candidate* as having virtually materialized from out of nowhere: "Something—something in
the story, something in the times, in the interplay of various people
caught up consciously in the story, and consciously, unconsciously, or
half-consciously in the times—came together."[1]

To hear Marcus tell it, no one associated with the project—not
its stars, not its director or screenwriter, *no one*—ever came close to
producing anything like it: "[In *The Manchurian Candidate*] we're seeing [director] John Frankenheimer, [screenwriter] George Axelrod,

the cinematographer Lionel Lindon, the production designer Richard Sylbert, the composer David Amram . . . [Frank] Sinatra, [Laurence] Harvey, [Angela] Lansbury, [Janet] Leigh . . . and a clutch of actors in smaller roles . . . working over their heads, diving into material they've chosen, or been given, and in every case outstripping the material and themselves."[2]

This impossibly romantic notion obscures more than it explains. And, as it turns out, there is plenty to ponder, for *The Manchurian Candidate*, a film Marcus rightly calls "the most exciting American movie from *Citizen Kane* to the first two *Godfather* pictures," as much as any film, is the product of its historical moment, and of the personal and political alchemy of the principals involved.[3] As we shall see, the remarkable thing is not so much that *The Manchurian Candidate* materialized out of nowhere for reasons we can't quite explain, but that it was shaped to such a large degree by the particular people who came together at a particular moment to make it.

For Frank Sinatra, 1960 was turning out to be one of those very good years. After seven successful years with Capitol Records, a partnership that had cemented his reputation as the foremost interpreter of American popular song, the singer was making plans to found his own record company, Reprise. He was becoming more and more friendly with John F. Kennedy, the young Massachusetts senator who wanted to be president. And he had a new film project in the works: an adaptation of William Bradford Huie's 1954 best seller *The Execution of Private Slovik*, the true-life story of the only American soldier executed for desertion during World War II—indeed, the only American soldier executed for such a crime since the Civil War.

The character of Eddie Slovik would have appealed to Sinatra for obvious reasons. Slovik was a hard-luck loser from Detroit who had been plucked from the home front in 1943, a troubled kid who had just begun to get his life together—he'd recently married, rented an apartment, bought some furniture to go with it—when fate stuck a foot out to trip him. Even Huie, who takes great pains to be sympathetic to the U.S. command in his book, describes the call-up of Slovik, and thousands like him, as the result of the meanest wartime logic:

The decision was this: despite all our sea, air, and possibly atomic power, it was decided [in late 1943] to stage mass infantry assaults, not only on Fortress Europe, but also on the main islands of Japan. This meant a wheatlike *[sic]* sea of dogfaces, floods of replacements— so the heat was put on the draft boards: scrape the barrel . . . relax requirements . . . don't examine his eyes, count them . . . fill the pipelines so that dogfaces can be funneled into the lines in Europe in August, 1944, and in Japan in November, 1945.[4]

And so it was that the reform-school graduate with a history of emotional disturbance, who had originally been classified 4-F, wound up in the U.S. Army. During a night action in France on August 25, 1944, Slovik reportedly failed to leave his foxhole and engage the enemy. Following the battle, the young soldier was separated from his platoon and not seen again for six weeks. Claiming a Canadian unit had temporarily absorbed him, he rejoined his own unit on October 8, only to go missing again later that same day. The following day, Slovik surrendered and confessed to desertion. He was executed on January 31, 1945, a little more than three months before V-E Day.

The little guy who got a bad break, who wouldn't (or couldn't) conform, and who was subsequently squashed by the state apparatus, bore more than a passing resemblance to the character, Angelo Maggio, Sinatra had portrayed in *From Here to Eternity* (1953), the film that had launched his comeback in the early 1950s. Like Slovik, the fictional Maggio was a working-class, white ethnic army grunt. And although he may not have been executed for desertion in combat— the film, like the James Jones novel on which it is based, is about life at Schofield Barracks in Hawaii in the days leading up to Pearl Harbor—Maggio's demise is the direct result of a dereliction of duty.

Sentenced to the stockade for leaving his guard post, he is placed at the mercy of the sadistic sergeant of the guard (played by Ernest Borgnine), with whom Maggio has a running feud. The sergeant exacts a daily revenge, beating the "tough monkey" methodically until, finally, Maggio attempts to escape by stealing away on the back of a truck leaving the stockade. He is killed when the truck hits a bump in the road and he is accidentally ejected. "I bounced. I think I broke something," he gasps as he dies in the arms of his friend, Private

Robert E. Lee Prewitt (Montgomery Clift). The role garnered Sinatra a best supporting actor Oscar and further solidified the persona Sinatra had already begun to stake out in his music—the nonconformist romantic willing to take his lumps and dish them out, too; the cultural type Sinatra biographer Pete Hamill dubbed "the tender tough guy."[5]

To write the screenplay for *The Execution of Private Slovik*, Sinatra hired Albert Maltz, a veteran screenwriter he had known for years and who had scripted the 1945 Academy Award–winning short *The House I Live In*, in which the singer had sung the Popular Front anthem of racial and religious tolerance to a diverse cast of dead-end kids. Since that time, Maltz had become well known to the public for other reasons. He had been one of the so-called Hollywood Ten, the group of Hollywood writers, directors, and producers who had refused to cooperate with the House Un-American Activities Committee's (HUAC) investigation of communist influence in the movie industry. For his lack of cooperation, Maltz was held in contempt of Congress and sentenced to a one-year prison term in 1950. After his release, he—like fellow Hollywood Ten members Dalton Trumbo, Ring Lardner Jr., and others—was blacklisted.

By 1960, though, the blacklist had begun to crumble in practice, if not in theory. Blacklisted writers, because they could work anonymously, had begun to find work in the movies.[6] Director Otto Preminger had already hired Trumbo to write the screenplay for *Exodus* (1960). Likewise, star/producer Kirk Douglas had commissioned the writer for the slave epic *Spartacus* (1960). In both cases, Trumbo's actual name would appear in the credits. Also during this time, producer Stanley Kramer acknowledged that writer Nathan E. Douglas, who had scripted both *The Defiant Ones* (1958) and *Inherit the Wind* (released in 1960) for him, was in fact blacklisted actor-turned-writer Nedrick Young. Sinatra's hiring of Maltz, though still a courageous stand, was by no means an isolated incident.

More to the point, it was completely in keeping with Sinatra's professed liberal beliefs. As several biographers have pointed out, the singer had grown up in an intensely political environment. His mother, "Dolly" (born Natalia Garavente, in Genoa), had been a ward heeler in the Hudson County political machine of Jersey City Mayor Frank Hague, serving as a liaison between the poor Italian immigrants

The "New Deal crooner" (right) helps publicize a New York City concert to benefit historically black Bethune-Cookman College in 1940. From left to right: Fred Norman, Bunny Berrigan, Tommy Dorsey, Eleanor Roosevelt, Lionel Hampton, and Frank Sinatra. (Bettmann/Corbis)

of Hoboken's Third Ward and city hall. On election day, she'd make sure her constituents toed the (Democratic) party line.[7]

His mother's unofficial duties as a ward heeler (her official occupation was running a tavern, a vocation that dovetailed perfectly with her political pursuits) provided the young Sinatra with object lessons in influence, power, and patronage at a time when the Democratic Party was not only the political, but something approaching the spiritual, home of working-class white ethnics and immigrants. "I've been campaigning for Democrats ever since I marched in a parade for Al Smith when I was a twelve-year-old kid [in 1928]," Sinatra liked to say as an adult, referring to the first Catholic nominated for the presidency by one of the major parties.[8]

Sinatra's affiliation with the Democrats grew with the advent of the New Deal. He would come to political maturity under Franklin Roosevelt, who was first elected when Sinatra was only sixteen, and who would remain president for the next twelve years, well after Sinatra's rise to cultural prominence. Sinatra idolized Roosevelt, even naming his son, born in 1944, after the president (Frank Sinatra Jr. isn't really a Jr., since Frank stands for Franklin, not Francis). But it wasn't until the fall of that election year that Sinatra finally got to meet his political hero. On September 28, legendary New York restaurateur Toots Shor dragged him along to a White House luncheon, where FDR reportedly teased the young singer by weighing in on the phenomenon the press had dubbed "Sinatrauma": "Fainting, which was once so prevalent, has become a lost art among the ladies," the president is supposed to have said. "I'm glad that you have revived it." Then he asked Sinatra what song he thought might climb to the top of radio's "Hit Parade" that week.[9]

It was a meeting the singer wouldn't soon forget—and not just because he had met the president. The anti-Roosevelt press began to ridicule Sinatra's White House visit almost before he exited 1600 Pennsylvania Avenue. Frank R. Kent of the *Baltimore Sun* called the visit "a cheap little publicity stunt." Republican Senator Kenneth Wherry of Nebraska—no doubt thinking of the general election six weeks away—took the opportunity to question FDR's priorities: "That crooner! Mr. Roosevelt could better spend his time conferring with members of the Senate who will have to pass upon his foreign policy." Hearst columnist Westbrook Pegler, too, mocked Sinatra as "The New Deal Crooner."[10]

It wasn't only Sinatra's White House visit that got under the collective skin of the right-wing press, however. It was his repeated appearances on behalf of such groups as Young America for Roosevelt and American Youth for a Free World, and his unflagging support of racial and religious tolerance. "The Negro loves his children with the same sort of devotion that the white man does," he told the crowd at the World Youth Rally in New York in 1945. "The Chinese likes laughter and friendship and good times just as much as you and me . . . No matter what their race, religion, or nationality is, [all people] are alike in their loves and their fears, their needs and their hopes."[11]

With his move to Hollywood in 1944, Sinatra became even more politically active, openly associating with leftist groups and causes.

Most conspicuous was his collaboration with Maltz and director Mervyn LeRoy on *The House I Live In*. In the short film—something like an early music video, really—Sinatra plays himself. Taking a break from a recording session, he steps into an alley and encounters a group of kids hurling insults at a Jewish youngster. After a short talk on the virtues of tolerance, he launches into the Lewis Allen/ Earl Robinson ballad. Profits from the film—LeRoy, Maltz, and Sinatra all worked for free—were donated to agencies involved in social work with adolescents.

Sinatra's political activities did not stop with such gestures. In 1946, he was elected vice president of the Hollywood Independent Citizens Committee of the Arts, Sciences, and Professions (HICCASP) at the same meeting at which the collective refused to adopt a resolution rejecting communism "as a desirable form of government for the U.S.A."[12] And the following year, he became an outspoken opponent of the HUAC hearings that targeted the movie industry.

"Once they get the movies throttled, how long will it be before [HUAC] gets to work on freedom of the air[waves]?" he asked in a press statement in support of the Committee for the First Amendment, a group of Hollywood stars—led by Humphrey Bogart—that had traveled to Washington to protest the hearings in 1947. "If you made a pitch on a nationwide network for a square deal for the underdog, will they call you a commie?"[13]

Sinatra wouldn't have to wait long before they called him a "commie." In fact, he didn't have to wait at all. The previous year, the leader of the ultraconservative America First party, Gerald L. K. Smith, had already used his appearance before HUAC to question Sinatra's allegiances.[14] Indeed, as Jon Wiener has pointed out, during the eight years that followed the release of *The House I Live In*, Sinatra was labeled a communist before the committee twelve times.[15] The conservative press, again, played no small part in the attacks. Sinatra was "one of Hollywood's leading travelers on the road to Red fascism," charged Hearst writer Lee Mortimer, who, along with fellow Hearst columnist George Sokolsky, would become a constant nemesis.[16]

Ironically, though Sinatra would survive the postwar witch hunts, it is these attacks from the right that appear to have morphed into the charge that would haunt the singer for the rest of his career, into

Frank Sinatra and Hearst columnist Lee Mortimer in court, 1947.
(Bettman/Corbis)

the rumors that he had intimate ties to the criminal underworld, or
"the mob." In an August 1951 article in the *New American Mercury*
titled "Frank Sinatra Confidential: Gangsters in the Night Clubs,"
Mortimer easily moved between the two allegations. Citing a "Trea-
sury [Department] file," he confided to his readers:

The report went on to state that Frankie was by no means a rare case. Many well-known entertainment figures had been "captured," either with or without their knowledge, by the underworld, the Communists or both. The Communists and the gangsters both have the same motive, acquiring respectability by association with prestige names. Frankie's contacts with both groups are numerous.

According to the report, Sinatra's close friendship and association with known narcotics peddlers and dope addicts was constantly advertised to propagandize kids with a taste for the fast life and surround dope-taking with glamour. How Frankie reached his present eminent position is a fairly complicated story and illustrative of the methods whereby the Mafia (as well as the Communists) exploits susceptible stars.[17]

The article was the continuation of a long-standing feud—in a highly publicized incident at Ciro's nightclub in Los Angeles in 1947, Sinatra had physically assaulted Mortimer after the columnist accused the singer, in print, of acting as a bagman for exiled gangster Lucky Luciano on a trip to Havana earlier that year; nevertheless, it highlights the antipathy that would endure between the press (particularly the Hearst chain) and the singer, bad blood that would rise to the surface in the spring of 1960.

Politically, Sinatra would remain an ardent liberal and Democrat throughout the 1950s. He sang the national anthem at the Democratic National Convention in 1956, the same convention where his future friend John Kennedy made a heroic but unsuccessful bid for the vice-presidential nomination. And as late as 1959, he was still flouting his New Deal credentials, slightly tinkering with the lyrics to the Ira Gershwin/Vernon Duke standard "I Can't Get Started" so that they came out: "Each time I chanced to see Franklin D. / He always said, 'Hi, Buddy' to me."[18]

For Sinatra in 1960, hiring Maltz to adapt *The Execution of Private Slovik*—thumbing his nose at the conservative establishment while giving an old acquaintance a much-needed break—was probably more temptation than he could stand. At least, certainly, it would turn out that way. The singer was appearing at the Fontainebleau Hotel in Miami Beach when the story of Maltz's hire broke in the *New York Times* on Monday, March 21, 1960. Other papers jumped on it immediately.

"Senator Calls It Shocking," blared the headline of the *Los Angeles Examiner* story the following day. The accompanying article quoted Senator Karl Mundt, a Republican from South Dakota and the only member of the House Un-American Activities Committee that had sentenced Maltz to still be serving in Congress. Mundt, who apparently hadn't lost a step—or a talking point—in the intervening decade and a half, wondered how, "In these uneasy times...people will grant new opportunities for the injection of Communist propaganda into motion picture fare."[19]

The *Examiner,* a Hearst paper, kept up the pressure in the ensuing days. "Maltz Toed Red Line on Art: Sinatra's Writer Abject Marxist," read the headline two days later, on March 24. Recalling a "groveling example...of [Maltz's] total allegiance to the Marxist line," the article recounted how the screenwriter had previously "abjectly accepted the Communist doctrine that all art...is a weapon in the class struggle and must always be used as a weapon." This, according to the article, was a special matter of concern since *The Execution of Private Slovik* was "made to order for the art-weapon treatment."[20]

Sinatra tried to defend his decision to hire Maltz—and assuage fears that communist ideology would be planted in the film—by issuing a statement on Friday, March 25: "Since I will produce and direct the picture, I am concerned that the screenplay reflect the true pro-American values of the story. I spoke to my screenwriters, but it was not until I talked to Albert Maltz that I found a writer who saw the screenplay in exactly the terms I wanted. This is 'the Army is right.'"[21] Then he went on to address what had to be one of the most delicate aspects of the growing controversy. "I would also like to comment," said Sinatra, "on the [newspaper] articles from certain quarters on Senator John Kennedy by connecting him with my decision of employing a screenwriter...I do not ask the advice of Senator Kennedy on whom I should hire [and] Senator Kennedy does not ask me how he should vote in the Senate."[22] Sinatra and Kennedy had by this time become intimately associated with each other in the public eye, thanks in no small part to Peter Lawford, the British matinee idol turned member of Sinatra's famed Rat Pack and husband to the senator's sister ("The Brother-in-Lawford" Sinatra supposedly called him).

The "certain quarters" to which Sinatra referred were, of course, the Hearst papers and even some Hollywood conservatives, such as John Wayne—"I wonder how Sinatra's crony, Senator John Kennedy, feels about him hiring such a man," offered the Duke, when approached by the papers.[23] But, then, even the *New York Times*'s Hollywood columnist had put forth the theory that Sinatra had wanted to keep his hiring of Maltz a secret until after that summer's Democratic National Convention, for fear of hurting Kennedy's chances for the nomination.[24]

The Hearst papers kept the pressure on, penning an open letter to Sinatra on Monday, March 28. "In hiring Maltz," the piece scolded Sinatra, "you are not giving employment to a poor little sheep who lost his way, but to a real Communist pro . . . Dump Maltz and get yourself a true American writer."[25] Industry gossip queen Hedda Hopper, writing in the *Los Angeles Times* on Friday, April 8, adopted a similarly personal, even more impassioned approach. "If Sinatra loves his country, he won't do this," Hopper cried.[26]

Later that day, from his home in Palm Springs, Sinatra, for one of the few times anyone could recall, gave in, issuing his last statement on the matter: "The American public has indicated it feels the morality of hiring Albert Maltz is [the most crucial point] and I will accept this majority opinion."[27] The next day, the *Examiner* ran the headline "Sinatra Ousts Maltz as Writer" above its own masthead.[28]

There was little doubt as to the motivating factor for Sinatra's reversal, or the price he paid. As biographer Arnold Shaw wrote only a few years later: "At the height of the campaign to elect [JFK], Sinatra faced the troubling choice of getting off the political bandwagon or firing a left-wing writer he had retained as a scripter. . . In backing down, he had to face demeaning comparisons with other producers who had stood pat when they were attacked for employing blacklisted writers."[29]

The singer paid off Maltz—seventy-five thousand dollars, the full fee—and turned his attention to other projects: fulfilling his remaining obligation to Capitol Records, the company he was leaving behind to launch Reprise; campaigning for Kennedy (Sinatra would even record a version of his Oscar-winning song from the previous

Frank Sinatra and Senator John F. Kennedy at a fund-raiser in Los Angeles on the eve of Kennedy's selection as the Democratic nominee for president, 1960. (Bettman/Corbis)

year, "High Hopes," as a campaign anthem for the senator); and jumping on another, infinitely less controversial movie project—a caper film about a group of old army buddies who rob five Las Vegas casinos, called *Ocean's Eleven* (1960).

The lingering effects of the Hollywood blacklist, media pressure, and his relationship to John Kennedy had conspired to sink *The Execution of Private Slovik*, but soon Sinatra would get a chance at exacting a symbolic revenge of sorts.[30] He would be approached about starring in a complex film about Cold War politics and the power of mass persuasion based on a recent, offbeat best seller: *The Manchurian Candidate*.

Richard Condon's 1959 novel, cultural critic Louis Menand has observed, was inspired in large part by the 1950s obsession with brainwashing, a phenomenon fed by accounts of American prisoners of war in Korea being subjected to psychological conditioning by their Chinese captors. As Menand recounts, a U.S. Army report issued in 1955, "POW: The Fight Continues after the Battle," concluded that a "shocking number of prisoners had, to one degree or another, succumbed" to brainwashing. Stories about the brainwashing of American prisoners were also featured in mainstream publications such as the *Saturday Evening Post* and *Life*.[31]

The Manchurian Candidate exploited these preoccupations with its conspiracy theorist's dream of a plot: Raymond Shaw is an American soldier during the Korean War who, along with his platoon, is taken captive to a site across the Manchurian border and brainwashed, turned by his captors—a team of Chinese and Soviet psychiatrists— into the perfect assassin, then returned to Korea, and, eventually, the United States. The men in the platoon, including Captain Bennett Marco, are made to memorize the details of a fictitious action in which Shaw saves their lives, an action that results in the soldier being awarded the Congressional Medal of Honor. Shaw thus arrives in the States the war-hero stepson of John Yerkes Iselin, a red-baiting U.S. senator and his ambitious wife (Raymond's biological mother), who, as the reader will discover, are in reality communist agents, with their eyes set on the 1960 presidential election. Shaw has been programmed to help them. It will ultimately be up to Marco to figure out the details, and to stop them.

"A human time-bomb is turned loose on an unsuspecting nation in this brilliant and startling novel, at once a spy story, a love story, a fascinating tale of adventure, and a savage satire," promised the novel's dust jacket, its language reminiscent of the Hollywood movie trailer, the latter a genre with which Condon was intimately acquainted, having worked as a studio publicist during much of Hollywood's golden age. Beginning his career at Walt Disney in 1936—he promoted *Fantasia* and *Dumbo,* among other classics—Condon had opted for the life of a writer in 1957.[32]

Oddly enough, despite Condon's studio system background—he boasted that he had watched more than ten thousand movies, gaining in the process "an unconscious grounding in storytelling"—*The Manchurian Candidate* was anything but adaptation-friendly.[33] For one thing, there was the relationship between Raymond and his overbearing mother. In the novel, her sins include not only the naked quest for power—"[she] sought power the way a superstitious man might look for a four-leaf clover"—and an addiction to heroin, but a fanatical love for her son that, replicating the relationship she had with her own father, crosses the line into incest. "Her long fingers dug into [Raymond's] shoulders and pulled him to her on the chaise," reads one particularly racy (and crucial) passage. "And as her left hand opened the Chinese robe she remembered Poppa and the sound of rain high in the attic when she had been a little girl, and she found again the ecstatic peace she had lost so long, long before."[34]

But even beyond the problem of working such taboo material into a script, another potential obstacle to adaptation might have been the fact that the book contained remarkably little character development for a work of fiction. Condon's novel might have been "a spy story, a love story, a fascinating tale of adventure," but it is its satirical edge that dominates, Condon's third-person narration often lapsing into pronouncements on the state of the culture and humankind in the mid-twentieth century, especially the new mass-media age.

Early in the book, the self-centered Shaw travels, despite himself, to St. Louis, to offer comfort to the family of Ed Mavole, a soldier he believes was killed in the action for which he received the Congressional Medal of Honor. (In reality, Shaw had been made to kill the man by his programmers, as a test.) Upon arriving at the airport, he is met not only by the soldier's father, but by a young female reporter and a photographer for the local paper. The latter is puzzled by Raymond's reluctance to have his photograph taken: "'Whassa matter?' [the photographer] asked [Raymond] in bewilderment—because he lived at a time when only sex criminals and dope peddlers tried to refuse to have their pictures taken by the press" (3).

The cynical attitude toward the media—and the people whose sensibilities are shaped by it—surfaces throughout the work. Describing Gomel, the Politburo man who had been present during Shaw's brainwashing, Condon explains that "[his] teeth made him carnivorously unphotogenic and therefore unknown to the newspaper readers of the West" (35). It is the point of the novel that the conspiracy to deliver the United States into the hands of the totalitarian left (disguised as the radical right) may succeed not simply because they have built an assassin capable of striking at America's leaders, but because they have perfected the art of mass manipulation. (In the novel, as in the film, the climactic assassination is scripted to play out on national television for maximum impact.) Thus, Raymond's visit to the White House to accept his Medal of Honor becomes an absurd photo op for his mother, Eleanor, and her husband:

> Raymond heard his mother ask for the honor of a photograph with the President, then moved her two tame photographers in with a quick low move of her left hand . . . The shot was lined up. Raymond's mother was on the President's right. Johnny was on Raymond's right. Just before the bank of press cameras took the picture, Mrs. Iselin took out a gay little black-on-yellow banner on a brave little gilded stick and held it over Raymond's head. At least it seemed [that way] . . . when the pictures came out in the newspapers the next day, then in thousands of newspapers all over the world beginning three and a half years hence, and with shameful frequency in many newspapers after that, it was seen that the gay little banner had been held directly over the President's head and that the lettering on it read: JOHNNY ISELIN'S BOY. (62)

If Condon plays the scene for laughs, it is perhaps only to offer the reader a momentary respite from the book's potentially depressing pronouncements on the overmediated, flaccid intellect of the American public. When, in an episode that would be replicated in the film, Iselin, in the midst of a campaign in which he daily accuses the government of harboring communist agents—screaming out a different number every day—asks his wife to help him come up with "one goddam figure he could remember," the choice is obvious: fifty-seven, because "all the jerks could remember it, too, as it could be linked so easily with the fifty-seven varieties of canned food that had been advertised so well and so steadily for so many years" (132).

Yes, the story of a brainwashed assassin was the stuff of potboilers—Menand likens the novel to "a very ripe banana, [delectable] for those who have the taste for it"—but *The Manchurian Candidate* was also a work of pop social criticism, and not only incidentally, but at its heart. It would require a particular sensibility to recognize its potential as a mainstream movie property. Indeed, as director John Frankenheimer remembered quite definitively years later, "[The book] was turned down by every studio in Hollywood . . . It had been around. It had been turned down and rejected."[35]

Born in 1930, Frankenheimer was a young director who had made a name for himself in live television drama in the 1950s, directing more than a hundred teleplays. As senior director of *Playhouse 90*, he had been responsible for such landmark programs as J. P. Miller's *Days of Wine and Roses*, with Piper Laurie and Cliff Robertson (adapted for the big screen by Blake Edwards in 1962), and a three-hour version of Ernest Hemingway's *For Whom the Bell Tolls*, starring Jason Robards, Maureen Stapleton, and Eli Wallach (budgeted at four hundred thousand dollars, it can rightly lay claim to being one of television's first blockbusters).[36] He had graduated to feature-length filmmaking with a couple of social problem films: *The Young Stranger* (1957), about a teenage boy's brush with delinquency and his strained relationship with his father, and *The Young Savages* (1961), in which Burt Lancaster (who would become a frequent Frankenheimer collaborator) played a DA confronting street gangs.

One might assume it was Frankenheimer's idea to tackle *The Manchurian Candidate*. He was, after all, well versed in drama; his first production for *Playhouse 90*, in 1956, had been a Cold War cautionary tale titled *Forbidden Area*, about an apparent Soviet nuclear attack on the United States. More important, he had spent the decade in the nascent television industry, learning firsthand the medium's potential for reaching and influencing millions. But in fact, it was screenwriter George Axelrod who approached Frankenheimer about translating the book to the screen. Years later, Frankenheimer discussed his friend's role in securing the property:

> The way that George Axelrod and I got the rights was that we went to a bookstore and bought two copies of the book. We read it in a single afternoon. It was George Axelrod's idea that this might make a good movie. I'd never heard of the book. I read it as he read it and we called his agent, Irving Lazar . . . and by the end of the afternoon . . . George and I owned the rights.[37]

George Axelrod, only eight years older than Frankenheimer, was already a veteran of both Broadway—where, as a playwright, he had authored the male midlife crisis farce *The Seven Year Itch* as well as the advertising industry send-up *Will Success Spoil Rock Hunter?*—and the movies. As a screenwriter, Axelrod specialized in light comedy and romantic repartee. His first screenplay was for *Phfft!* (1954), a laugh-a-minute affair starring Jack Lemmon and Judy Holliday. In 1955, he adapted *The Seven Year Itch* for director Billy Wilder. A few years later, he earned an Academy Award nomination for his screen adaptation of Truman Capote's *Breakfast at Tiffany's* (1961).

Although the absurdist humor of Condon's book would certainly have appealed to Axelrod, it appears that he, and Frankenheimer, responded at least as much to the book's topical subject matter and critique of the culture. As Frankenheimer recalled in the late 1960s:

> We started to get absorbed in the story and realized that what we had was something that could very well be a lot closer to the truth than many people imagined. We consulted every book written about brainwashing, and I remember reading one called *In Every War But One*, about American prisoners of war in Korea . . . It was the story about how the Chinese brainwashed these men, what they did to them, and things like that; and while it wasn't quite as total as the brainwashing in *The Manchurian Candidate*, it was nevertheless a very distinct type of brainwashing that they'd known. On another level we believed that we lived in a society that was brainwashed. And I wanted to do something about it.
>
> I think that our society is brainwashed by television commercials, by advertising, by politicians, by a censored press . . . with its biased reporting. More and more I think that our society is becoming manipulated and controlled.[38]

As written by Condon, and summed up by Frankenheimer, the gist of *The Manchurian Candidate* is one that would have struck a chord with Sinatra, whose career, to as great an extent as that of any star of the twentieth century, had played out in the pages of the press. The media, Sinatra must have known, had helped make him. And, in the spring of 1960—for neither the first time nor the last—it had tried to break him. At least segments of it had. Bullied by the Hearst papers and the political right into dumping Maltz (proof of his lingering re-sentment was a well-publicized run-in the singer had with John Wayne a month after firing Maltz; "Sinatra, John Wayne Tiff over Maltz at Star Party" the headlines read the next day), Sinatra might have been somewhat predisposed to undertake a project that would appear, on at least one level, as an indictment of the disproportionate influence wielded by the mass media.

Indeed, one wonders what joy it might have brought Sinatra had Axelrod preserved, in his screenplay, a particular passage from Condon's book, naming some of the singer's long-standing detractors. Describing the costume party at the Iselin house (in the film, the affair at which Raymond is reunited with his long-lost love, Jocie), Condon wrote: "Many of the uniforms were quaint American Legion uniforms so like that of the *squadristi* of former days in Italy, encasing various sizes of fleshy prejudice which exchanged opinions they rented that week from Mr. Sokolsky, Mr. Lawrence, Mr. Pegler, and that fascinating younger fellow who had written about men and God at Yale" (259).

The fact that *The Manchurian Candidate* was about presidential politics, an overheated fantasy about the fate of the nation and the men who could save it from threats both internal and external, at precisely the moment that Sinatra felt most secure about his own status in the republic, also must have appealed to him. After Kennedy's election, Sinatra—who had not only campaigned for JFK but had been the architect of the star-studded inaugural gala—was viewed by the public as something approaching a member of the extended (and extensive) first family (although the reality, as we will see in chapter 8, was far more complicated). A film in which he would play a quintessential Kennedy-era hero must have seemed like a natural fit.

"George had heard that Frank Sinatra wanted to do this picture," Frankenheimer remembered. "We went down to see Sinatra in Florida, where he was singing at the Fontainebleau Hotel . . . [By the time] we arrived at Sinatra's door, there was this great smile on his face and he said, 'God, I just can't wait to do your movie.'"[39]

Although Sinatra would ultimately prove an eager participant, negotiations appear to have been more complex than Frankenheimer's sanguine recollection. A story in the March 29, 1961, issue of *Variety* announced not only that Sinatra would star in the adaptation but that he had purchased the property outright from Frankenheimer and Axelrod.[40] Two weeks later, the showbiz bible recanted, claiming that negotiations for the sale of the property between the parties had fallen through.[41] As late as May 18, there was no agreement between

Frankenheimer and Axelrod—who retained the rights to the story—and Sinatra, whom they, as coproducers, still hoped to cast in the film. Sometime that summer, the three reached a compromise—Sinatra would star, and, along with Frankenheimer and Axelrod, coproduce the film; Howard Koch would serve as executive producer.[42]

But obstacles remained. One was the geopolitical geometry of the novel's plot, which implicated not only the Chinese but the Russians in the conspiracy to murder a U.S. presidential nominee. "United Artists said, 'We're scared to make this thing,' because they said it was so anti-Russian," Axelrod recalled in a 1988 interview. "[But then Sinatra] said, 'I just came down from Hyannis Port [the site of the Kennedy compound in Massachusetts] and I saw the president and the president said, "What are you going to do next?"' and [Sinatra] said '*The Manchurian Candidate*.' And he said 'Great, who's going to play the mother?'"[43]

JFK's enthusiasm for a story of foreign intrigue shouldn't surprise; he had, after all, publicly professed his love for the books of Ian Fleming early in his administration. Sinatra's September 1961 meeting with the president assuaged the fears of United Artists (UA) president Arthur Krim (who also happened to be the national finance chairman of the Democratic Party). The project got the green light. Filming would begin in California and New York in January 1962.[44]

There was still the question of gaining the approval of the Production Code Administration (PCA), Hollywood's governing censorship board. Given the nature of Condon's novel, any attempt to faithfully adapt it for the screen was bound to raise eyebrows—and red pens—in the PCA offices. In a letter dated September 19, Geoffrey M. Shurlock of the PCA wrote to Koch, detailing the PCA's chief objections to Axelrod's initial draft. Not surprisingly, some of the agency's concerns had to do with sex, or, more accurately, the implication of sex. The PCA took issue, for example, with showing the "upstairs portion" of Miss Gertrude's establishment—a Korean bar frequented by the American platoon—because "it has the clear identity of a brothel. In this connection, the business of Private Mavole and the Korean girl being in bed together will likewise be eliminated."[45] The board also objected to showing Shaw in bed with Mardell (in the first few pages of the novel, the young reporter Shaw

seduces in St. Louis, during his visit to console Mavole's parents).
Nor did the relationship between Marco and Rosie, his love interest,
escape the PCA's attention: "We ask that you eliminate [the scene]
showing Rosie in bed and Marco tightening his tie in the mirror."[46]

These objections were undoubtedly anticipated by Axelrod, a sea-
soned screenwriter, and easily corrected, either through omission of
the scene, as in the case of Shaw's encounter with Mardell (a character never referenced in the film), or through symbolic substitution.
(In the finished film, is there any doubt, even without showing the
upstairs, that there is more than beer being served up by the hostesses
at Miss Gertrude's?)[47]

Violent representations were another area of concern for the PCA:
In both the case of Mavole being strangled and of Bobby Lembeck
being shot through the forehead (another member of the platoon
whom Shaw executes as part of his "programming"), the agency
asked that the action "be indicated out of frame." The PCA, though,
was most preoccupied—at least judging by Shurlock's memo—by
what it viewed as "unacceptable profanity": repeated utterances of
"damn," "hell," "Oh, God," and, in one instance, the phrase "We're
in like Flynn," spoken by Mrs. Iselin.[48] Quite good at spotting the
devil in the details, the PCA would appear, at least in this case, to
have ignored the devil that was all around. Shurlock closed his letter
to Koch by reminding him that, specific recommendations aside, the
PCA's final judgment would be based on the finished picture.[49]

Having agreed to a distribution deal with UA and secured the
blessings of President Kennedy and, at least for the moment, the PCA,
all that remained for Sinatra and Frankenheimer was to settle on a
cast. Sinatra, of course, would star, but not as Raymond Shaw. Instead, he would play Marco. It would be Sinatra's last great role as an
actor. Making movies had always been primarily a sideline for the
singer and after this would become, almost exclusively, an excuse
to get friends together or a way to take maximum advantage of extended concert commitments in attractive locales (as in the late
1960s, when he would make two detective films based in Miami, at
the same time that he was appearing at the Fontainebleau Hotel's La
Ronde nightclub). Not that he hadn't been convincing—even com-

pelling—as an actor in a number of films: *From Here to Eternity*, *Suddenly* (1954; another film with a presidential assassination plot and one that we will take up in greater length in chapter 3), *The Man with the Golden Arm* (1955; playing a heroin addict, he received a Best Actor Oscar nomination), and *Some Came Running* (1959), the Vincente Minnelli Technicolor soap opera that would become a favorite among the French New Wave, to name a few.

The casting of the other principals followed. On September 7, *Variety* announced that Laurence Harvey would costar with Sinatra.[50] He would play Shaw, the aloof, doomed protagonist whose own mind is turned against him. The Lithuanian-born Harvey had been a popular leading man since scoring a best actor Oscar nomination as a ruthless social climber in *Room at the Top* (1959), a performance he had followed with a supporting role opposite Elizabeth Taylor in *Butterfield 8* (1960), and an appearance in the John Wayne–directed western epic *The Alamo* (also 1960).

On November 29, it was announced that Janet Leigh also had been signed to the project.[51] Leigh, who had not had a starring role in a film since being immortalized in Alfred Hitchcock's *Psycho* two years earlier, was perhaps Frankenheimer's secret good-luck charm—one of Hitchcock's classic, icy blondes in a film that would ultimately owe more than a little to the Master of Suspense. She had also been—along with husband Tony Curtis—an active, and highly visible Kennedy supporter during the 1960 campaign. Leigh would play Sinatra's enigmatic love interest, Rosie.

Sinatra, Leigh, and Harvey were an accomplished trio, to be sure, but the most inspired casting choice might well have been tapping Angela Lansbury to play the mother. A veteran actress even though she was only in her late thirties, Lansbury had made her screen debut almost twenty years earlier, in George Cukor's *Gaslight* (1944), playing a sinister maid, a role for which she was nominated for a best supporting actress Oscar. She graduated almost instantly to playing sometimes flighty, sometimes strong-willed, matronly women.

In 1961, she appeared as Elvis Presley's mother in the restless-son-comes-home-from-the army musical *Blue Hawaii* (this, despite the fact she was barely nine years older than the rocker). And she had played a mother (Warren Beatty's) in the Frankenheimer-directed *All Fall Down*, a film shot in 1961 but not released until the following year. Together with *The Manchurian Candidate*, it would cement Frankenheimer's career. *All Fall Down* also led, indirectly, to Lansbury's hiring for *The Manchurian Candidate*. Sinatra originally had wanted Lucille Ball for the role of the mother; it was only after previewing *All Fall Down*—at Frankenheimer's insistence—that he agreed to Lansbury.[52]

Lansbury—in the film, snarling, manipulative, and vindictive— would prove ideally cast as Shaw's poisonous mother, the incest plot greatly enhanced by the fact that, like her last few screen sons, Laurence Harvey was closer in age to her than any offspring could possibly be (the actor was only three years younger than Lansbury).

Rounding out the ensemble were stalwart character actors James Gregory and John McGiver. The former, best remembered by a younger generation as the perpetually cynical and trench-coat-clad Inspector Frank Luger on 1970s cop sitcom *Barney Miller*, was a Frankenheimer favorite dating back to the director's days in television. Gregory would play Iselin as a thinly veiled Joe McCarthy (so thinly, in fact, that it is hardly worth making the distinction), a boozing, vulgar opportunist. McGiver would play Senator Thomas Jordan, Iselin's liberal adversary. A ubiquitous character actor in the 1950s and 1960s, McGiver specialized in portraying good-hearted (and sometimes kooky) characters. In 1961, he had played a small, but crucial, role in *Breakfast at Tiffany's* (for which, again, Axelrod had written the script). As the understanding counter salesman at the exclusive jewelry store, he sympathizes with the predicament of the young lovers (Audrey Hepburn and George Peppard) who would like to purchase a trinket to commemorate their visit, but whose budget consists of only a few dollars. Agreeing to engrave a Cracker Jack prize ring for the couple, it is he who makes the store Holly Golightly's idea of heaven on earth.

Rather than an example, then, of "people working over their heads," *The Manchurian Candidate* would appear to have been the product of shrewd assembly, of some good, some very good, and—on occasion—some great talents joining forces, swimming not only in "the material they were given," but in the swirling currents of their historical moment. The finished film (which stuck surprisingly close to Axelrod's earlier script drafts) turned out to be as wild a ride as the novel that had inspired it.

The opening scene takes place in Korea in 1952; Captain Marco and Sergeant Shaw pull up in a jeep in front of Miss Gertrude's, where the rest of the platoon has assembled to partake of drinks and female companionship. Shaw enters and rounds up the men for action; resentful and dismissive of the sergeant, they nevertheless collect themselves. In the next scene, it is nighttime, the platoon is in the field, and bullets are flying all around. They rely on Chunjin, their Korean interpreter and guide, for an escape route. He recommends proceeding in single file. Marco objects on tactical grounds, but ultimately defers. As the men advance, foreign soldiers emerge from the shadows, ambush them, and load them onto waiting helicopters.

The next scene (following the opening credits) begins with Shaw emerging from an airplane that has just landed in Washington, D.C. A voice-over explains that he is there to be decorated with the Congressional Medal of Honor. Almost before he steps onto the tarmac, he is the victim of another ambush: in an echo of the episode from the novel, his mother and Senator Iselin set upon him, unfurling a banner that reads "Johnny Iselin's Boy!" Later, Shaw informs his mother and Iselin, for whom he has nothing but contempt, that he will be taking a job as personal assistant to a prominent political columnist. When his mother asks him why he would go to work for "that communist," Shaw answers, "Well, for one thing, we discovered that we both loathe and despise you and Johnny."

Meanwhile, Marco, who has been promoted to major and reassigned to army intelligence in Washington, suffers from an odd, violent recurring dream: He and the rest of the platoon are waiting out a rainstorm in a hotel lobby in New Jersey, at a meeting of a ladies garden club, where a lecture on hydrangeas is being delivered. The ladies, though, soon morph into Chinese and Soviet officials, and the locale shifts to a very institutional-looking auditorium. (Frankenheimer would achieve this cinematic trick by utilizing a railroad track setup, which allowed him to replace the hotel-lobby set with the

auditorium set while he panned 360-degrees around the room; while
the camera was pointed away from them, the actors simply jumped
off one set and onto the other, assuming their same seated positions.)

At the front of the auditorium, surrounded by the platoon and
speaking from a stage that includes huge portraits of Mao Zedong
and Joseph Stalin, is Yen Lo of the Pavlov Institute, who explains to
his audience that the Americans have been brainwashed. The officials
gathered are chiefly interested in Shaw, who is ordered by Yen Lo to
strangle Ed Mavole to death. Shaw complies, while the rest of the
platoon sits idly. At this point in the dream, Marco awakens, screaming, in a cold sweat.

When Marco describes his repeating nightmare to his military
superiors, they dismiss it as a stress-related reaction to his tour in
Korea, and reassign him temporarily to the public relations corps,
hoping the cushy job will act as a tonic. On one of his first assignments, however, Marco runs into trouble: Iselin interrupts a press
conference by the secretary of defense to accuse him of harboring 207
communists in his agency. While Marco, who is acting as the secretary's aide, looks on in disbelief, unable to prevent the secretary from
engaging Iselin in verbal warfare, Mrs. Iselin watches a television
monitor in the room, to see how her husband's grandstanding is playing to the masses.

In the ensuing scene, Al Melvin, another member of the platoon,
lies in bed with his wife, and has a similar dream to the one Marco
has been experiencing: In Melvin's dream, the ladies (in his version,
they are, like him, African-American) turn into the same Chinese
and Soviet agents who inhabit Marco's nocturnal world. Yen Lo drills
Marco on the details of the military action they have all been conditioned to believe took place—the action for which Shaw will eventually be awarded his medal—then orders Shaw to shoot the youngest
member of the platoon, cherubic Bobby Lembeck, through the forehead. Again, Shaw complies while the platoon looks on disinterest-
edly. Melvin, like Marco, awakens screaming. His wife encourages
him to write to Shaw and tell him about the dream, which Melvin
has been having for weeks. "You like [Shaw] a lot, don't you?" she asks
him. "Raymond Shaw is the bravest, kindest, warmest, most wonderful

human being I've ever known in my life," he tells her. It is, verbatim, what Marco had earlier told his superiors, when he was asked what the men in the platoon thought about Shaw. Melvin's recitation of the line is the first indication, within the world of the film, that the dream may have some basis in fact.

At his New York City apartment, Shaw receives a phone call; the man on the line suggests "passing the time by playing a little solitaire," then hangs up. Shaw reaches for a deck of cards he keeps by his phone and begins to deal. After turning over a few cards, he produces the queen of diamonds. The phone again rings, and the same voice informs him that, in a few days, he will be taken to a local sanitarium for "a checkup." Shaw is clearly in a trance. At the sanitarium, Yen Lo, flown into the United States under "embassy quota," inspects Shaw and determines that "his brain has not only been washed . . . it has been dry-cleaned." Just to make sure, though, Shaw is ordered to murder his columnist-boss, a test that has the added advantage of elevating Shaw into that prominent position and providing the communists with an influential opinion shaper.

Meantime, Marco is on the verge of a nervous breakdown. Relieved of duty (after the debacle involving Iselin and the secretary of defense), and more convinced than ever that "there's something phony about me, about Raymond Shaw, about the whole Medal of Honor business," he takes a train to New York, where he hopes to track down Shaw, whom he has not seen since Korea. Aboard the train, he meets an attractive young woman named Rosie, who comes on to Marco, despite his clearly troubled state. (The relationship will be taken up at length in chapter 7.)

From here, the action moves quickly. Marco arrives at Shaw's door only to discover that Chunjin is now working for him (as Shaw's valet, the better to monitor him); from his dreams, Marco knows that Chunjin is part of the plot that is unfolding. He lands a hard right to Chunjin's jaw and a brawl ensues, one ultimately broken up by the police. At the station, Rosie shows up to bail out Marco.

When Marco finally catches up with Shaw, he tells Marco of the letter he received from Melvin. Although the letter gave only the broad outlines of the nightmare that Melvin and Marco share, it's

enough to confirm Marco's suspicions. After Marco successfully identifies two of the foreign officials in his dream (matching Melvin's
earlier testimony), the army makes him the head of a task force in-
vestigating Shaw.

Marco subsequently becomes the lonely Shaw's constant compan-
ion, hoping to uncover the mystery of what his subject has "been
built to do" before it is too late. Meanwhile, Mrs. Iselin continues to
orchestrate her husband's meteoric rise. She conspires to reunite her
son with a former flame, Jocelyn Jordan, the daughter of a liberal
U.S. senator. It was Raymond's mother who had sabotaged the relationship a few years earlier; now, she has her eyes set firmly on securing the vice presidential slot on the party ticket for Iselin, and she
thinks the marriage will guarantee Senator Jordan's cooperation—or,
at least, neutralize his antipathy for her husband.

At the costume party meant to reintroduce Raymond and Jocie to
each other—and provide Mrs. Iselin with a setting for broaching the
subject of Iselin's candidacy with Senator Jordan—Axelrod reveals
the narrative shocker. "Why don't you pass the time by playing a little
solitaire?" Mrs. Iselin asks her son, confirming that she is, indeed, his
"American operator."

Shaw and Jocie, their romance rekindled, elope; by the time Marco
arrives at Shaw's apartment, to ask Shaw to place himself under
observation, he discovers that the two are married. Reluctantly, Marco
allows them to go on their honeymoon. During their stay at an inn,
Shaw and Jocie turn on a television and discover that Iselin has
launched a vicious attack on Senator Jordan (who had vowed to block
Iselin's nomination, despite his daughter's marriage to Shaw). Raymond returns to New York to confront his mother and Iselin. Instead,
he is sent by his mother to assassinate Senator Jordan in his home.
While in the act, he is interrupted by a distraught Jocie and—following Yen Lo's prior instructions (to eliminate any witnesses)—he kills
her as well.

A few days later, an inconsolable Shaw calls Marco from a cheap
hotel opposite Madison Square Garden, where the convention will
be held. (In the film, it is, presumably, the 1956 convention, not, as
in the book, the convention of 1960.) Shaw tells him he's been hav-

ing the same dreams Marco described to him. Marco hustles over to the hotel, carrying a loaded deck of fifty-two red queens. Using the cards to unlock Shaw's psyche, he grills him about what really happened in Korea. (In the scene, Marco is slightly out of focus, giving the impression that we are seeing him from Raymond's point of view. In fact, Frankenheimer simply screwed up, and, when he was unable to re-create the scene to his satisfaction, decided to use the flawed take anyway.) Shaw tells Marco about the conditioning, and confesses to murdering his boss, Senator Jordan, and Jocie. Just then, they are interrupted by a phone call. It's Mrs. Iselin; Raymond should report to her for his final instructions. After Shaw hangs up, Marco gives him a contact number, and assures him he can marshal enough federal forces to prevent his mother's plan from succeeding.

Back at the Iselin residence, Mrs. Iselin unveils the plot: Two minutes into the presidential nominee's acceptance speech, Raymond, from a secure location in Madison Square Garden, is to shoot him through the head. Iselin will then rise heroically, lift the nominee's body in his arms, and address the television audiences. "Johnny will relieve those microphones and those cameras," his mother, growing increasingly excited, tells Shaw, "... rallying a nation of television viewers into hysteria, to sweep us up into the White House with powers that will make martial law seem like anarchy." After adding that she did not know her communist collaborators would choose him to be her remote-controlled assassin, she leans in and kisses him hard on the lips. It is not the incest so richly detailed in the novel, but it hardly matters—the image is shocking.

When Marco doesn't hear from Shaw, and the convention inches toward its conclusion and what Marco suspects will be the climax of the communist plot, he heads to the Garden. Looking around during the national anthem, he sees a clue: a spotlight booth, high above the main floor, remains lit while all others are dark. Instinctively, he knows: that's where Shaw is. He's right. Shaw, carrying a disassembled high-powered sniper's rifle in a small suitcase, had sneaked into the building earlier in the day by masquerading as a priest. Marco rushes to reach him before it is too late. Just before Marco gets to the booth, Shaw fires his gun, but not at the nominee.

Instead, he coolly shoots Iselin, and then his mother, both fatally through the forehead.

"You couldn't have stopped them, the army couldn't have stopped them, so I had to," he explains, as Marco throws open the door to the booth. Then Shaw, wearing his medal, turns the rifle on himself. The film ends with Marco reading from a book listing Congressional Medal of Honor winners. He improvises an entry for Shaw: "Made to commit acts too unspeakable to be cited here, by an enemy who had captured his mind and his soul. He freed himself at last and, in the end, heroically and unhesitatingly gave his life to save his country." Then Marco turns toward the window, and the screen fades to black.

It didn't take Frankenheimer long after filming had begun (on January 22, 1962, at the Goldwyn Studios in Hollywood) to realize the project might amount to something quite special. In 1998, he recalled the first day's shoot:

> I was quite nervous about [the scene in which Marco's commanding officer places the major, fraying at the edges because of his recurring nightmares, on temporary leave; the first scene filmed] . . . Frank was nervous about it, too.[53]

Neither man need have been concerned. "It took only about two hours to film the whole scene . . . Sinatra really amazed me," remembered Frankenheimer. "This was a delightful, glorious first day. It was after this scene, that I thought 'Wow, we have a real chance with this.'"[54]

By all accounts, the rest of the production went just as smoothly. On February 5, Sinatra, Harvey, Leigh, and Henry Silva (cast as Chunjin) traveled to New York for a week of on-location filming.[55] Sinatra, who had by this stage of his career acquired a reputation as being difficult to work with on a movie set, remained completely committed. "This is a suspense story, and you need a feeling of movement around the city," he explained to a *New York Times* reporter. "We have the actors we wanted—Angela Lansbury is the mother, the McCarthy character who turns out to be the villain, and Larry Harvey is perfectly cast. That's a lot going for us, so now we have to make it good."[56]

They not only made it good, they made it quickly. Six weeks later, on March 23, 1962—five days ahead of schedule[57]—principal photography wrapped. Although years later Sinatra would speak of the shoot with exceptional fondness ("I remember the wonderful enthusiasm on the part of everybody involved in the film . . . I think it only happens once in a performer's life"),[58] it is unlikely that even he could have imagined just how culturally enduring the final product would prove to be.

2

A Culture of Contradiction
Affluence and Anxiety

If John Iselin were a paid Soviet agent, he could not do more
harm to this country than he's doing now.

—*Senator Thomas Jordan (John McGiver) to*
Eleanor Iselin (Angela Lansbury)

The narrative plot of *The Manchurian Candidate*, like the fanciful
political plot residing at its center, is founded on a series of contradictions and paradoxes that are obscured behind a veil of stark, black-
and-white polarities. This is a Manichaean drama of good and evil,
to be sure, but the two are never as easily sifted as they first appear:
the anticommunist crusade *is* a communist plot, most fundamentally;
Medals of Honor are dreamed up and bestowed in treachery; good
men die at the hand of conspiracies whose existence they have
doubted; manipulators are manipulated, and assassins, assassinated.
The logical twists and reversals of *The Manchurian Candidate* are not
merely clever, but grow organically from a Cold War culture whose
own patterns of polar extremity masked an array of unsettling—if
perhaps unsettled—contradictions. Both the brilliance of the film's
satire and the resonance of its central themes derive in large part

from the tale's natural gestation, as it were, within a culture whose own unforgiving polarities were in fact paradoxical and, at moments, self-collapsing.

By "Cold War," for the moment, let us confine ourselves to the years between the mid-1940s, when "superpower" status and the epic rivalry of the United States and the Soviet Union first began to take shape, and the early 1960s, when *The Manchurian Candidate* appeared (and, significantly, when the Vietnam commitments that would later unravel Americans' Cold War consensus began to claim some dim public attention). One might point out that the U.S.–Soviet alliance during World War II was a marriage of convenience to begin with, and that the mutual dislike was expressed even during wartime—as, for example, in President Franklin D. Roosevelt's and Soviet leader Joseph Stalin's heated exchanges over when and where the United States would open up a second front against Germany, and in the tense discussions at Yalta and Potsdam over precisely what shape the post-war world might assume. A steady beat of disquieting events marked the ratcheting up of the contest in the years and decades after the war, from British Prime Minister Winston Churchill's "iron curtain" speech in Fulton, Missouri, in March 1946; to the Czech crisis of 1948; to the Soviets' unexpected atomic test, the "fall" of China, and the formation of NATO in 1949; to the Soviet invasion of Hungary and the launching of Sputnik in 1956 and 1957.[1]

But the complex of competing interests, entrenched insecurities, and institutionalized mentalities that we now know as the Cold War crystallized in 1950, upon the formulation of a national security white paper called NSC-68, and its newly expansive doctrines of global threat and national resolve. As opposed to American diplomat George Kennan's earlier notion of an anticommunist "containment" that satisfied itself with defending a few key "strongpoints" from Soviet advance, NSC-68 asserted that "the assault on free institutions is worldwide now, and in the context of the present polarization of power a defeat of free institutions anywhere is a defeat everywhere." Virtually any extension of Soviet influence, no matter where, "would raise the possibility that no coalition adequate to confront the Kremlin with greater strength could be assembled."[2] The stakes in any given contest were high indeed, historian John Lewis Gaddis points out, as "considerations of [national] image, prestige, and credibility" now entered the calculus of policy planning, and the doctrines and discourses of national security policy began vastly to multiply "the number and variety of interests deemed relevant to the national security, and to blur the distinctions between them."[3]

If NSC-68 articulated a new national resolve, then the first proving ground would be Korea. As President Harry Truman told a radio audience in September 1950, effectively translating the arcane policy universe of NSC-68 into what would become the domino logic of the American vernacular, "If aggression were allowed to succeed in Korea, it would be an open invitation to new acts of aggression elsewhere ... We cannot hope to maintain our own freedom if freedom elsewhere is wiped out."[4] Convinced that the North Korean invasion of South Korea could not have occurred without Soviet authorization, and, further, that therefore events in Korea represented a proxy contest in this much larger standoff (in their 1951 "Review of the Current World Situation," the Joint Chiefs depicted Korean hostilities as a fairly uncomplicated instance of Soviet ambition; and U.S. propaganda directed at Koreans, too, portrayed North Korean leader Kim Il Sung as a groveling Soviet slave), the Truman administration determined to meet North Korea directly and militarily.[5] Although the United States had already committed itself to a certain outcome in far-off Vietnam, it was really here, with the direct military intervention in Korea, that U.S. commitments to "national" security became truly global; it was here that "defense" became an overriding obsession and an eleven-digit budget line ($48 billion in 1951); it was here that the culture itself was mobilized and set on a permanent war footing.[6]

George Bernard Shaw once quipped that the United States was the first society in human history that had gone directly from barbarism to decadence without ever passing through a stage of civilization. The joke had a particular resonance in the postwar years. The late 1940s and the 1950s represented the nation's moment of arrival as a supreme power on the world scene, economically, culturally, politically, militarily—it was the nation's world premiere, some liked to think, as a leading civilization. Hadn't *Time* magazine founder Henry Luce, in his famous 1941 essay, confidently inaugurated an "American Century" in human affairs? And yet a range of social scientists, poets, writers, avant-garde artists, and filmmakers were expressing profound disquiet, and were already noting some disturbing signs of decline.

Cold War culture, then, was a culture of vexing contradiction. Perhaps the founding contradiction of them all was that this was a jubilant postwar period whose mood of encroaching apprehension, as the *Washington Post* reported in 1948 ("to put it bluntly") seemed more "a pre-war atmosphere."[7] As the United States and the Soviet Union squared off, in national consciousness the demise of the Axis powers quickly gave way to the emergence of new threats and World War II quickly gave way to the possibility of World War III. President Truman captured both the dire stresses of the moment and the melodramatic scripting of its rivalries in his "Truman Doctrine" speech of March 12, 1947, an effort to secure both congressional and popular backing for the anticommunist struggles then taking place in Greece and Turkey:

> At the present moment in world history nearly every nation must choose between alternative ways of life. The choice is often not a free one. One way of life is based on the will of the majority, and is distinguished by free institutions, representative government, free elections, guarantees of individual liberty, freedom of speech and religion, and freedom from political repression. The second way of life is based upon the will of a minority forcibly imposed upon the majority. It relies upon terror and oppression, a controlled press and radio, fixed elections, and the suppression of personal freedoms. I believe that it must be the policy of the United States to support free peoples who are resisting attempted subjugation by armed minorities or outside pressures.[8]

Ironically, then, so high were the perceived stakes in the coming war that this was a period in which repression was widely accepted as the price to be paid for freedom. Precisely because of its life-and-death rivalry with an unfree enemy, the nation embarked upon an energetic campaign to crush perceived subversions of every kind. We tend to remember the harsh lights of the McCarthy hearings; but the House Un-American Activities Committee (HUAC), headed by Martin Dies and then J. Parnell Thomas, had been issuing subpoenas and grilling witnesses since 1938, long before Joseph McCarthy burst onto the scene; and that "ism" devised by the Wisconsin senator owed its long leash and its extraordinary political teeth to the era's already revised definitions of "sedition," already narrowed notions of legitimate dissent, innovations in surveillance already developed within J. Edgar Hoover's FBI, and the security and loyalty programs already put in place by Truman. In 1946 Truman had instructed Hoover to make a top priority of potential "subversion" within the federal bureaucracy; a year later he issued an executive order establishing a Temporary Commission on Employee Loyalty (likely in response to Republican charges). Now "membership in, affiliation with, or sympathetic association with any foreign or domestic organization, association, movement, group or combination of persons designated by the Attorney General as totalitarian, fascist, communist, or subversive" would be weighed in the assessment of any federal employee's "loyalty." The power which the order granted the attorney general in developing his list, as well as the breadth of illicit activities implied in phrases like "affiliation" and "sympathetic association," convey a great deal about the degree of restriction which Americans would tolerate in the name of defending their freedoms. Between World War II and the end of the Vietnam era, the FBI alone employed more than thirty-seven thousand informers to report on the activities of American citizens.[9]

This was a period that also placed an impossible premium on both individualism and conformism. Individual liberty was said to set American society apart from the totalitarianisms of either left or right—indeed, it made America exceptional in all of human history, it was the hallmark of national superiority. And yet, as embodied by the fads, the styles, the suburban rhythms, and the politics of the time, the weight of social convention and the imperatives of conformity were severe. "The forces of the times," lamented social critic Vance Packard, "seem to be conspiring to squeeze individuality and spontaneity from us."[10] The "standard operating procedure" in the postwar rat race, according to the protagonist in Sloan Wilson's *Man in the Gray Flannel Suit* (1955), was "a little like reading fortunes. You make a lot of highly qualified contradictory statements and keep your eyes on the man's face to see which ones please him. That way you can feel your way along, and if you're clever, you can always end up by telling him exactly what he wants to hear." Once his "business education" is complete, he remarks, "I'll be able to suspend judgment entirely until I learn what [the boss] thinks, and then I'll really and truly feel the way he does. That way I won't have to be dishonest anymore."[11]

Despite the nation's self-flattering and self-congratulatory discourse of liberty and individualism, sociologist William H. Whyte Jr. charted the rise of a new political animal, "the organization man":

> The corporation man is the most conspicuous example, but he is only one, for the collectivization so visible in the corporation has affected almost every field of work. Blood brother to the business trainee off to join Du Pont is the seminary student who will end up in the church hierarchy, the doctor headed for the corporate clinic, the physics Ph.D. in a government laboratory, the intellectual on the foundation-sponsored team project, the engineering graduate in a huge drafting room at Lockheed, the young apprentice in a Wall Street law factory... Listen to them talk to each other over the front lawns of their suburbia and you cannot help but be struck by how well they grasp the common denominators which bind them... The word *collective* most of them can't bring themselves to use—except to describe foreign countries or organizations they don't work for—but they are keenly aware of how much more deeply beholden they are to organization than were their elders. They are wry about it, to be sure; they talk about the "treadmill," the "rat race," of the inability to control one's direction. But they have no great sense of plight.[12]

Whyte went on, with an extraordinary directness, to insist that "the Bill of Rights should not stop at the organization's edge," and to warn that, while the organization might indeed insist on the individual's "superlative work... it should not ask for his psyche as well."[13] "Organization impersonalizes all it touches," warned historian Arthur Schlesinger Jr.; and "if organization corrupts, total organization corrupts totally." The postwar order's new economies of scale, its new depths of mass production and mass organization, in Schlesinger's view, had taken "the guts out of the idea of property. The basis in day-to-day experience of private property and of the free contract has disappeared." At worst this presaged a kind of "capitalist suicide," threatening death to the very liberation that was capitalism's genius. Sociologist C. Wright Mills saw the new "white collar" men as "cogs in a business machinery that has routinized greed and made aggression an impersonal principle of organization."[14] David Riesman, likewise, summed up the herdlike conformity and the social atomization of American life in this period in the evocative shorthand *The Lonely Crowd* (1950). This was the "comfortable, smooth, reasonable, democratic unfreedom" with which Frankfort School philosopher Herbert Marcuse would later begin his critique *One-Dimensional Man* (1964).[15]

It was further a period whose unbounded material wealth, some feared, was equaled only by its boundless spiritual poverty. The United States, alone among the major combatants, had emerged from the war virtually unscathed in its productive capacity, its infrastructure, its ability to get goods to market. On the contrary, the war had been a "technological piñata" for the United States, in John McPhee's apt phrase, whose loosing of creativity, production, and scale now poised the nation for a new economic epoch.[16] The American Dream seemed to be coming true, in material terms, and yet a number of observers in the arts, the social sciences, and the clergy worried over signs of inner rootlessness and crass materialism. As Packard had it, Americans possessed a "packaged soul." Industrialism, wrote Schlesinger, "has burned up the mortgage, but at the same time sealed us in a subtler slavery. It has created wealth and comfort in undreamed-of abundance. But in the wake of its incomparable economic achievement it has left the thin, deadly trail of anxiety." Anonymity, standardization, and emptiness were among the "savage wounds" that advanced industrial development had inflicted on the human sensibility.[17] Beat poet Allen Ginsberg, for his part, decried America's "Robot apartments. Invisible suburbs. Skeleton treasuries."[18]

Nor, indeed, was the dark side of affluence spiritual only: as economist John Kenneth Galbraith memorably wrote in *The Affluent Society* (1958):

> The family which takes its mauve and cerise, air-conditioned, power-steered and power-braked automobile out for a tour passes through cities that are badly paved, made hideous by litter, blighted buildings, billboards and posts for wires that should long since have been put underground. They pass on into a countryside that has been rendered largely invisible by commercial art. (The goods which the latter advertise have an absolute priority in our value system. Such aesthetic considerations as a view of the countryside accordingly come second. On such matters we are consistent.) They picnic on exquisitely packaged food from a portable icebox by a polluted stream and go on to spend the night at a park which is a menace to public health and

morals. Just before dozing off on an air mattress, beneath a nylon tent, amid the stench of decaying refuse, they may reflect vaguely on the curious unevenness of their blessings. Is this, indeed, the American genius?[19]

It was a period in which, having weathered the all-too-public commitments of the war years, massive numbers of Americans re-treated to the private sanctuary of hearth and home—a newly *priva-tized* sanctuary for many, in fact, given the rise of the postwar suburb and its demographic formula of nuclear families ensconced in row upon row of single-family dwellings. Hence the baby boom. But so too was this a period when, ironically, the "private" took on an increas-ingly *public* significance nonetheless. If the "fight against communism settled into the cultural bones" of the nation, as political scientist James Morone puts it, the very marrow of this emergent Cold War politics was in the "private" realm of motherhood, fatherhood, family values, and procreative heterosexuality as at once the creation and the rigorous defense of a new, patriotic "normal." "In America the family is in special trouble," warned J. Edgar Hoover. "Unfortunately the home no longer provides the inspiration for right living," and the consequence was nothing less than a "juvenile jungle." Children "need the firm moral backing of . . . a good Christian home," he said. "Strong morals" are the *"major obstacles in the path of communist prog-ress."*[20] Under such a regime of cultural mobilization, remarks histo-rian Elaine Tyler May, "Domesticity was not so much a retreat from public affairs as an expression of one's citizenship."[21] The Cold War battlefield extended outward to every corner of the globe, but also in-ward to hearth and home: private sanctity was public duty. In this con-nection one of the greatest "national security" threats on the scene, according to tracts like Philip Wylie's *Generation of Vipers* (1942), was the overweening American "mom," whose smothering protec-tiveness threatened to neuter an entire generation of American boys.[22]

And finally, in this catalog of contradictions, the era was deeply touched by both the undeniable promise and the Promethean men-ace of modern technology. There were ranch-style houses with well-appointed kitchens; there were ostentatious cars, gaudily chromed and finned; there were TVs, hi-fi's, neon jukeboxes—all the things that would prove to the Soviets, in Dwight Eisenhower's estimation,

Vice President Richard Nixon and Soviet Premier Nikita Khrushchev during the famous "kitchen debate" in Sokolniki Park, Moscow. The relative merits of the superpowers' competing systems came down to a question of color television sets and kitchen appliances. (Corbis)

that the American worker "is not the downtrodden, impoverished vassal of whom Karl Marx wrote." But there was also the bomb. Even within a week of Japan's surrender in 1945, newsman Edward R. Murrow noted that "seldom, if ever, has a war ended leaving the victors with such a sense of uncertainty and fear, with such a realization that the future is obscure and that survival is not assured."[23]

The American Dream, it turned out, would be defended by a policy of Mutually Assured Destruction and punctuated by periodic civil-defense drills. Here again, Galbraith warned that, although "Western man has indeed escaped for the moment the poverty which was for so long his all-embracing fate," still the "unearthly light of a handful of nuclear explosions would signal his return to utter deprivation if . . . he survived at all." Nor, for Galbraith, did the new affluence and the new terror simply *coincide* at a particular historical moment: rather, "the weapons culture which underlies the macroeconomic stabilization of the economy... plays a deeply functional role in underwriting technology." Since a market-driven "consumer goods economy is limited in the resources it can allocate to research and development," the United States had come to depend on the "weapons industry to [sustain] such effort on a vastly greater scale."[24] Critic Dwight Macdonald, too, saw the bomb as "a natural product of the kind of society we have created. It is as easy, normal and unforced an expression of the American Way of Life as electric ice-boxes, banana splits, and hydromatic-drive automobiles."[25] The good life and unthinkable death were strangely one and the same. So fitting, then, that one of the era's most intriguing and public political debates on the relative merits of the world's two competing giants—between Soviet Premier Nikita Khrushchev and Vice President Richard Nixon—should take place in an exposition mock-up of a modern American kitchen.[26]

These currents and crosscurrents of thought and feeling influenced American cultural production of all sorts—the visual arts, film, drama, literature, popular forms like television and comic books, and nonfiction genres like social-science literature (Whyte's *Organization Man* and Galbraith's *Affluent Society*, to name two). In this context of contradiction and uncertainty, *anxiety* was among the dominant themes in cultural and artistic expression—"the official emotion of our time," as Schlesinger put it.[27] On one level, Americans experienced a political anxiety about the fragility of liberty and the onslaught of totalitarianism; and on another, a broadly social anxiety about the postwar transformations of American life and the perceived human costs of the new affluence.

Most pronounced was the widespread political anxiety regarding the communist threat itself, as the dramatic polarities of the Truman Doctrine speech quickly became commonplaces in the American worldview. Leftist ideologies by definition represented "attempts at subjugation"; and they imperiled the United States by their capacity to gnaw from within or to encircle from without. In the realm of politics proper, anticommunist vigilance played out in the HUAC and McCarthy hearings and in State Department purges; internationally it played out in proxy wars on battlefields from Korea to Guatemala to Cuba to Vietnam. In the realm of American *culture*, meanwhile, stark Cold War visions and their underlying anxieties surfaced in popular films such as *Invaders from Mars* (1953) and *Invasion of the Body Snatchers* (1956), in which the United States is subjugated by enemies who are literally alien; *My Son John* (1952), in which the boy next door turns out to be a red; or *The Caine Mutiny* (1954), a protracted meditation on questions of loyalty and duplicity, directed by one of the persecuted filmmakers of the blacklist era, Edward Dmytryk, a member of the Hollywood Ten.

A second political anxiety of the time—actually a shadow of the first—was a suspicion of the threat that anticommunism *itself* posed to real Americanism and to individual liberties. The abuse of congressional rights on the part of HUAC, according to Schlesinger, "has done much to discredit one of democracy's most valuable instruments."[28] Others went further still. In a 1949 *Atlantic Monthly* article, Archibald MacLeish predicted that some future historian would look back on the late 1940s and see nothing less than "the conquest of the United States by the Russians." But the conquest he predicted was not at all what so many Americans had braced themselves for. Rather, it was a de facto subjugation founded upon Americans' obsession with the communist threat to the virtual exclusion of everything else. "Never in the history of the world," writes MacLeish's imaginary historian, looking back from some distant future, "was one people as completely dominated, morally and intellectually, as the U.S. by Russia." American policies—both foreign and domestic—were crafted according to "a kind of upside-down Russian veto": nothing could be done, no one could be elected, no proposal could go through, unless it was first demonstrated that the Russians would not like it. Nor was this debilitating obsession confined to the realm of the strictly political. MacLeish's fancied historian went on to describe how writers had stopped writing in order to convene massive colloquiums on Russia and the Russians, until the very substance of American culture became a ponderous reflection on the problem of Russian culture. Even religious dogma was Russian dogma turned about: the first duty of the Christian was not to love his enemy, but to hate the communists (yet also to pray for them, if at all possible).[29]

This kind of anti-anticommunist anxiety was neither as common nor as freely expressed as anticommunism itself; but one recognizes

A docile and herdlike populace looks on as a televised authority declares martial law in *Them!* (1954). However anticommunist in intent, science-fiction and other B movies from the period often betrayed a creeping unease with the unprecedented powers of the national security state.

this current not only in anti-McCarthyite productions like Arthur Miller's *The Crucible* (which drew on the precedent of the Salem witch trials to explore issues of suspicion and persecution), but in far less "serious" modes of cultural work: *My Son John,* for example, whose depiction of the totality of the FBI's surveillance apparatus conveys a creeping disquiet, even despite the film's pronounced anticommunism; or even a science-fiction B feature like *Them!* (1954), in which Americans repulse an invading army of giant ants by becoming entirely antlike themselves—regimented, soulless, mechanical, and submissive to authority. The pre-battle scene, when a docile public watches a cavalcade of military vehicles stream by in the street before them just as a televised "authority" announces the imposition of martial law from a department-store window behind them, remains one of the most ghoulish visions of state power in the history of this democracy's cinema. Even if the film never fully relinquishes its faith in the state, *Them!* is nonetheless a muted fable of authority and governance whose titanic, Manichaean struggles can never be as cleanly emplotted as it initially appears: 1954 turns out to be, as the closing line proclaims, "later than you think"—a mere stone's throw from *1984*—and almost in spite of itself the film suggests that perhaps the greatest menace of all is not *Them* but *Us*.[30]

The vortex of frankly political anxieties swept the "high" arts as well. By the 1940s, artistic production itself had become overtly and increasingly politicized: on the one hand, many Depression-era visual artists had been active in the Popular Front left, and had long identified art as an important venue for political expression; and, on the other hand, an array of critics, curators, and even government officials had seized upon art for political purposes of their own. During the war, for instance, one Museum of Modern Art bulletin described the museum's collection as "a symbol of the four freedoms for which we are fighting—the freedom of expression."[31]

Such concerns carried easily into the Cold War period: in the highly charged climate of the postwar years, amid fierce political crosswinds, could any work of art claim neutrality? The growing experimentation with Abstract Expressionism, some have argued, was in part a response to precisely these conditions: proletarian realism, which had been popular before the war, was now politically dangerous; "safer" genres, like regionalism, were ripe for co-optation by propagandistic nationalism. Naturalism, as Dwight Macdonald averred, was "no longer adequate, either esthetically or morally, to cope with the modern horrors." Abstraction represented an attempt, as one critic put it at the time, "to hang around in the space between art and political action."[32] But abstraction, as it turned out, could be pressed into the service of Cold War doctrine, with or without the artist's consent. Although the abstract aesthetic might indeed suggest something subversive, cold warriors recognized in it a perfect example of precisely what made America great: its commitment to individualized expression. The U.S. Information Agency and even the CIA self-consciously adopted abstract art as a weapon in the war for the hearts and minds of Europe, sponsoring and mounting several international tours of Abstract Expressionism as a traveling commercial for both a freedom and a genius that were said to be distinctly American.[33]

All of which is simply to emphasize how thoroughly politicized the culture had become during the Cold War years—how thoroughly various cultural forms had been mobilized around questions of communism and anticommunism, liberty and tyranny. But in addition to these overtly political currents, American culture in this period also embodied a sneaking suspicion that, politics aside, the nation's economic triumph was *itself* giving birth to a new brand of tyranny. In his influential tract on Cold War liberalism, *The Vital Center* (1949), Schlesinger described "totalitarian man" as "tight-lipped, cold-eyed, unfeeling, uncommunicative . . . as if badly carved from wood, without humor, without tenderness, without spontaneity, without nerves."[34] In retrospect, one of the striking features of American culture at the height of the Cold War is the frequent misgiving expressed by various commentators that Americans, too, were becoming, essentially, "tight-lipped, cold-eyed, unfeeling, uncommunicative . . . as if badly carved from wood." Thus it was, for instance, that a film like *Invasion of the Body Snatchers* could play so deliciously upon the interchangeability of alien pods with suburban Americans.

The toys that came tumbling out of the technological piñata of World War II were as troubling in some respects as they were bedazzling and even liberating in others. Along with the consumer goods, the information and communication technologies, the advances in transportation, the innovations in the area of mass amusement, came a "postindustrial" order based on bureaucratization on an unprecedented scale—a bureaucratization, as Whyte pointed out, that engulfed and transfigured huge sectors of the national economy, including the corporation, the professions, the knowledge industries such as publishing and the modern university, the research sciences, government, and the military along with its mushrooming array of consultive, intelligence, and research-and-development agencies. The result of this economic transformation was not simply a new way of working, some now remarked, but a new way of *being* in the world. Riesman's *Lonely Crowd* was one response to the rising order: individuals were no longer stayed by an inner moral and intellectual ballast, but had become "other-directed"—their work was routinized, and the people themselves had become anxiety-driven, hyperalert to outside cues, politically indifferent, and easily tyrannized in being so utterly naive to everyday tyrannies. The individualism that had governed social life for most of the nation's history, Whyte concurred, no longer squared with economic realities.

So, while the right and what remained of the left might worry over the fate of the individual in an era of Stalinist or McCarthyite authoritarianism (depending on one's view), a slightly muted but no less urgent discussion was taking shape regarding the fate of an individual who had quietly become fettered by postwar affluence and the postindustrial economic order that created and sustained it. The constraints of the moment generated their own opposition, not just in social criticism by people like Riesman, Whyte, Mills, or Betty Friedan, but also in the protests of the Beat poets, for instance, or in the mass nonconformism of early rock and roll. Alienation, in fact, became a staple of cultural expression right alongside anxiety. Individuality in crisis indeed marked the culture—high, low, and middle—in recurring motifs of isolation and fragmentation; in the blending of the mechanistic with the organic; in alternating evocations of violence, ennui, and imprisonment. Clearly, there are psychodynamic dimensions to the anxiety and alienation treated in works like Ginsberg's epic *Howl* (1956), Paul Goodman's *Growing Up Absurd* (1962), Friedan's *The Feminine Mystique* (1963), or Bob Dylan's "The Times They Are A-Changin'" (1964); but broad, structural features of American culture united an array of artists and commentators in their concern for individuality in the face of mass commodification, humanity in the face of technological progress, critical insight in the face of stultifying comfort, and political acuity in the face of repression and popular complacency. Sculptor David Smith was perhaps conveying as much about the culture at large as he was about his own personal vision when he wrote of a landscape filled with "things I desire and despise." John Steinbeck, returning to the United States in 1959 after a long absence, remarked, too, "If I wanted to destroy a nation I would give it too much, and I would have it on its knees, miserable, greedy, and sick."[35]

The Manchurian Candidate certainly does not share in the spaciousness or the opulence (however unsettled) of many classic Cold War narratives—one thinks precisely of Ginsberg's "invisible suburbs," Nixon's model ranch kitchen in Moscow, or the inhumanly manicured lawns of *Invasion of the Body Snatchers*. On the contrary, the film is dark and claustrophobic throughout, its coloration more gothic than postindustrial. The point here is not to depict either Richard

Condon's novel or John Frankenheimer's film as a direct expression of the identical social visions and anxieties that surfaced across the genres, from Schlesinger's *Vital Center*, to Whyte's *Organization Man*, to Wilson's *Man in the Gray Flannel Suit*, to Ginsberg's *Howl*, to Fred Sears's sci-fi film, *Earth vs. the Flying Saucers* (1956). Rather, it is to paint Cold War culture in general as a culture deeply structured in contradiction, and to situate *The Manchurian Candidate* as an extraordinary exemplar of *that*.

The Manchurian Candidate does offer provocative meditations on some of the common, vexed themes of the age: the text's meditations on the familial/national drama of "proper" lines of authority and allegiance (the perversely matriarchal Iselin family) or on the lost idyll of a truly "private" sphere (Raymond's short-lived romance with Jocie), as we shall see, align it with a variety of Cold War texts, from *My Son John* to *Generation of Vipers*. But most striking, finally, is not the text's fossilizations of this or that Cold War theme, but rather its bedrock rendering of—one wants to say *reveling in*—the era's peculiar, even uniquely developed, realm of social and political paradox.

What does the film say, finally? Where does it sink its hooks? The film's core paradox, of course, is that the communist threat and the anticommunist witch hunt—the structuring opposition of Cold War politics and sensibility—turn out to be one and the same. The declarative logic of the film is thus something like the visual trickery of a Nekar Cube, that simple line drawing that appears at first glance to be oriented down and to the right, and on second, up and to the left. Does *The Manchurian Candidate* indict McCarthyism, or vindicate it? Both the ACLU and the John Birch Society could find their strongest warnings ratified here. When Senator Jordan declares that, "if John Iselin were a paid Soviet agent, he could not do more harm to this country than he's doing now," he is recapitulating a most powerful— and common—denunciation of McCarthyism. The missing piece in Jordan's mental jigsaw is that Iselin *is* the wedge of the imminent Soviet takeover that Jordan himself does not suspect. If McCarthy is both the figure of the communist fifth column *and* the nation's lone anticommunist Cassandra, then his detractors, like Jordan, lay claim to both righteous vindication and grievous—and deadly—misperception. Jordan will be murdered by a conspiracy whose existence he would "spend every cent I own and all I could borrow" to deny—which just goes to show how right he was in his distrust of Iselin. This foundational paradox speaks directly to the submerged Cold War anxiety that *Them!* had merely hinted at.

But this is but one in a series of paradoxes that structure the movement of *The Manchurian Candidate*. The vexing question of American superiority or inferiority, for example, also haunted the period and the film: if the country is really so far superior to all the world's known alternatives—in its animating commitment to liberty, its technological ingenuity, and the genius of its free-market organization—then how can it possibly lose a global competition to a two-bit dictatorship like the Soviet Union? Are not the very notions of "American superiority" and "Soviet threat" incompatible, in that the "threat" posed by one implies the possible *inferiority* of the other, in some dimension or another? In *The Manchurian Candidate* this ambiguity is mapped as an ambiguous geography of evil—Manchuria itself, first of all, a Sino-Soviet frontier whose hazy contours only cloud the issue of the locus of villainy; but not Manchuria alone, but rather Manchuria *plus its American operatives*. Like those earlier American myths that Sitting Bull actually had white ancestry and a Harvard education, the "threat" gathered here is threatening precisely because of American superiority: Soviet and Chinese leaders might contribute their particular brands of villainy—the one "red," and the other, chiefly, "yellow"—but without the steely genius of American participation all this villainy would come to naught.

And so, also like the Sitting Bull myths, this rendition of villainy is mapped racially as well as geographically. As one Eisenhower administration official put it, "I always thought the Yellow Peril business was nonsense...Now I can visualize that Asiatics teamed up with Slavs could indeed conquer the world!" Or again, during the Korean War one U.S. general spoke of the "typical Mongol-Slav manner" by which North Korea dealt with prisoners.[36] *The Manchurian Candidate* makes the most of such racializations, overlaying its portrait of communist machination with a brand of Orientalized villainy whose roots in American culture run even deeper. "I can see that Chinese cat standing there smiling like Fu Manchu," says Marco, beginning to recall the Manchurian brainwashing operation. But the circuitry could not be complete without the steady nerve of the white American—the "Anglo-Saxon," as Condon put it in his novel: "If a normally conditioned Anglo-Saxon could be taught to kill and kill, then to have no memory of having killed . . . he could feel no guilt." Such a killer would "remain an outwardly normal, productive, sober, and respectful member of his community"—as one of Raymond Shaw's "handlers" puts it, nearly "police proof." "Normal, productive, [and] sober," here, are traits that are keyed to the designation "Anglo-Saxon," just as Eleanor Iselin's icy reliability as an operative is rooted in her "Norse" character, by Condon's account.[37] Typical "Mongol-Slav" treachery may author this campaign, in other words, but its ultimate success depends on significant doses of "Anglo-Saxon" and "Norse." When pitted against its own superiority, America may indeed be in trouble.

This racialized alliance of the Soviet Berezovo, the Chinese Dr. Yen Lo, and Eleanor Iselin (ingeniously, stand-ins for a fanciful alliance of Stalin, Mao, and McCarthy) raises yet another spectral paradox: when it comes to pressing psychological questions of autonomy and control, Manchurian brainwashing and American-style public relations (embodied chiefly in Iselin's McCarthyesque media manipulations) are of a piece: Madison Avenue and the Pavlov Institute are joined at the hip. The term "brainwashing" had entered Americans' popular lexicon precisely during the Korean War, via *Saturday Evening Post*, *Life*, and *New Yorker* accounts of more specialized tomes like *Brain-washing in Red China: The Calculated Destruction of Men's Minds* (1951).[38] But so had the American public become recently attuned to *capitalist* efforts in thought control—an unholy marriage of psychiatry and marketing, Madison Avenue's new "depth probers of merchandising," as Packard called them, whose "extreme attempts at probing and manipulating" minds had brought us "from the genial world of James Thurber into the chilling world of George Orwell." In this new media universe, one University of Michigan analyst had warned, "A world of unseen dictatorship is conceivable, still using the forms of democratic government."[39] In this respect, *The Manchurian Candidate* repays a close reading against both *Brain-washing in Red China* and *The Hidden Persuaders*. The technologies of the "free market" themselves threaten a new totalitarianism.

Which brings us back to the fate of the beleaguered individual: Packard's "manipulated" consumer, Riesman's hapless specimen of "other-directedness," Whyte's "organization man," Mills's "cog" in the corporate machine, Wilson's "man in the gray flannel suit," Schlesinger's poorly carved "totalitarian man"—Raymond Shaw, passing the time by playing a little solitaire. When Bennett Marco reads the citation for Shaw's Medal of Honor at the close of the film (now that Shaw has in fact earned it), we are confronted anew with the unsettling fact of the automaton as hero. That the protagonist is likely to be an automaton in this era Packard, Riesman, and Whyte have already explained. But does an automaton have to be the *hero*? Evidently so, and this is the final contradiction for an age whose official moods are anxiety and alienation. "You couldn't have stopped them, the army couldn't have stopped them," Raymond tells Marco after he has turned his sniper's rifle on his mother and Johnny Iselin. "So I had to." The strange truth is that freedom can only be rescued by the enslaved, humanity by the dehumanized, America by the Soviet-controlled assassin. No one else possesses the necessary power. When Raymond dons his medal of distinction, all other distinctions—the distinctions between free will and total surrender, and between the nature of the two superpowers, for example—hopelessly blur.

If Condon and Frankenheimer had not bequeathed us *The Manchurian Candidate* as a document of mid-century sensibilities, then surely we would have had to invent it: the film at once embodies and critiques the dominant Cold War ethos in such a way as to render it uniquely legible. Cultural historian Tom Engelhardt has commented that the film comes across today "not as tense, dark, anti-Communist melodrama, but as outright camp." No one watching the brainwashing scene today, argues Engelhardt, "could doubt that the anti-Communist story was [by 1962] in tatters, or that the very idea of 'brainwashing,' taken quite seriously in the wake of the Korean War, could no longer carry its cultural weight."[40] On the contrary, what is most striking in screenings of *The Manchurian Candidate* for a twenty-first century audience is how well the film plays on two distinct planes: as "outright camp," to be sure, but in equal measure as straight thriller. In its rendering of a besotted McCarthy or of Yen Lo's imagined transformation into a frumpy New Jersey matron, the film presents itself as too intelligent to be taken in by the Cold War's platitudes or its melodramatic simplifications. This is undoubtedly what Frankenheimer and screenwriter George Axelrod were referring to when, in a 1988 interview, they adamantly insisted that the film was not reflexively "anti-Soviet."[41] But other elements—its Orientalism, for example, or the perverse iciness of Angela Lansbury's Eleanor Iselin and the seamless weave of matters political and sexual—invite us to read the film as a "straight" Cold War expression nonetheless. *The Manchurian Candidate* seems to emanate at once from within and without Cold War culture—it both plumbs and reflects.

Engelhardt notwithstanding, at most screenings even today some members of the audience gasp or groan audibly when Raymond shoots Thomas and Jocie Jordan, and most sit riveted through the assassination scene until the final credits roll. One suspects that the film retains this kind of power not only because of its remarkable narrative technique, but precisely because so many of its vexing social and political contradictions are still alive and in play. Today's audiences invariably laugh when Raymond commands Jocie to "make like a housewife"; but in fact there is little else in the film that strikes quite this register. Where the formerly serious strikes us as funny ("make like a housewife") or the formerly funny strikes us as serious (a racist stereotype in a 1930s comedy, say), we are seeing social change right before our eyes. What *The Manchurian Candidate*'s enduring power to entrance seems to indicate, then, is significant social *continuity*.

Politically, for one thing, the Cold War has rolled over with disturbing ease into the War on Terror. "There is no more exciting time in which to live," wrote Schlesinger at the onset of the Cold War, "—no time more crucial or more tragic. We must recognize that this is the nature of our age: that the womb has irrevocably closed behind us, that security is a foolish dream of old men, that crisis will always be with us."[42] Perhaps every generation has felt its own legitimate version of this, from antiquity on down. But in the era of the ICBM its salience was, shall we say, impressive; the era of the box cutter and the suicide bomber has only made it more so. In its very discomfort, Schlesinger's statement comfortably characterizes the American prospect in all but a few of the years between 1949, when he uttered it, and the early twenty-first century—perhaps only the eyeblink between the fall of the Berlin Wall and the first Gulf War being exempted. Certainly in the post-9/11 era, Schlesinger's words, two generations stale, ring like a pronouncement from this very day's punditry. Which is only to suggest that, in their endless and epic encounters around the globe, Americans have been beautifully situated for many decades to be transfixed—either in skepticism or in fear—by the kind of political melodrama depicted in *The Manchurian Candidate*.

But more profoundly, the strictly political shades off toward the more broadly psychosocial—and here, perhaps, is where *The Manchurian Candidate* exercises most its continued hold over the modern American imagination. Americans' point of pride in the U.S.–Soviet rivalry—just as in the U.S.–Islamic conflict, as a matter of fact—is in being a self-governing democracy as opposed to a dictatorship or a theocracy; but this, ironically, in a social and technological setting where it is nearly impossible to feel "self-governing" at all; for if Schlesinger gave voice to the political concerns of a generation in perpetual political crisis, so too did he notice the more generalized structures of "modernity," the substrate of modern discontent, and their portent for the pursuit of happiness. "Industrialism," he wrote,

> is the benefactor and the villain of our time: it has burned up the mortgage, but at the same time sealed us in a subtler slavery. It has created wealth and comfort in undreamed-of abundance. But in the wake of its incomparable economic achievement it has left the thin, deadly trail of anxiety. The connecting fluids of industrial society begin to dry up; the seams harden and crack; and society is transformed into a parched desert, "a heap of broken images, where the sun beats, and the dead tree gives no shelter, the cricket no relief, and the dry stone no sound of water"—that state of social purgatory which Durkheim called "anomie" and where Eliot saw fear in a handful of dust.[43]

The Manchurian Candidate is not exactly about "industrialism," but it does speak to precisely this world of hardened tissues and broken images—subtle enslavements. It is about distinctively modern struggles over individual agency and free will, about governance and the mass, about baffled attempts to compose one's own thoughts and actions, and about our vain, impossibly gauzed glimpses at "truth" in a world not just of deceit or intrigue, but a world whose chief episteme is mediation of one sort or another *from without*. The Cold War has closed—merely a chapter, it turns out, in a more enduring epic which Schlesinger called "industrialism" but which our current political crisis might prompt us to label "the age of petroleum," a shorthand as workable for our ozone-ripping lifeways as for our proprietary geopolitics. Some of Bennett Marco and Raymond Shaw's dire dilemmas reflect not just Cold War culture, but the deep contradictions of this longer enduring epoch as well.

3

Five from the Fifties

Threat, Containment, and the Rise of the
Security State in Postwar Film

I tell you there's a bomb here, a time bomb, that's just waiting
to go off.

—*Bennett Marco to Colonel Milt (Douglas Henderson)*

Where does *The Manchurian Candidate* come from, other than the
fertile imaginations of Condon, Axelrod, and Frankenheimer? Greil
Marcus, for his part, sums up—really, almost dismisses—the film as
consisting of "bits and pieces of Hitchcock and Orson Welles, of *Psycho*
and *Citizen Kane*, most obviously—perhaps less obviously, but more
completely, taking *Invasion of the Body Snatchers* out of science fiction
and returning it to history."[1]

While pegging *Psycho* (and, one assumes, Norman Bates's overheated identification with his mother) as a main source of inspiration
may be taking these things too literally, Marcus is not entirely wrong.
As we will see in chapter 7, a close reading of the train scene in
which Marco and Rosie meet, Hitchcock's influence, stylistically and
ideologically, can be felt throughout.[2] And, true, *The Manchurian Candidate* is indebted to several movies of the era—*Invasion of the Body
Snatchers* among them—but not, as Marcus's breezy description sug-

gests, by way of pilfering an image here or an idea there. If Richard
Condon's novel was a highly aware work—consciously contemplat-
ing the mass-mediated quality of American life in the mid-twentieth
century—John Frankenheimer's film adaptation would appear to be
no less aware of its cinematic antecedents.

Certainly, the case could be made that no other film of the era is
quite like *The Manchurian Candidate*, but it very clearly reaches out,
both symbolically and more directly, to an assortment of cinematic
texts that in the previous decade had helped construct the idea of
the Cold War in the popular imagination. Five films, in particular,
stand out: Elia Kazan's *Panic in the Streets* (1950), Leo McCarey's *My
Son John* (1952), Lewis Allen's *Suddenly* (1954), Robert Aldrich's *Kiss
Me Deadly* (1955), and Don Siegel's *Invasion of the Body Snatchers*
(1956). Individually, each contributes cinematic DNA to *The Manchurian Candidate*: The sight of Dr. Clinton Reed (Richard Widmark)
running around New Orleans in his U.S. Public Health Service uniform, trying to find the carrier of a deadly plague (in *Panic in the
Streets*), for example, very much anticipates that other governmental
organization man, Bennett Marco, racing through Madison Square
Garden, trying to reach Raymond Shaw before he "goes off." Other
generic fragments leap out: the figure of the alienated son (Robert
Walker) in *My Son John*; the icy, emotionless stares of the pod people
in *Invasion of the Body Snatchers*; in *Suddenly*, would-be assassin John
Baron (played, ironically, by none other than Frank Sinatra) perched
high atop the spot where the president is scheduled to appear; the
mysterious femme fatale (Gaby Rodgers) who holds the key to the
mystery in *Kiss Me Deadly*.

Collectively, these films construct a world in which things and
people are not as they appear, there are both internal and external
threats to the family, secrecy is a powerful state apparatus, and the
fate of the republic forever hangs in the balance; indeed, such is the
case in all five films, though the threat (plague, treason, presidential
assassination, atomic annihilation, alien invasion) differs from film
to film. Although no five films can fully represent the era, consider
the range of genres here: the social problem film, the detective film,
science fiction, and film noir, all staples of the 1950s. *The Manchurian
Candidate*, in its ambitions, effectively mined those diverse genres,

and, more than any single film, channeled, reworked, and critiqued the ethos and anxieties of the period. Like the "time bomb" Marco warns about, the cultural and creative impulses that would ultimately produce *The Manchurian Candidate* had been long in the making.

Panic in the Streets (1950)

Elia Kazan's *Panic in the Streets* is not, on its surface, about geopolitics or questions of national security. Instead, the plot of the film revolves around the threat posed by a plague loosed on the city of New Orleans. Dr. Clinton Reed, with the U.S. Public Health Service, is called in to perform an autopsy on a man—of "Armenian, Czech, or mixed blood"—found shot to death on the city's docks. Reed determines that, the immediate cause of death notwithstanding, the man suffered from pneumonic plague, a variant, he warns civic leaders, of the "Black Death" of the Middle Ages.

Reed pleads with city officials and a police department skeptical of his diagnosis to find the killers, since he believes it's likely they've been contaminated with the plague and will begin spreading it in forty-eight hours. Teamed with a hard-boiled plainclothes policeman named Warren (Paul Douglas), who thinks the doctor's sensational diagnosis may be more indebted to Reed's desire for career advancement than medical science ("Why shouldn't I believe you, doctor?" Warren asks Reed. "You're a smart fella, a college man. You probably wouldn't make something out of nothing just to be important."), the good doctor quickly strikes out on his own. Immersing himself in the city's underclass—in ethnic restaurants, tenements, and waterfront bars—he manages, with the eventual help of Warren, to wheedle, coax, and threaten leads out of members of New Orleans's Eastern European immigrant community.

In the end, Reed and Warren trace the murder to a local hood named Blackie (Jack Palance), cornering him on the docks at the port of New Orleans. Blackie tries to escape by stowing away on a ship bound for sea. Working his way up the mooring, he makes it as far as the hawser, the round guard designed to prevent rats from climbing aboard. Weakened from his exposure to the plague, unable to hang on to the mooring, Blackie falls into the water.

Although not a political thriller, *Panic in the Streets*, which won an Academy Award for best story, nevertheless participates in the narrative economy of the early Cold War, elevating the threat of plague from the symbolic realm to the literal. Communism was often cast as a disease in popular culture; Kirsten Ostherr, for example, has shown how public health films from the period—specifically, *Hemolytic Streptococcus Control* (1945), a U.S. Navy training film, and *The Eternal Fight* (1948), a United Nations film—"[revealed] a paranoia about maintaining organic boundaries that [underlay] the supposed confidence of the globally hegemonic postwar United States."[3] *Panic in the Streets*, as its title would imply, made the paranoia explicit, while steadfastly advocating for a policy of quarantine, or "containment" when dealing with the threat of contamination. The term "containment" had been introduced into bureaucratic speak less than three years earlier, by George Kennan, writing anonymously in *Foreign Affairs* magazine. "It is clear," Kennan offered, "that the main element of any United States policy toward the Soviet Union must be that of a long-term patient but firm and vigilant *containment* of Russian expansive tendencies."[4]

Indeed, seen from the perspective of more than fifty years, Kazan's film is only coincidentally *not* about communism. The elements that would later inform a number of Cold War movies, including *The Manchurian Candidate*, are already in place: the threat of foreign infiltration and national crisis; the omnipresent state apparatus, and the dependence on the government expert. "Pneumonic [plague] can be spread like a common cold, on the breath, sneezes or sputum of its victims," Reed explains early in the film. Later, his warnings will take the form of—indeed, anticipate—the domino theory. "Community?" Reed inquires of the mayor, who is advocating for public disclosure of the potential epidemic. "What community? Do you think you're living in the Middle Ages? Anybody that leaves here can be in any city in the country within ten hours. I could leave here today and I could be in Africa tomorrow. And whatever disease I had would go right with me."[5] Four years later, President Dwight Eisenhower would suggest that communism was similarly contagious, but, instead of medicine, he turned to the family parlor for his metaphor. "You have a row of dominoes set up," Eisenhower told reporters, explaining the importance of what was then French Indochina (now Vietnam) to American interests in Southeast Asia. "You knock over the first one, and what will happen to the last one is the certainty that it will go over very quickly."[6] For Reed in the film, as for the U.S. government at the time, the globe was shrinking.

The appropriate response to this new world order, *Panic in the Streets* makes clear, is an increase in state authority. In the film, the muscle of the state is perpetually flexed, underwritten by the idea that the government knows best. It also controls the flow of information to the public. When a newspaperman (depicted as a bothersome snoop), following the plague death of an immigrant's wife, confronts Reed with a moral question—"If the doctor had known what was going on, couldn't he have saved her?"—Reed is at a loss: "I don't know." Still, it doesn't prevent Warren from having the reporter arrested to prevent his putting the story in the morning paper. What are the charges? asks the reporter. "Loitering, public nuisance, anything you like," Warren tells him. A character that might have come off as a bully or rogue cop in a film of the 1930s or 1940s is here constructed as a hero. (In the ensuing scene, Reed will tell his wife that Warren is "four times the man [Reed will] ever be" for risking the ire of the newspapers.)

Like *The Manchurian Candidate* later, Kazan's film unashamedly embraces the postwar culture of the expert (in this case, Reed), and its attendant secrecy. When Reed, worried that the cops and reporters in the morgue—where the murdered man's body had been brought—could have been exposed to the plague, he orders them to line up for inoculation. "Hurry up, Paul," he whispers to his assistant, "before they start asking questions." One man, though, does ask:

> "What's in them things, Doc?"
> "A little serum."
> "Serum for what?"
> "I told you—precautionary measures."
> "Yeah, precautionary, but for what?"
> "Well, it's possible the dead man may have had some communicable disease . . ."

Unsatisfied with Reed's answers, the man balks: "I don't want to have to take one of them shots." Reed, however, has the last word: "I can

Dr. Clint Reed (Richard Widmark) takes charge in Elia Kazan's *Panic in the Streets* (1950).

quarantine you for ten days." The man submits. Later in the film, when Warren asks him how he's going to keep the cause of death in a plague case a secret, Reed assures him: "[The] doctor put down a ten-tative diagnosis of pneumonia with complications. That'll do for now."

This very culture of secrecy, so central to the Cold War, is what would eventually make the story line of *The Manchurian Candidate* imaginable, even as a dark farce. As cultural historian Tom Engel-hardt has written: "There was an undercurrent of doubt about what the various curtains, walls, and parallels were actually separating... It was a world in which the fiercest boundary builder for one side might be secretly suspected of building for the other... from this shared secret world, the enemy, contained by nothing, might sud-denly emerge, looking and acting just like 'us.'"[7]

But *Panic in the Streets* resembles *The Manchurian Candidate* in an even more crucial—though less obvious—regard: in the manner in which it positions the nuclear family as a potential casualty of the struggle against America's "foreign" enemies. In *The Manchurian Can-didate*, the link is a direct one—the corruption at the core of the Shaw/Iselin clan is what makes it available to communist infiltration. In

Panic in the Streets, the chief threat to the family appears to come not from the plague itself—Reed, for example, does not consider moving his wife and child out of New Orleans to protect them from contamination—but from Reed's overwhelming responsibilities.

On the surface, the Reeds would appear to be living an idealized version of postwar suburban life. The doctor has a pretty young wife (Barbara Bel Geddes), a precocious son named Tommy, and a house in a middle-class neighborhood. But, as will become abundantly clear, it is not an altogether happy existence. Money is tight, Reed's wife will not give him a second child, and there are tensions over how to raise their son. The trouble, the film makes clear from the start, springs directly from Reed's job, which, while not paying him enough to support his family as he would like, has the added effect of keeping him away from home for too many hours a day and too many days a week.

The threat to the family's long-term survival is neatly conveyed by the presence of an overly friendly neighbor, the provocatively named Mr. Redfield. (The name may be read as a something like a shorthand for the threat posed by communism—"Red-field"—or, at the very least, as a "doubling" of Reed—Red/Reed.) When we first encounter the doctor, he and Tommy are painting a dresser in the family driveway. "Things get dull, just drop right on over, you hear?" Mr. Redfield shouts to the boy, as he climbs into his car, parked across the street from the Reed house. When Reed asks his son who the stranger is, the boy tells him that "he's a painter. He lives in the big house, down on the corner. You oughtta see it, Pop. It's full of all kinds of stuff. He has electric trains and everything." Getting up to go for a can of paint thinner, Reed looks over his shoulder at Redfield getting into his car, shakes his head and mutters to himself, "Electric trains yet."

Redfield's presence in the film is intended to be disruptive. It isn't simply that he has symbolically supplanted Reed as Tommy's father figure—in Reed's absence, the boy clearly spends a good deal of time over at Redfield's—or that Redfield is financially better off than the doctor ("He lives in the big house, down on the corner"), an obvious sore point for Reed. Redfield is constructed, albeit vaguely, as a deviant: a middle-aged bachelor who fancies toy trains, and who takes an almost unseemly interest in the neighborhood children. When we (and Reed) first encounter him, he is dressed as a dandy, wearing white pants with his sports coat. Even after he removes the sports coat to reveal that he is actually wearing white overalls (the tools of his trade), the initial image lingers.

Within the logic of 1950s Hollywood, are we supposed to regard Redfield as a homosexual, or possibly a pedophile? Perhaps. Certainly, the film is not above trafficking in homophobia. In a scene in which Warren and Reed are interviewing the members of a ship's crew—they suspect the ship (*The Nile Queen*) of having brought the murder victim, an illegal alien, into the country—a perpetually smiling Chinese cook plops himself down and inquires, playfully, of Warren, "Now you ask me the questions?" Warren, regarding the cook's behavior as a sexual flirtation, sighs, "I suppose we're apt to wind up at a policeman's benefit, but I'll have to." The scene is played for laughs, but its presence in the film, and its clear intended meaning (Asians had long been associated with the feminine in American culture, a subject we will explore in chapter 5), serves as a signifier of that "other" threat in the film—the threat to normative masculinity. The threat is exemplified by Reed's professional frustrations and his inability to adequately provide for his family, and it's embodied by Redfield, who, significantly, appears at both (and only) the beginning and the end of the film, essentially bookending the domestic subplot. When, having cracked the case, Warren drops Reed off at home, Redfield is himself just arriving. "Say," Redfield remarks to Reed, "Tommy tells me you haven't been around in a couple of days... You oughtta spend some time with that boy... Your own son comes first, you know." When Reed agrees with him, Redfield taps the top of the dresser, which has sat in the driveway the past two days, and delivers one final, ominous-sounding bit of advice: "Ought not leave this out, either. Wood rots, you know." So, too, presumably, do boys abandoned by their fathers and exposed to corrupting influences.

Reed nods and goes up the walkway to meet his wife. After some teasing, he kisses her, and they walk toward the house together. The moment has all the trappings of the happy ending, but little has changed. If the plague has been effectively contained—at least for now—other threats to the family (Redfield, Reed's hours and low pay) remain. As at the conclusion of *The Manchurian Candidate*, the need for eternal vigilance endures.

My Son John (1952)

The family and the state are also at odds, albeit in more direct fashion, in *My Son John*, a film Nora Sayre calls "the most feverish of the anti-Communist films [of the period]."[8] It would be hard to argue the point. In the film, John (Robert Walker) is the eldest son of an idealized version of the American family named (what else?) the Jeffersons: the father is a schoolteacher and American Legionnaire; the mother, a devout, churchgoing woman; the two youngest boys, former high school football stars.

From the beginning, John is defined as an outsider. Unlike his father, who repeatedly refers to himself as being "not too bright," John is a college graduate. ("He has more degrees than a thermometer," brags his mother.) Unlike his mother, he has no time for religion. ("That's a nice life you have, Father. We take care of you in this world and you promise to take care of us in the next," he tells the family's parish priest.) And, unlike his two younger brothers, Chuck and Ben, John never played football, which, the film will show, is a sin only slightly less egregious than communism.

The family dynamic is easily established in the opening minutes of the film, when, at a family dinner that is also a send-off for Chuck and Ben—"the fighting halfbacks," already in uniform, are headed for Korea. John, who has a high-profile (but undefined) position in the federal government, is noticeably absent. When he eventually shows up the following week, we are informed that it is his first visit in almost a year. Almost instantly, he proceeds to charm his mother (Helen Hayes)—he is very much "her son"—and subtly deride his father (Dean Jagger) for his patriotic platitudes.

It will soon become apparent that John has a secret. "What's the matter with you, son? You seem nervous about something," his father tells him. His mother inquires if "he's got a girl." John, forever the intellectual, shrugs: "Well, sentimentalizing over the biological urge isn't really a guarantee of human happiness, dear." Although the

implication that John might be another of the era's "sad young men"
is present (helped along by the casting of Walker, who, as we will see
in chapter 7, had already played a homosexually coded character in
Hitchcock's *Strangers on a Train*), that is not what raises suspicions.[9]
"You sound to me like one of those guys that we should be alert about,"
his father tells him, after John tinkers with a speech he'd written for
his American Legion meeting, and challenges his mouthing of canned
patriotic sentiments. The old man dismisses the idea, but only because
he can't stand the thought. He issues John a warning: "If I thought
that you really were [a communist], I'd take you out in the backyard
and I'd give it to you both barrels," he tells him. Despite John's re-
assurances to his doting mother—he goes so far as to place his hand
on a Bible and recite that he "is not now or ever [has] been a member
of the Communist Party"—he, in fact, is a communist, under investigation by the FBI.

The solidly named Agent Stedman (Van Heflin) infiltrates the family by taking advantage of—or engineering—a fender bender with
John's parents. He comes over to the house to present the family
with a bill for the damage to his car and ends up ingratiating himself
to John's mother, and pumping her for information about her son.
Eventually, the G-man will reveal his true identity, and confess to
Mrs. Jefferson that he has a professional interest in her son. Still loyal
to John, though increasingly suspicious, she declines to cooperate.

The turning point in the film comes when John, who returned to
Washington, D.C., unexpectedly, calls home and asks his mother to
retrieve a pair of pants she had donated to the local church. (The
pants were torn when, in one of the film's most celebrated scenes,
John's father, returning intoxicated from his Legion meeting, lashed
out at his too-smug, too-glib, possible traitor of a son, striking him
over the head with a Bible, then sending him flying over the kitchen
table.) Finding a key in the pocket of the pants, John's mother hops a
flight—her first ever—to Washington, D.C., to confront her son.

In his office, John denies that the key means anything, telling her
it opens his apartment. Not believing him and distraught, she leaves
and finds a park bench overlooking the Jefferson Memorial. There,
she is approached by Stedman (the FBI has been tracking her since
she landed in D.C.), who tells her that her son is the subject of an

investigation into a communist cell. "Hunt Higher-Ups in Red Spy
Ring; Convicted Courier Refuses to Name Confederates; FBI Check-
ing," reads the front page of the newspaper the agent hands her. After
getting her to agree to identify the voice of the "convicted courier"—
Mrs. Jefferson had spoken with this woman when she tried reaching
John at his parents' home—Stedman drops her off on a Washington
street.

The next scene begins with a young agent setting up a movie
screen, and briefing Stedman on what happened after he left Mrs.
Jefferson, information the Bureau's field agents captured on film.
There's footage of Mrs. Jefferson walking over to the convicted
woman's apartment, "We had two hidden cameras outside [the] apartment," narrates the young agent. "See, one was hung from the fire
escape . . . we picked [Mrs. Jefferson] up in the middle of the hall." In
the film, Mrs. Jefferson begins to insert the key in the lock. "Look at her
hand shake," says Stedman. "I don't blame her; mine would, too." A
surveillance shot from the interior of the apartment shows the despair
on her face as the door swings open. "[The interrogation] will be
quite a test," concludes Stedman. "God and country, or her son John."

By this point in the movie, it's no contest. John will lose out not
only to God and country, but to the modern security state. Back at
the house, Mrs. Jefferson, disgusted by her son, pledges to John that
she will tell all she knows. Displaying that he really has no love left
for his mother, John threatens to take advantage of what others per-
ceive to be her delicate condition—the fact she's at "that time" in
her life, sick with worry because her two sons are headed for Korea,
and on medication for her nerves. When Stedman shows up, Mrs.
Jefferson tries one last time to get John to confess (as all good Catholics
should). Holding a photo of her two fighting halfbacks, she urges
him, "Listen to me, John. You've got to get in this game and you've
got to carry the ball yourself . . . Take the ball, John . . . John, time's
running out . . . John, take the ball . . . I'm cheering for you now . . .
My son John! My son John! My son John!" But, alas, John never
learned to play football. "Take him away, take him away," she says to
Stedman, when her son refuses to confess.

Although John manages to get out of the house, his mother's final
attempt to save his soul—her "Hail Mary," as it were—will prove

successful. He will attempt to inform on his comrades ("Name names," as the young FBI agent puts it, echoing the infamous phrase). But it will never happen, as John is rubbed out, Mob-style. On his way to the Bureau, a black sedan pulls up next to the taxi he is riding in and riddles it with bullets, causing it to crash, of all places, on the steps of the Lincoln Memorial.

Stedman takes John's confession, and grants his final wish, playing John's taped confession at his alma mater's commencement ceremony, where he had been scheduled to speak.

In the film's final scene, a heavenly light shines down on the vacant podium, while John's voice plays over the sound system. In his address—like the speech his mother gave him, a cross between a church sermon and a locker-room pep talk—he compares intellectualism and communist ideology to opiates and warns the smiling faces that Soviet agents ("snakes lying in wait") are no doubt already scouting them, ready to take advantage of their decent impulses and good, liberal intentions.

As his parents exit the commencement hall of the Catholic university, the sound of a choir singing builds to a crescendo, and Mrs. Jefferson suggests to her husband that they enter the chapel across the courtyard: "Let's pray for John . . . Let's hope they forget what he did, and pray they remember what he said . . . today."

My Son John has long been considered one of the most absurd films of the 1950s. It may also be, at least in spirit, one of the most absurd films of the 1930s. Its director, Leo McCarey, did his best work in that era, earning his first best director Oscar for the Cary Grant–Irene Dunne screwball classic *The Awful Truth* (McCarey would win again in 1944 for the sentimental favorite *Going My Way*, starring Bing Crosby as—not surprisingly—a kindly priest). But more than that, the characters, with the exception of John (who is demonized for having different ideas), feel like holdovers from McCarey's earlier (funny) films.

As Sayre writes, "Even in this desperately solemn movie, the director of [the Marx Brothers'] *Duck Soup* . . . reveals himself in sudden bursts of burlesque, as when a parish priest turns playful, or when the enraged father—drunk because his wicked son has upset him—falls downstairs, sings, and falls again."[10] Watching *My Son John*, one gets

Leo McCarey's *My Son John* anticipates the overheated mother–son dynamic of *The Manchurian Candidate*.

the feeling that McCarey started out to remake *Knute Rockne, All-American* as a right-wing musical, but forgot the songs.[11]

Of course, to only concentrate on the film's anachronistic characters is to miss the manner in which it contributes, in fundamental ways, to the cinematic construction of the domestic Cold War. Like *Panic in the Streets*, it positions the nuclear family as a central political unit, a synecdochic stand-in for the state. Within this model, the mother is both privileged and suspect—if she can produce outstanding citizens like the fighting halfbacks, her excessive mother love is also capable of producing a traitor like John. Indeed, Mrs. Jefferson may well be the most obvious manifestation in the films of the decade of what Michael Rogin calls "the simultaneous glorification and fear of maternal influence within the family."[12]

Then, too, there is *My Son John*'s infatuation with the new national-security state. As Rogin reminds us, "Although liberals blamed McCarthyite attacks on responsible policymakers for the cold war Red scare, the rise of a new security-oriented state bureaucracy was the most important new factor in the modern history of counter-subversion."[13] As in *Panic in the Streets*, there is the affirmation of the government expert, of state authority, and of the culture of secrecy. "We *gather* information," is Stedman's terse reply to John when he asks him what he's doing in his mother's house. "We don't give it out."

The most chilling example of the security apparatus is the filming of Mrs. Jefferson as she makes her way to the convicted woman's apartment. Aside from what civil libertarians might say about the practice, ideologically, within the film, it functions as retribution; that is, although the agents purport sympathy for her plight ("Look at her hand shake . . . I don't blame her; mine would, too"), the film appears to be encouraging a voyeuristic (and somewhat sadistic) delight in "mom's" humiliation. Along with her impending breakdown (a gendered one, brought on, we are told, by the strain of menopause), it would appear to be one of the pitfalls of momism, her just reward for having coddled a communist.

These are all tropes that *The Manchurian Candidate* would both channel and upend. But there is other, less obvious symbolism in *My Son John* that Frankenheimer (whether intentionally or not) will borrow. When Mrs. Jefferson visits John at his D.C. office, prominently displayed behind his desk is a photo of Abraham Lincoln. (A photo of Washington hangs, less conspicuously, next to the door.) The portrait is directly behind John when he stands over his mother, his arms around her, trying to comfort her even as he lies to her.

If McCarey suggests that subversives may wrap themselves in the flag to avoid detection, Frankenheimer, as with so much of the Cold War symbolism he inherits, will take that idea to its (il)logical extreme, to an obsessive preoccupation with patriotic imagery bordering on the manic. In *The Manchurian Candidate*, it is Lincoln (again) who is chosen to represent the republic at risk. The scene in which Eleanor and John Iselin settle on the easy-to-remember number of 57 (the number of communists Iselin should accuse the Defense Department of harboring) begins with a medium shot of Lincoln or rather, a portrait of Lincoln. Iselin, staring at it as he speaks, and plots, is reflected in the glass. It is not a flattering comparison. During the flashback sequence in which Raymond recalls his summer romance with Jocie, Lincoln is again present; when Eleanor confronts Raymond, forcing him to end the affair, Lincoln watches from both the foreground and the background (in the foreground, there is a bust of

Honest Abe, framed, fancifully enough, by a lamp shade that suggests a stovepipe hat; in the background, the portrait we've already seen, this time over the fireplace). Later, at the costume party at the Iselin house, Johnny dressed as Lincoln plunges a cake cutter into a plate of caviar (arranged in the pattern of an American flag). When, during that same party, his mother leads Raymond into the den (and we learn that she is his American operator), prominently displayed are more busts of Lincoln. Indeed, so identified (as a counterpoint) is Lincoln with the travesties being perpetrated that, by the end of the film, as Frankenheimer explained years later, it was enough simply to show Lincoln, and the audience would know what was coming. Recalling the scene in which Raymond reports to his mother (who will order him to assassinate Senator Jordan), the director explained, "Shooting this thing through a window was a choice to make, and bouncing [the shot] off [a bust of] Lincoln . . . Because we know what this scene is going to be . . . you just don't want to see it."[14]

Significantly, there are no references in Condon's novel to the Lincoln imagery that Frankenheimer employs so ubiquitously; at the costume party, to name one instance, Iselin dresses up not as Lincoln, but, like his wife, as a dairy farmer.[15] But the use of Lincoln is not an invention of Frankenheimer's, either. Like so much of the film's hyper-patriotic imagery (the American eagles that hang in the Jordan home, for example), it's borrowed from the less self-aware films of the decade, films like My Son John, only blown up. In Frankenheimer's film, Lincoln is not a prop, he's a *character*, a martyr (again) for the cause.

Suddenly (1954)

Home invasion was a particularly powerful metaphor in the Cold War, given the conflation of public and private space so dominant in the era. Threats to the family and the home were seemingly everywhere in the films of the 1950s, not simply, as we have seen, in *Panic in the Streets*, but in noirs like Fritz Lang's *The Big Heat* (1953; starring Glenn Ford as a police detective whose wife is killed and his family ripped apart after he leans on the wrong hoods), dramas like William Wyler's *The Desperate Hours* (1955; in which an escaped con played by Humphrey Bogart takes refuge in a middle-class family's home), and even in such minor melodramas as *The Unguarded Moment* (1956; starring Esther Williams as a high school teacher terrorized by an unstable student). *The Manchurian Candidate* would eventually both mine this particular strain of cinema (for what is *The Manchurian Candidate* about, at its core, if not the dangers of home invasion?) and subvert it. The home-invasion film that it would most rely on, symbolically, was Lewis Allen's *Suddenly*.

In the film, a team of hired killers led by John Baron (Sinatra), has been tipped off that the president of the United States, traveling by train, will be making an unannounced stop in a small, out-of-the-way California town named Suddenly. Posing as FBI agents, they gain entry to the most strategic (and symbolic) location in town—a house on a hill, overlooking the depot.

The residents of the house are Pop Benson, an old man who was once Calvin Coolidge's personal bodyguard, his daughter-in-law, Ellen, and Pidge, his grandson. Pop's son, we learn early on, was a soldier killed in battle (one assumes Korea), an event that, more than any other, informs the family dynamic. Ellen, still mourning the loss of her husband, is overprotective of Pidge, and doesn't want him playing with guns. The grandfather, a staunch patriot, is at odds with his daughter-in-law over how his grandson should be raised. An exchange during the first scene at the house sums up the family tension and the larger ideological conflict the film will attempt to resolve:

POP: I read about an experiment once [that] kept germs away from a kid. Raised him pure and scientifically. First time he got out in the rough, he caught cold and died of pneumonia . . . The kid hadn't been exposed; he had no immunity. There's cruelty and hatred and tyranny in the world; you can't make believe they aren't there. And Pidge has gotta learn what is the law and what isn't the law, so he can defend it.

ELLEN: Defend it? So he can become a soldier and go out and be murdered like his father was?

POP: My son was killed in the performance of his duty, Ellen.

ELLEN: Duty—being blown to bits on some godforsaken battlefield thousands of miles from where he was born. You call that duty?

POP: Yes, Ellen.

ELLEN: Is that what you'd like for Pidge? Would that make you happy?

POP: If Pete [his son and her husband] could hear you now, I think he'd be ashamed of you ... When the old boys wrote those words, "life, liberty, and the pursuit of happiness," they sounded mighty nice, but they wouldn't have been worth a plug nickel if somebody hadn't made them stick.

In the political landscape of the early 1950s, Ellen, the film makes clear, is a double threat, representing both isolationism and the threat of momism. To a large degree, the rest of *Suddenly* will be devoted to her reeducation, and to strengthening the idea of the family as the primary defense against America's enemies.

Indeed, the family is placed at the center of the drama from the very beginning. After a shootout in the house that results in the death of a Secret Service agent and in the town sheriff, Todd Shaw (Sterling Hayden), being wounded, Baron tells Pop: "I don't want any more shooting around here. I want it nice and quiet and cozy ... explain to [Ellen] that one phony [move] and she's got a kid with his throat cut ... That's simple enough."

Baron's request that everything remain "nice and quiet and cozy" in the home while he plans his dirty work, his arranging of the family members and the sheriff (who has been pursuing Ellen romantically and stands in for the absent father) in the living room forms an ironic tableau—a picture of domestic bliss, under threat of death.

Not surprisingly, we will discover that Baron is the product of a dysfunctional family. "You got any food in the house?" he asks Ellen at one point. "Of course I have," she responds defensively, seeming almost as upset by the questioning of her homemaking skills as she is by the fact that her family is being held captive. Baron follows her into a gleaming white kitchen, its clean-scrubbed pots on top of the range and a well-stocked fridge constituting a shining vision of postwar middle-class abundance, the kind of normative ideal that Baron threatens to subvert.

When realizing the knife Ellen has just produced from a kitchen drawer could become a weapon, Baron sneaks up behind her and takes it away. She lashes out:

ELLEN: Haven't you any feelings?

BARON: No I haven't, lady. They were taken out of me by experts. Feelings are a trap. Show me a guy with feelings and I'll show you a sucker. A weakness ... makes you think of something besides yourself. If I had any feelings left in me at all, it'd be for me. Just me.

ELLEN: Don't you ever think of your mother, your father?

BARON: Think of them? I used to think of them a great deal. My mother wasn't married. My old man was a dipso. They left me in a home ... a *home* ...

Baron spits out the last word ironically. The point is made: If momism produces soft sons who will grow into communist sympathizers or communists themselves (as in *My Son John*), the absence of a home life produces psychopaths like Baron.

Later, Baron, sounding like a pop sociology primer on fifties alienation (William Whyte's *The Organization Man* meets David Riesman's *The Lonely Crowd*), details the extent of his rootlessness:

Before the war I drifted and drifted and ran, always lost in a great big crowd. I hated that crowd. I used to dream about the crowd once in while. I used to see all those faces scratching and shoving and biting and then the mist would clear and somehow all those faces would be me. All me, and all nothing.

The war, he says, gave him direction, a purpose. "I did a lot of chopping in the war ... killed twenty-seven Gerries ... I won a Silver Star," he brags on more than one occasion. After his discharge from the army (for mental instability, or, as the sheriff offers, for being a "psycho in charge of killing"), Baron became an organization man of a different sort: "The fingers said where and how much and Johnny Baron did the job."

In his self-absorption, ambition, worship of violence, and hatred of weakness, Baron (the name itself implies a superiority complex) is reminiscent of the fascist dictators who ruled Europe in the 1930s. In his isolation, friendlessness, and stunted emotional life, he could well be lineal ancestor to Raymond Shaw. "I knew guys like you in the army," the sheriff tells Baron, trying to anger him into letting his guard down. "You'd rather kill a man than love a woman." (Shaw, in Condon's novel, was a virgin; in Frankenheimer's film, beginning with the opening brothel scene, he is depicted as frigid and largely uninterested in sexual adventure.)

Baron is a more complex character than his hostages are capable of comprehending. When Judd, the young TV repairman who unwittingly stumbles into the scenario, accuses the would-be assassins of being "commies, enemy agents," Baron laughs disdainfully.

> "All right, who is behind it, Baron?" asks the sheriff.
> "I haven't the slightest idea . . . I got no feeling against the president. I'm just earning a living."
> "By treason," counters Pop.
> "Ace, deuce, crap! Don't give me that politics jazz. It's not my racket."

Perhaps Judd's accusation springs from watching too many movies. As Michael Rogin has pointed out, "Anti-Communist films [of the early 1950s] like *I Was a Communist* warned against a political danger, [but] they depoliticized the appeals of Communism by using the conventions of the gangster movie and equating Communism with crime."[16] *Suddenly* would appear to be swimming in the same cultural current: if movie communists acted like gangsters, it wouldn't take much to assume that gangsters like Baron might be communists (and, here again, the gangland-style execution at the end of *My Son John* is worth considering).

At the same time, by constructing Baron as a figure who stands outside the Cold War dichotomy of patriot/communist, *Suddenly* is, in some ways, a more sophisticated (though no less reactionary) film than many of its contemporaries. "[In a war], you can knock over a whole platoon, or a guy invents a bomb and kills a hundred thousand people—just like that—and maybe gets more medals," Baron tells the sheriff, making a point about the tangled morality of warfare. But because it comes from the already-discredited Baron, it is a perspective that hardly needs to be addressed.

Still, *Suddenly*, despite its story line and Sinatra's effective, menacing portrayal, never comes close to imagining a conspiracy on the scale of *The Manchurian Candidate*. At one point, Baron makes the hard-boiled observation that he's being paid "a half a million clams for absolutely nothing. Because tonight at five o'clock, I kill the president and, one second after five, there's a new president. What changes?

Nothing. What are they paying for? Nothing." This, of course, is a premise *The Manchurian Candidate* will reject outright.

What *Suddenly* does bequeath to the later film, besides its ideology of the family and the image of Sinatra in a story line involving a presidential assassination attempt, is the idea that a man (like Raymond Shaw, a decorated veteran) with a gun—and a plan—could alter the fate of the nation. Watching *Suddenly* now, the view from the window of the Benson home is impressive. One can easily imagine the president stepping into the frame—back when presidents still did things like get on and off trains, and ride in convertibles—and being cut down. In 1963, the probability that such a thing could happen, even in the modern security state, would be established in fact. When *The Manchurian Candidate* was made, however, the subject was still the stuff of pulp potboilers and Hollywood B movies. No film mapped out the scenario more powerfully than *Suddenly*.

The assassination, of course, is foiled. By the time the train approaches, both of Baron's accomplices have been killed—one in a shootout in town, the other when he got too close to a metal table that Pop and Judd had rigged with electrical current. Undeterred by this, or by the fact that the Secret Service is on to him, Baron positions himself behind the rifle and waits, staring through the window in shock when the train bolts by the station. His incredulous cries of "It didn't stop! It didn't stop!" are interrupted by a bullet fired from a gun Baron had assumed was one of Pidge's toys but that was, in fact, the real thing. The shooter is Ellen, now fully recruited into the war against America's enemies. The sheriff finishes the job.

Killing Baron, exorcising the threat to the state, turns out to be just the thing the sheriff and Ellen needed. The next morning, she meets him at the hospital, to check on the condition of Judd (whom Baron had shot) and of a deputy injured during the shootout in town, then offers, uncharacteristically, to pick up the sheriff the next morning for church. He kisses her and tells her, "That'd be swell."

Suddenly, participating in the same logic as *My Son John* (which conflates home life and the life of the nation), not only makes the case that the American family is the bulwark against threats to the state, but that the Cold War may actually be capable of producing better families, in this case, in all probability providing Ellen with a new husband and Pidge with a father. Less than a decade later, *The Manchurian Candidate*—both the book and the film—would approach this scenario from a different direction. Radically rethinking the assumptions of the home-invasion narratives of the 1950s, Frankenheimer's film asks the question, "What if mom had cooperated?"

Kiss Me Deadly (1955)

"I can't think of another movie that in its smallest details is so naturalistic and in its overarching tone is so crazy," Marcus has written of *The Manchurian Candidate*.[17] And it's true: Frankenheimer's film does feel like a combination of gritty film noir and something approaching the weird tale, which H. P. Lovecraft defined as follows:

> The true weird tale has something more than secret murder, bloody bones, or a sheeted form clanking chains according to rule. A certain atmosphere of breathless and unexplainable dread of outer, unknown forces must be present; and there must be a hint, expressed with a seriousness and portentousness becoming its subject, of that most terrible conception of the human brain—a malign and particular suspension of belief or defeat of those fixed laws of Nature which are our only safeguard against the assaults of chaos and the daemons of unplumbed space.[18]

If *The Manchurian Candidate* is not a weird tale in the strictest sense—because everything, in the end, can be "explained" in terms of the natural world—it nevertheless does share the genre's preoccupation with the idea that things are rarely as they appear, that there are "other," darker forces at work. In this respect, the film that Frankenheimer's creation may most directly both borrow from and invert is Robert Aldrich's offbeat thriller *Kiss Me Deadly*.

As J. P. Telotte has pointed out, "*Kiss Me Deadly* exaggerates even the baroque patterns of most other noirs, so that it can seem simultaneously the most fantastic film in the noir tradition and...the most realistic as well."[19] For Telotte, this quality—which he dubs "fantastic realism"—while present in film noir as a whole, achieves its most open articulation in *Kiss Me Deadly*, where such conventions of realism as on-location shooting are wedded to an "excess of distortion," reflexive moments where the film attempts to communicate to viewers that what they are watching should not be confused with reality, at least as normally defined by the classical Hollywood cinema.

Kiss Me Deadly opens with a woman running down a deserted highway at night. The action is presented in a series of alternating shots—medium shots from the waist down show her running over the white line in the middle of the road, long and upper-body shots show her clearly running by the side of the road, well away from the white line. "[These shots] subtly signal ... that the ensuing narrative might not be playing by the normal rules, that they may well be out to depict a very different sort of world than we are used to seeing on film, even in the strange realm of film noir," writes Telotte.[20]

The woman turns out to be Christina, the archetypal (or so it would appear at first) damsel in distress. Her murder will send detective Mike Hammer (Ralph Meeker) off on a case quite unlike any other he's ever had, a point the film will convey both narratively and visually.

Walking down an abandoned city street at night, on his way to question an acquaintance of Christina's, Hammer realizes he's being followed and, to buy himself some time, pauses to purchase popcorn from a street vendor. Behind the two men, off to the left of the frame, is a neon clock. At the moment Hammer stops, it reads 2:10. The camera cuts to another angle, a different perspective on the transaction: the clock is now in the center of the frame and reads 2:17. Hammer walks away and we have alternating shots of his feet and of his stalker's feet. When the camera cuts to a medium shot of Hammer's pursuer passing in front of the same neon clock, only a few seconds later, the clock reads 2:22. We are clearly meant to interpret this as continuous action, occupying thirty seconds of screen time, yet the clock informs us that, inexplicably, twelve minutes have elapsed.

The film, Telotte astutely argues, is trying to tell us something: "If we are watching with care, we see Hammer, a figure drawn from the conventional world of the detective film and in the midst of a familiar suspense situation, step into a kind of narrative black hole, where the basic laws of both genre and nature seem at times simply to have been suspended."[21]

Eventually, the mystery itself will turn out to be more than Hammer—or the viewer—might have bargained for. The object of Hammer's pursuit, or, as his secretary Velda puts it, "the great whatsit," in a Cold War twist, will not be heroin (as was the case in the Mickey Spillane novel on which the film is based), but atomic matter that a syndicate is attempting to peddle to foreign buyers. It is a scenario that defies Hammer's limited powers of deduction. (Spillane's hero, never a disciple of the Sherlock Holmes school of detection, is here reduced to the genre's lowest common denominator—a beefy, somewhat obtuse, bedroom dick.)

Hammer never does crack the mystery completely. Instead, his friend Pat Murphy, a Los Angeles police detective who's been furtively working the case, has to explain it to him: "Now listen, Mike. Listen carefully. I'm going to pronounce a few words. They're harmless words, just a bunch of letters scrambled together, but their meaning is very important. Try to understand what they mean: Manhattan Project. Los Alamos. Trinity."

Hammer is powerless not only to understand the depths of the mystery in which he is embroiled, but also to prevent its catastrophic conclusion: a nuclear explosion that, apparently, claims the lives of both Hammer and Velda (and who knows how much of Southern California?).[22] It is an apocalyptic vision, one that Telotte argues serves to deconstruct the traditional detective film and acknowledges the limitations of the form to grapple with the complex postwar nuclear age.[23]

Like *Kiss Me Deadly*, *The Manchurian Candidate* combines stylistic elements that aspire to realistic representation—on-location shooting, depth-of-field photography, and realistic depictions of violence (has a man ever been strangled more realistically on film than Ed Mavole?)—and reflexive moments that appear to be winking at us. These moments, however, function differently than in the first film. *Kiss Me Deadly* attempts to tip off the viewer that not everything is what it appears to be in order to set up a previously unthinkable turn of events. *The Manchurian Candidate* is built around the premise that *nothing* is as it appears (Raymond Shaw didn't really save his platoon, Eleanor Iselin isn't really a patriot, Bennett Marco isn't, as the army brass believe, going crazy)—the unthinkable has already happened.

Those scenes or elements, then, that deviate from the hyperrealism that Marcus identifies have the effect not of making us doubt what we are seeing—the conspiracy—but to more strongly believe in it, no matter how absurd it might seem. (Brainwashing? A ladies' garden club? The red queen as a trigger mechanism?) The most obvious example of this may be the scene in which Al Melvin awakens from his own version of "the dream," and his wife urges him to contact Shaw—"You like him a lot, don't you?" Melvin agrees, telling her that "Raymond Shaw is the bravest, kindest, warmest, most wonderful human being I've ever known in my life." We've heard the line before, of course. It is the exact description given by Marco a few scenes earlier when the army psychiatrist asked him what he thought of Shaw.

The difference is that Marco delivered the line while remaining in character, giving the sense that it really was what he believed (even though it does not jibe with what we have already seen of the less than likable Shaw). Melvin recites the words in an eerie monotone, as if possessed (which, in fact, he is). Certainly, the line didn't need to be delivered that way. We would have remembered that it was what Marco had said, down to the last word, even without the exaggerated prompt. The moment thus comes off as slightly comical, yet functions to corroborate Marco's theory that the platoon was brainwashed even before the film itself admits any such thing. (Shaw receives his first phone call from his controllers in the ensuing scene.)

The same principle may be said to be at work in the film's smaller details. Consider the fleeting glimpses of the elevator operator in Shaw's building. Marcus has observed:

> Far more than the sight of late-fifties, early-sixties cars on screen, or the use of the Korean War as a social fact it's assumed everyone understands, or Joe McCarthy as a monster or a hero everyone only recently reviled or applauded, this is odd: we know elevator operators can't do that anymore, that even if we get another Korean War, another Joe McCarthy, we won't get any more elevator operators smoking in elevators. Such tiny details, as we see them today, make the movie safe, today—protect us from it.[24]

Marcus's point is that the unfamiliarity of the image, its anachronistic quality, somehow helps render the movie less threatening, helps mitigate the awfulness of its most disturbing moments with a certain charm. But perhaps the opposite is true. Marcus's reading assumes that the elevator man's presence, in the context of the early 1960s, is unproblematic. But is it? For one thing, Shaw's apartment building is not the kind of place one would expect to find an elevator operator, in any era. When Shaw pulls up in front of the building for the only time in the film, its exterior is rather forlorn, a gray mass against an even grayer sky, giving the impression that, if it was once a signature Manhattan address, it has fallen on hard times. The interior shots, coupled with David Amram's exceedingly sad score, only corroborate this sense: before he ever emerges from the elevator, an establishing shot of Shaw's hallway reveals dingy, dark walls and peeling paint on the elevator door.

When the door opens, we catch a glimpse of the operator. His double-breasted uniform coat hangs open, a cigarette dangles from his mouth, and he exchanges not a word with his passenger. One would be surprised if he *didn't* smell of alcohol. In his only other appearance, when Marco steps off the elevator on his way to see Shaw (only to find Chunjin), the man again says nothing, instead directing Marco to the right door with a "There you go, bub" gesture.

In a different film—one directed, say, by Billy Wilder—this textbook image of shiftlessness might provide comic relief. In this film, it only disturbs further: the elevator operator is not only an oddity from the perspective of the present day, his presence in the film would have been somewhat curious in 1962 as well.

The same is true of many of the casting choices. "We did all sorts of strange things, but we did them so automatically," screenwriter George Axelrod recalled years later. "I mean, it's rather strange that Angela Lansbury was one year older than Larry Harvey and played his mother."[25] Indeed. Also odd was the selection of actor Joe Adams to play the army psychiatrist. "This [was] one of the first instances where a black actor, or an African-American actor, was cast in a part that specifically didn't say that the character was black," Frankenheimer later remembered.[26]

Adams playing the psychiatrist, Lansbury as Eleanor Iselin, a seedy elevator operator in an even seedier building, New Jersey matriarchs who morph into Chinese and Russian agents: all of these are the equivalent of the neon clock in *Kiss Me Deadly*, cinematic semaphores telling us that we should pay extra-close attention, not because (as in *Kiss Me Deadly*) they hint at some rupture in the classical Hollywood narrative apparatus, but because they are proof that we have, indeed, gone through the looking glass.

Although they proceed through different logics, the two films— *Kiss Me Deadly* by assuming something like a collective innocence on the part of its audience, *The Manchurian Candidate* by inscribing us within its dark knowledge—inevitably end up at the same place: the apocalypse. For isn't Raymond Shaw's act of matricide the emotional equivalent of *Kiss Me Deadly*'s nuclear blast? Don't they both, in their own way, signal the end of the world (within the cosmology constructed by each film)?

Certainly, Hammer and Marco would appear, in the end, to be equally impotent. "OK, I blew it," Marco chastises himself, following his attempt to deprogram Shaw. "I blew it. 'My magic is better than your magic.' I should've known better. 'Intelligence officer'? 'Stupidity officer' is better. If the Pentagon ever wants to open up a Stupidity Division, they know who they can get to lead it."

Although he doesn't know it, Marco did succeed in deprogramming Shaw, but he won't be able to prevent him from killing his mother, or Iselin, or himself. Like Hammer, he can only stand by and watch as the contents of the postwar Pandora's box spill out.

Invasion of the Body Snatchers (1956)

Taking the genre of home invasion and extending it to the area of mind control (or something like it), Don Siegel's *Invasion of the Body Snatchers* would appear to be the final, almost necessary step in the evolution toward *The Manchurian Candidate*.

The film begins with Dr. Miles Bennell (Kevin McCarthy), wild-eyed and disheveled, proclaiming his sanity to a group of doctors: "At first glance everything looked the same. It wasn't. Something evil had taken possession of the town." The story of how Bennell came to this place, in this state, will be told in flashback. Anticipating the brainwashing sequences in *The Manchurian Candidate*, Bennell's account takes on almost dreamlike quality, the screen fading to the small-town California physician being met at the train station by his secretary, who informs him that an unusually high number of his patients have come around. Arriving back at his office, Bennell finds that suddenly no one needs him. No one except Becky Driscoll (Dana Wynter), an old flame of the doctor's who has recently divorced and moved back to Santa Mira. She tells Bennell that her cousin, Wilma, has a problem: she doesn't believe that her Uncle Ira is really her Uncle Ira. Bennell stops by Wilma's and tries to reassure her that Uncle Ira is, indeed, himself. "There is no difference you can actually see . . . there's something missing," Wilma insists. Bennell encourages her to see Dr. Kauffman, a psychiatrist. Later that night, Bennell and Becky run into Kauffman, who's well aware of the phenomenon sweeping the town. "What is it?" Bennell wants to know. "I don't know . . . a strange neurosis, evidently contagious, an epidemic of mass hysteria," offers Kauffman, going on to speculate that its root cause may be "worry about what's going on in the world."

At dinner, Bennell receives an emergency call, from Jack (King Donovan) and Teddy (Carolyn Jones), a couple he knows. He and Becky drive over to the couples' home and are ushered into the den, where, on the pool table, is a corpse, or, more accurately, a full-grown, but yet to be fully formed body. "It's like the first impression that's stamped on a coin . . . it isn't finished," says Jack. Bennell takes its fingerprints—blank splotches. "This isn't you yet, but there is a structural likeness," he warns Jack, telling him to stay up with the body, and call him if anything happens.

Later that night, something does happen. The body, looking more and more like Jack, develops a cut on its hand, in the identical place Jack had cut himself earlier in the evening. Bennell eventually discovers the truth: large green pods are morphing into bodies, taking the place of the people they resemble. "So much has been discovered these past few years, anything is possible," says Bennell, speculating on where the pods may have originated. "Maybe it's the result of atomic radiation on plant life or animal life. Some weird alien organism, a mutation of some kind."

It soon becomes clear that the pod people have taken over Santa Mira. Fearing for their lives—because they are the last two humans in the community—Bennell and Becky take refuge in a cave on the outskirts of town. Becky, though, makes the mistake of falling asleep. When she awakens, she, too, has been "changed." (Pods replaced people, Bennell and Becky had already learned, during sleep.) "He's in here! He's in here!" she screams to the townspeople searching for her and Bennell. "Get him!"

Bennell makes it to the highway, where drivers swerve to avoid him, ignoring his cries: "You're in danger!" He climbs up on the cab of a truck and is pushed off. "You fools! You're in danger!" he warns them. "Can't you see? They're after you! They're after all of us! They're here already! You're next! You're next!"

The flashback ends. The attending physicians don't believe a word of his story. But then, a fortuitous development: a man is wheeled into the hospital after crashing his truck into a bus. "We had to dig him out from under the most peculiar things I ever saw," the orderly tells the doctors. "Looked like great big sea pods." The doctors spring into action, dialing up the FBI, while Bennell, exhausted, but vindicated, collapses against the wall.

Invasion of the Body Snatchers, in film scholar Peter Biskind's view, is a right-wing document. "The pod society is the familiar mechanistic utopia usually (and rightly) taken as a metaphor for Communism," writes Biskind. "This is a world in which 'everyone is the same,' a collectivist millennium..."[27] Of course, it could be read from the other end of the spectrum as well, as a critique of the overly restrictive imperative to conform dictated by the anticommunist struggle (the tendencies identified by Packard, Whyte, et al.). In this sense, *Invasion of the Body Snatchers* shares a certain ideological ambiguity with *The Manchurian Candidate*, which holds McCarthyism up to ridicule while confirming—indeed, exceeding—our worst fears about the Communist menace.

Despite Biskind's limited reading of the film's politics, he does put his finger on one of the direct links between Siegel's film and Frankenheimer's: "Possession by pods—mind stealing, brain eating, and body snatching—had the . . . advantage of being an overt metaphor for

Dr. Miles Bennell (Kevin McCarthy, right), after a sleepless night of
dodging pod people in Don Siegel's *Invasion of the Body Snatchers* (1956).
Actor Whit Bissell (left) plays an incredulous doctor.

Communist brainwashing, which had just turned GIs into Reds in
Korea."[28] And, indeed, do not the glassy-eyed, expressionless counte-
nances of the pod people—without "love, desire, ambition, faith," as
Dr. Kauffman explains in the film—approximate the look that comes
over Raymond Shaw whenever he's invited to play a game of solitaire?

Certainly, Bennell's attempts to get the doctors to believe him are
eerily reminiscent of Marco's own efforts. (In his condition, Bennell,
like Marco, would appear to be a textbook case of masculinity in crisis, a subject to which we will return in chapter 7.) As we've already
pointed out, there is a dreamlike quality to the story as it unfolds in
flashback, told from Bennell's point of view. As was the case with
Marco, who is to say that Bennell isn't the one going mad? This is a
point acknowledged even by the film's producers, who, over the objections of director Don Siegel, insisted on the coda in which Bennell's
allegations are independently corroborated by the hospital orderly.
(Siegel wanted to end the film with Bennell on the highway.) In an
amazing coincidence, the actor who plays one of the two doctors in
Invasion of the Body Snatchers, Whit Bissell, would also play the skepti-

cal army medical officer who diagnoses Marco as "suffering a delayed reaction to eighteen months of continuous combat in Korea."

If not exactly "taking *Invasion of the Body Snatchers* out of science fiction and returning it to history," then, Frankenheimer, would appear to have in part traded on the conventions of the science-fiction film—or, as with *Kiss Me Deadly*, the near-fantastic tale—to craft his particular commentary on the Cold War.

These five films (and the countless others they represent) helped to construct the cultural geometry of the Cold War in the 1950s, helped define the symbols Frankenheimer would appropriate—symbols he ingeniously took far too literally and literally too far. If *My Son John* implicitly argued that obsessing, doting mothers produced communists by accident, *The Manchurian Candidate* would assure us that it was no accident. If the residents of Santa Mira could be turned into automatons through some freak natural occurrence, why not the stepson of a U.S. senator through brainwashing? If an assassin could get a clear shot at the president of the United States, why did something have to ultimately go wrong?

The films of the 1950s—the cultural currents that informed them and that they, in turn, fed—in many ways prepared us, to the degree anything could, for *The Manchurian Candidate*'s dark, biting vision. That Frankenheimer's film was (and is) capable of shocking us only speaks to how completely it absorbed, reflected, and reshaped those currents.

4

Bullwhip and Smear

Reading McCarthy

I am United States Senator John Yerkes Iselin, and I have here a list of the names of two hundred and seven persons who are known by the secretary of defense as being members of the Communist Party.

—*Johnny Iselin (James Gregory) at a press conference*

The figure of Johnny Iselin is so patently Joseph McCarthy himself that to say he is "a McCarthy *type*" would be a ludicrous misrepresentation. This is no small matter, as *The Manchurian Candidate*'s depiction was among the very first full-throated satires of McCarthy, and it remains among the very best. But what is the method of this satire, and what precisely is its significance? Measuring the meaning of McCarthyism in 1960, Richard Rovere wrote that McCarthy had "held two presidents captive—or as nearly captive as any Presidents of the United States have ever been held; in their conduct of the nation's affairs, Harry S. Truman and Dwight D. Eisenhower, from early 1950 through late 1954, could never act without weighing the effect of their plans upon McCarthy and the forces he led, and in consequence there were times when, because of this man, they could not act at all."[1] Rovere could not know then that at least two more presidents, Kennedy and Lyndon Johnson, would also be left to wrestle with McCarthy's enormously powerful ghost—and in a sense, to lose to it. One thinks of the ready-made McCarthyesque smear and the force it exerted on these liberal presidents' sensitivities to being "soft on communism" in places like Cuba and Vietnam. To recall Kennedy's acquiescence in the CIA's fanciful plot at the Bay of Pigs, or Johnson's determination not to "lose" Vietnam to communism as an earlier administration had "lost" China, is to footnote Joseph McCarthy, long dead though he was.

The Manchurian Candidate thus appeared at a peculiar juncture in the nation's political life—that moment when McCarthy had been so thoroughly discredited that a sound satirical thrashing was possible, but yet when the communist threat and the McCarthyite vocabulary for discussing it retained enough salience that a communist plot to take over the White House could provide the stuff, not just for camp, but for a plausibly compelling political thriller. The Manchurian Candidate plays both deliberately and mirthfully with this seeming contradiction. That McCarthy's rise coincided with the Korean War was crucial for the anticommunist tilt of the nation's political culture: "if China preoccupied conservative elites," as Michael Rogin noted, "the Korean War attracted the attention of the population as a whole," at once bringing to a head "amorphous cold war anxieties" and intensifying popular "concern over communism." McCarthy and McCarthyism reaped the political benefits of this invigorated concern.[2] The Manchurian Candidate twists this reality to suit its needs, setting McCarthy's rise some years *after* soldiers like Raymond Shaw and Bennett Marco have returned from the war. But in doing so the film makes full use of the political atmosphere of the dawning Vietnam era, bringing both McCarthy and an elaborate Asian conspiracy to life for a rendition of the 1956 election to be presented to a 1962 audience. The film has it both ways on the McCarthy question, as it were, just as the nation itself had it both ways in the early 1960s: although McCarthy was an ideologue and a buffoon, he was not altogether wrong about the conspiratorial immensity of communism and the peril it represented.

Although common parlance seizes upon Joseph McCarthy to summon and give name to the anticommunist fervor of the era, the convenient simplification "McCarthyism" scarcely does justice to the dense political weave of the phenomenon. As historian Ellen Schrecker writes, "the 'ism' with which he was identified was already in full swing" by the time McCarthy appeared at a Lincoln Day event in 1950 in Wheeling, West Virginia, brandishing his famous "list" of 205 communists in the State Department. The Wheeling speech itself, Schrecker notes, was essentially a knockoff of a speech that Richard Nixon had given a few days earlier; and as for anticommunist zealotry and its chosen technologies, had observers known in the 1950s what they have since been able to discover thanks to the Freedom of Information Act, "'McCarthyism' would probably be called 'Hooverism.'"[3] The Manichaean logic of the Truman Doctrine, and the president's Federal Employee Loyalty Program, had since 1947 been creating in some quarters precisely the persecutory climate whose invention McCarthy is credited with; and many of the most dramatic trials of conscience and commitment unfolded not before McCarthy's Senate committee, but before the House Committee on Un-American Activities, especially in the days when a hectoring J. Parnell Thomas of New Jersey served as its chairman. The Hollywood Ten predated McCarthy's emergence on the national scene by a good three years. Trade unions and universities were already in retreat. As Ted Morgan puts it, "McCarthy arrived on the battlefield after the battle was over to finish off the wounded."[4]

It was not the tenor or the ferocity of his politics, then, but his considerable gifts as a demagogue and his penchant for show business that garnered so much attention—both at the time and in retrospect—for the senator from Wisconsin. As blacklisted writer Walter Bernstein wrote:

> The House Committee on Un-American Activities was minor-league bigotry; Senator Joseph McCarthy was big-time show business. Television, the new arbiter of discourse, loved him. He combined two elements that had always brought shows high ratings: he was a gangster in a soap opera. He lay over the country like one of those disease-ridden blankets that white settlers had given the Indians. He sickened the body politic. The few voices against him were weak and ineffectual. McCarthy went his brutal, demagogic way, swinging his sockful of shit, doing the necessary dirty footwork of the cold war.[5]

McCarthy was thus a natural target for anyone wishing to lampoon the politics of peril—what one critic called Americans' 1950s bout with "phobofilia."[6] Arthur Miller, of course, had explored the psychology of the witch hunt in *The Crucible* (1953), a treatment of the Salem witch trials whose modern-day referents were transparent to all. As critic Eric Bentley wrote in response to *The Crucible*, "at a moment when we are all being 'investigated,' it is moving to see images of 'investigation' before the footlights." Such a play "by an author who is neither an infant, a fool, or a swindler, is enough to bring tears to the eyes." Miller had also examined the spiritual malady of the informant in *A View from the Bridge* (1955), the story of a jealous wretch who turns a personal rival—an illegal alien—over to the Immigration and Naturalization Service (INS) for reasons that are equally transparent and decipherable.[7] Throughout 1953, too, blacklisted writers Arnold Manoff, Abraham Polonsky, and Walter Bernstein were able, through their various "fronts," to put before the public several episodes of the television show *You Are There* that were unmistakable parables on McCarthyism: "The Execution of Joan of Arc," "The Crisis of Galileo," "The Death of Socrates," and "The First Salem Witch Trial."[8] But, as Richard Condon was writing in 1958, and even as John Frankenheimer set up shop a few years later, the full parody of McCarthy *as McCarthy* had never yet been mounted (with the possible exception of Bob and Ray's 1954 radio show *Mary Backstayge, Noble Wife*, in which Skunkhaven's commissioner Carstairs prosecuted minor building-code infractions in the dead-on badgering and stammer of the Wisconsin senator).

The Manchurian Candidate accomplishes its devastation of McCarthy with breathtaking economy. Johnny Iselin appears in ten scenes, most occupying only a minute or less—some, far less: (1) a photo op at the Washington airfield where Raymond Shaw is being feted, then into a limo with Raymond and Eleanor; (2) the Iselin/Shaw family in their private airplane leaving Washington; (3) a press conference clearly playing on the collective televisual memory of McCarthy in action, where Iselin challenges the secretary of defense on the "207" known communists in his department, and afterward in the vestibule of the Senate hearing room, changes the number to "104" and then

Johnny Iselin knocks ketchup out of a Heinz bottle, thereby arriving at the
solid figure of "57" communists in the Department of Defense.

"275"; (4) Iselin and Eleanor in private: the senator begs his wife to
give him one number of "known communists" to hold constant, and
then arrives comfortably at a figure as he pours a bottle of Heinz;
(5) once again in the Senate, Iselin now bellows that "there are exactly 57 card-carrying members of the Communist Party in the Defense Department . . . Point of order!"; (6) in semiprivate (an entourage
of barbers and aids hover about) Eleanor orders Iselin simply to "keep
shouting 'point of order, point of order' into the television cameras,
and I'll handle the rest"; (7) at the costume party, where Iselin appears in the garb of Abraham Lincoln—an assassination reference,
to be sure, but also perhaps a reference to McCarthy's Lincoln Day
address; (8) in Raymond and Josie's living room, the fleeting, televised image of Iselin charges Senator Thomas Jordan with "high treason" and urges impeachment and a civil trial; (9) with reporters,
Iselin offers somber regrets after Jordan's death; and (10) at the
party's nominating convention, Iselin himself is assassinated.

The film sinks its teeth into McCarthy, first, by the manner in
which it plays with the senator as a distinctly *televised* political icon.
If McCarthy's rise against the backdrop of the Korean War represents
one significant confluence in the history of U.S. anticommunism,
another, perhaps greater one is the timing of his rise alongside the
rise of American television. When McCarthy burst onto the national
scene in 1950 with his spectacular allegations at that Lincoln Day

Middle America watches the Army–McCarthy hearings, April 1954. Although McCarthy had begun his crusade during the print era, he was to become the television era's first political juggernaut—and its first political casualty. (Bettman/Corbis)

dinner in Wheeling, there were only 98 television stations nationwide, serving 3,700,000 households. By 1954, when McCarthy's political arc had crested and army lawyer Joseph Welch was castigating him, asking him whether at long last he had no sense of decency, 413 stations were serving 35 million sets in 273 American cities. And the cameras were rolling.[9] Joseph McCarthy emerged in the twilight of the hegemony of print; he began as a creature of the news wires, and he ended, sputtering and shuffling, as one observer put it, the wretched, slain monster of the television exposé.[10] Hence, when Eleanor Iselin refers to Johnny's sweeping in to take charge of "a nation of television viewers," she is referencing a very specific aspect of McCarthy's moment, and not just the general, mass-mediated civic malaise of the latter twentieth century: a nation of newspaper readers may have watched McCarthy's rise, but indeed something very like "a nation of television viewers" witnessed his fall.

Johnny Iselin, as seen on TV.

McCarthy, as seen on TV during his filmed reply to CBS newscaster
Edward R. Murrow. McCarthy called Murrow "a symbol—the leader and
the cleverest of the jackal pack which is always found at the throat of
anyone who dares to expose communists and traitors." (Bettmann/Corbis)

If it is true that for a time television loved McCarthy—if there was momentarily something winning, by its sheer spectacle, in what Richard Fried called the "brute soap opera" of McCarthy's tactics as they came beaming across the airwaves—finally television itself contributed a great deal to McCarthy's undoing.[11] The most significant development here was the attention Edward R. Murrow turned on McCarthy and McCarthyism in 1953, and the documentary techniques he deployed in exposing the senator. Beginning in late 1953, Murrow and Fred Friendly's *See It Now* ran a cycle of programs that came at McCarthyite politics from a number of angles, all unflattering: "The Case of Milo Radulovich, A0589839" (October 20, 1953) covered the case of an air force lieutenant who was deemed a "security risk" because of his ongoing connection with his own immigrant parents; "An Argument in Indianapolis" (November 24, 1953) treated a controversy that had erupted when a group of citizens in that city set out to establish a chapter of the American Civil Liberties Union; "A Report on Senator Joseph R. McCarthy" (March 9, 1954), the most direct in the cycle, examined the senator and his tactics up close—it was here that Murrow passed on the characterization of McCarthyism as proceeding by the blunt techniques of "bullwhip and smear"; and "Annie Lee Moss before the McCarthy Committee" (March 16, 1954) reported on a code clerk for the Army Signal Corps who had been wrongly dismissed from her position because of her alleged ties to the Communist Party. (This case became momentarily humorous once it was clear that the race of Annie Lee Moss and other African-American principals in the investigation rather obviously failed to match up with the prosecution's descriptions and "positive" identifications.)[12]

Each of these telecasts had its trenchant moments. In the segment on Annie Lee Moss, for instance, as this impeccably mannered black woman fought to set the record straight before the committee—the consummate image of the underdog in 1954—the camera swung over again and again to show the empty chair of her chief accuser, Joseph McCarthy, who was evidently already on to other game. More famously, at the close of "A Report on Senator Joseph R. McCarthy," after showing McCarthy himself merrily quoting Shakespeare to win some point or other, Murrow directed his gaze into the camera: "Had

Edward R. Murrow defends his *See It Now* piece on Joseph McCarthy in 1954. (Bettmann/Corbis)

he looked three lines earlier in Shakespeare's *Caesar*, [the senator] would have found this line, which is not altogether inappropriate: 'The fault, dear Brutus, is not in our stars but in ourselves.'" Murrow went on to admonish:

> As a nation we have come into our full inheritance at a tender age. We proclaim ourselves—as indeed we are—the defenders of free- dom, what's left of it, but we cannot defend freedom abroad by deserting it at home. The actions of the junior senator from Wiscon- sin have caused alarm and dismay amongst our allies abroad and given considerable comfort to our enemies, and whose fault is that? Not really his. He didn't create the situation of fear; he merely exploited it, and rather successfully. Cassius was right: "The fault, dear Brutus, is not in our stars but in ourselves."[13]

The Murrow broadcasts are uniformly cited for their contribution to McCarthy's demise, though Murrow's techniques are not uniformly applauded. One critical observer argues that throughout the *See It Now* cycle, "Sections of McCarthy's speeches were taken out of context, and certain sequences seem to have been included more because of the expression on the senator's face or the tone of his voice—at one point a silly little laugh makes him appear to be insane—rather than the substance of what he had to say. Other sequences—his response to a testimonial dinner, for example, where he sputters and shuffles his feet for a minute or two before admitting to be speechless—seemed to have been included primarily to embarrass McCarthy."[14] Another account of Murrow's "Report on Senator Joseph R. McCarthy" notes that at one point,

> instead of cutting in what would be conventionally recognized as the "right" place . . . *See It Now* lingers on the senator for a moment longer. It is a deadly, revealing moment. McCarthy pauses, he looks about, his eyes seem to bulge. Nervously, he licks his lips, purses them, licks them again. The closeup microphone catches loud smacking as he opens and closes his mouth.[15]

But whether or not this represents "good" journalism—one thinks here of the similar charges leveled against Michael Moore's *Fahrenheit 9/11*—the images of McCarthy generated by television in 1953 and 1954 were critical in turning the tide of public opinion against him. Looking back on McCarthy's televised debacle, Arthur Miller recalled, "it was hardly ten minutes into the program [*See It Now*] when one knew it was the end of McCarthy, not altogether for reasons of content but more because he was so obviously handling subjects of great moment with mere quips, empty-sounding jibes, lumpy witticisms; it had not seemed quite as flat and ill-acted before."[16] Most important in the present context, these televised images were crucial to the lingering public memory of who McCarthy was and what he had done—they largely *constituted* the collective memory that *The Manchurian Candidate* would conjure up and toy with.

Soon after, in April and May 1954, the Army–McCarthy hearings sealed his fate: here, without even the bias of Murrow's deliberately prying camera and his unflattering editorial technique, McCarthy was done in by his own arrogant tenacity. It was here that, when McCarthy irrelevantly sought to besmirch one of the lawyers in Hale and Dorr (the firm representing the army) as a Lawyers' Guild member and therefore as a communist, army counsel Joseph Welch ripped into the senator in the apolitical but deeply human and affecting terms of cruelty, recklessness, and indecency. Having patiently explained that the attorney in question had been removed from this case—not because he was in fact a communist or any such thing, but merely because Welch anticipated that McCarthy might try to make an issue of his Lawyers' Guild membership—Welch now scolded the senator: "Little did I dream you would be so reckless and so cruel as to do an injury to that lad [even in his absence] . . . I fear he shall always bear a scar needlessly inflicted by you." When McCarthy persisted in the attack, Welch cut him off: "Let us not assassinate this lad further, Senator. You have done enough. Have you no sense of decency, sir, at long last? Have you left no sense of decency?" Amid long and loud applause, Welch quit the chamber, leaving a bumbling and befuddled McCarthy shrugging into the cameras.[17]

As James Reston wrote in the *New York Times* in the wake of this episode, television had "demonstrated with appalling clarity precisely what kind of man [McCarthy] is."

> One cannot remain indifferent to Joe McCarthy in one's living room. He is an abrasive man. And he is recklessly transparent. The country did not know him before, despite all the headlines. Now it has seen him. It has had a startling but accurate presentation of his ideas, his tactics, his immense physical power, and it is at least basing its judgments now on firsthand observations. The things that have hurt him and have cost him support are his manner and his manners.[18]

After that appearance, and in particular after McCarthy's televised dismantling by Joseph Welch, "people started to laugh at him" according to another *Times* reporter. "He became a joke, then a bore."[19]

This is the memory that was in play for most viewers, when *The Manchurian Candidate* opened, eight years after McCarthy's downfall. This, significantly, is exactly the McCarthy presented in the film— the McCarthy of the hot lights and television cameras, Arthur Miller's ill-acted McCarthy, the McCarthy of lumpy witticism and empty jibe. But in its narrative conflation of two distinct historical moments—its transporting of the slain-monster McCarthy of the Army– McCarthy hearings (1954) back to the originary, Wheeling moment of "205 known communists in the State Department" (1950)—the

film bends the reflection of McCarthy's career and the entire phenomenon of McCarthyism, as in a funhouse mirror.

This is the first maneuver in the satiric method of *The Manchurian
Candidate*. On the one hand, the depiction creates a certain ambiguity when it comes to Murrow's question of whether the fault "is not
in our stars but in ourselves": this telescoped image of McCarthy at
once as an emergent political juggernaut and a toppling buffoon may
articulate the smug notion on behalf of the audience that Americans
had had this scoundrel pegged all along, but if so, it also raises the
deeply uncomfortable challenge, how could they have let him get so
far? Here his crusade looks more ridiculous than it possibly could have
on Lincoln Day, 1950. But, on the other hand, what this conflation
does for sure is to render McCarthy the butt of an immense joke. His
accusations are patently absurd, and—worse, perhaps—they lack all
art. He plainly has nothing on the secretary of defense, for instance,
nor is there anything the least bit compelling about the case he puts
forward. Bullwhip and smear become transparency and sham. In any
case, to note that the McCarthy figure provides the only comic relief
in this tense thriller is probably to say enough.

Which brings us to the second maneuver in the film's satiric method: its careful manipulation of, and alternation between, McCarthy's
public and private personae. Iselin/McCarthy's public front and his
private conniving—or, more damning still, his private wheedling before the towering figure of Eleanor Iselin—are brilliantly modulated
throughout the narrative. A public appearance at the airfield gives
way to private family moments in limo and airplane; a dramatic (and
televised) public appearance in the Senate hearing room gives way to
the semiprivacy of the vestibule and then the full privacy of the
Iselin library. This private moment itself—where, significantly, a
puppet-like Iselin begs his wife to let him pick his own number of
"known communists"—then gives way to a dramatic public announcement, once again under the harsh lights of the Senate chamber, that there are "fifty-seven card-carrying members of the Communist Party in the Defense Department." Iselin's next appearance is
back in private, where for the first time his wife's total power and dis-
dain are fully revealed: "I keep telling you not to think," she says
coldly. "You're very, very good at a great many things, but thinking,

hon, just simply isn't one of them. You keep shouting 'point of order, point of order' into the television cameras, and I'll handle the rest." Iselin's next appearance is at the costume party, a sequence that itself alternates between public moments of drunken clownishness— Iselin's most authentic self, we are led to conclude—and quieter, private exchanges with his puppet master Eleanor ("Run along," she tells him, "the grown-ups have to talk"). And finally, his last three, fleeting appearances are public—his televised image charging Jordan with treason, the interview with reporters where he expresses condolences upon Jordan's death, and his appearance at the convention.

There are two things to note about the staccato, alternating rhythm of the public and the private here. One is the absolute bifurcation between the two realms, and the corresponding disjunction between what *seems* to be (what is revealed in public—on television, for example) and what *actually is* (what is revealed only quietly, behind the scenes). The film's depiction of McCarthy is in fact built upon the jarring incongruity between his brash and confident public charges on the one hand, and his cowering and uncertain deference to Eleanor on the other. The second noteworthy point, then, is that, as McCarthy/Iselin's public moments in the film are so carefully crafted from the actual historical record—and in particular the televisual record—the effect is to *suggest* an exposé of McCarthyism itself, an account of the behind-the-scenes actuality of the Wisconsin senator and his meteoric moment in the nation's political life several years earlier. That is indeed part of the humor—Frankenheimer's invitation to consider that, ahhh, perhaps *this* is what was taking place off camera each time McCarthy surfaced with more charges.

A signal moment in this connection is Iselin's comically borrowing the "57" from a ketchup bottle for his next round of accusations. This would be a funny gag in any case, but it becomes especially so when one recalls—as many members of the 1962 audience surely did—that fifty-seven is in fact one of the numbers that McCarthy had harped on in his melodramatic calculations of communists in the State Department during the Truman years. In the original Wheeling speech, McCarthy had used the number 205, a figure he evidently arrived at simply by taking "284 individuals" whose security reviews had resulted in "adverse recommendation," according to a letter by Secretary of State James Byrnes, and subtracting the "79" whose services had been terminated. Neither the 284 nor the 79 *necessarily* had anything to do with communism or the Communist Party, but the Byrnes letter at least explains McCarthy's original arithmetic. But he later revised that figure—in his public statements, in a forceful telegram to the president, and even in later accounts of his original Wheeling speech, including the one he entered into the *Congressional Record:* "I have in my hand 57 cases of individuals who would appear to be either card carrying members or certainly loyal to the Communist Party, but who nevertheless are still helping to shape our foreign policy."[20]

The joke in the Heinz scene, then, becomes not simply "this demagogue will pull his numbers from *anywhere*," but rather, "*that's* where McCarthy got that number." Like medieval astronomers whose task it was to "save the appearances"—to make what was observable in the firmament square with the "facts" of a particular cosmology—Condon and Frankenheimer made the observed public presence of McCarthy some years earlier square with a fantastic and occasionally comic theory of the actual principles of his political orbit. And, like medieval astronomy, the power of the theory derives in no small part from the airtight totality by which it matches the observed phenomena—the extent to which "appearances" are indeed "saved." To read the post-Murrow, post-Welch accounts of the televised McCarthy—the bulging and the smacking, the bumbling and shuffling, the hollow jibes and empty witticisms—is to read a perfect description of Johnny Iselin as played by James Gregory. But having re-created this collective and very public memory, Frankenheimer then publicizes the private, as it were, revealing the intervening off-camera moments to which even the prying lens of Edward R. Murrow could not make us privy. In so doing, *The Manchurian Candidate* marries Americans' collective memory of McCarthy to a new, parodic conspiracy theory of his intentions and motives.

Which is where *The Manchurian Candidate* begins to turn inward on itself, where comedy becomes tragedy and where purported anti-anticommunism becomes, in fact, *McCarthyism*. The bifurcation of public and private that operates in the depiction of Iselin is precisely the bifurcation that McCarthyism had thrived upon and that Cold

War Hollywood film had reveled in: a shocking hidden identity lies behind the placid public mask of the State Department employee (the Wheeling speech), an army lawyer (the Army–McCarthy hearings), one's kindly suburban neighbor (*Invasion of the Body Snatchers*), or one's own urbane offspring (*My Son John*)—and now, the demagogic Wisconsin senator. *The Manchurian Candidate* may parody Joseph McCarthy fairly gleefully, but it nonetheless adopts his modus operandi, and in doing so the film endorses his vision and authenticates his thesis. Although the film lambastes McCarthy, it also unwaveringly proceeds according to the epistemology of McCarthy*ism.*

It may be fruitful, in this regard, to set the workings of "public" and "private" in this purportedly anti-McCarthyite parody within the broader context of a political discourse of "privacy"—and particularly the *loss* of privacy—which was taking shape in the 1950s and early 1960s. As legal and literary scholar Deborah Nelson has observed, in these years the American concern for privacy as "a lost thing" surfaced "in an astonishing variety of locations—journalistic exposés, television programs, law review articles, mass-market magazines, films, Supreme Court decisions, poems, novels, autobiographies, corporate hiring manuals, scientific protocols, government studies, and congressional hearings," and it surfaced "in response to an extraordinary range of stimuli—satellites, surveillance equipment such as 'spike mikes' and telephoto lenses, job testing, psychological surveys, consumer polls, educational records, data-bases and computers in general, psychoanalysis, suburbs, television, celebrity profiles, news reporting, and more."[21] Such concerns were not exclusively linked to Cold War politics—questions of sexuality, birth control, and consent figured here too, as in court cases such as *Griswold v. Connecticut* (1965)—but the Cold War's ideological coordinates were decisive: on the one hand, the erosion of privacy was among the hallmarks of totalitarianism, including "red fascism"; and, on the other, the very war against communism had "created a rationale for surveillance that was infinitely expandable."[22] The powers and the prying eyes of the state were showing up in more and more areas of everyday life—a potentially troubling development even within the anticommunist formulations of *My Son John* and *Them!*, as noted earlier. Politically, then, the debate over privacy proceeded according to a vexing conundrum: "either privacy was stable and the United States would remain free, or privacy was dying and the nation was headed down the road to totalitarianism"; and yet the most vigorous defense of the private realm—as mounted, say, by Hoover's FBI—also threatened its erosion.[23]

This cultural conversation actually crested slightly after *The Manchurian Candidate* appeared in 1962. One charts its progress by milestone works like Morris Ernst's *Privacy: The Right to Be Let Alone* (1962), Myron Brenton's *The Privacy Invaders* and Vance Packard's *The Naked Society* (both 1964), and Allen Westin's *Privacy and Freedom* (1967).[24] But the discussion was well under way in the 1950s, beginning, perhaps, with Hannah Arendt's analysis of the political valences of privacy in *The Origins of Totalitarianism* (1951). Totalitarian government, she wrote, "certainly could not exist without destroying the public realm of life" and thereby people's "political capacities"; but "totalitarian domination as a form of government is new in that it is not content with this isolation and [it] destroys private life as well." Its incursions into the private constitute, in effect, the *total* in "totalitarian."[25]

This is precisely where Cold War film had made its contribution to the vernacular understanding of politics, surveillance, and privacy, even years before books like Brenton's *Privacy Invaders* appeared. But the logic of films like *Invasion of the Body Snatchers* and *Kiss Me Deadly* was convoluted and complex. As Michael Rogin wrote,

> Cold War films present themselves as defending private life from Communism. Like domestic ideology, however, these movies promote the takeover of the private by the falsely private. They politicize privacy in the name of protecting it and thereby wipe it out. Domestic and Cold War ideologies not only dissolve the private into the public; they also do the reverse. They depoliticize politics by blaming subversion on personal influence.[26]

"Counterpoised to the fears of penetration," adds Nelson, "is the anxiety that private space affords sanctuary to the enemies of privacy."[27]

And, like many far less intelligent films of the Cold War era, this is precisely where *The Manchurian Candidate* casts its lot philosophically, notwithstanding its biting caricature of McCarthy: if the most chilling aspect of the narrative is the extent to which Raymond Shaw's very *self* has been annexed as public (Soviet) property—a chill experienced most vividly at that moment when he shoots Jocie—still that annexation itself derives from the "sanctuary" that "private spaces" have afforded to those who would exploit them. This is ultimately Johnny Iselin's greatest political capital—not his brash tactic of bullwhip and smear, but the "sanctuary" he is accorded to conceal his true operations, and his consequent ability to don the public mask of the crusader without much danger of his actual mission being surveilled and exposed.

That anticommunism itself could be "un-American" was a formulation of wide currency in the early Cold War years—hence the acronym HUAC, for instance, whose altered order (the entity was actually called the House Committee on Un-American Activities, or HCUA) purposely and playfully suggested that it was the *House committee* that was behaving in suspect ways. As Ring Lardner Jr. prepared to say before HUAC in 1947 (but was barred from saying by Chairman Thomas, so the remarks were printed only decades later), "The atmosphere [in Hollywood] is considerably different than that of the small segment of Washington to which I have been exposed in the last ten days. Compared to what I have seen and heard in this room, Hollywood is a citadel of freedom. Here anti-American sentiments are freely expressed and their spokesmen heartily congratulated."[28] Truman himself once referred to McCarthy as "the greatest asset the Kremlin has."[29] This is in fact the position articulated in the film by Senator Thomas Jordan, though his anti-McCarthyite insight cannot save him from the Soviet conspiracy whose existence he so vigorously denies.

It may thus be tempting to view the McCarthy-as-communist paradox in *The Manchurian Candidate* with a certain bemusement—as a comic if extreme twist on dissenters' typical challenges to the received meaning of the term "un-American." But this plot element of a communist McCarthy, and particularly the method by which the McCarthy figure at once enacts and conceals his political intentions, runs far deeper. In its parodic approach to the memory of Joseph McCarthy the film leans decidedly left, signaling, it would seem, that its over-the-top anticommunism is merely campy (as some have read it) and nowise truly "dark." But in its epistemology *The Manchurian*

Candidate is dark indeed, sharing far more with classic Cold War films like *My Son John* than with the cinema of emergent dissent—*Dr. Strangelove* (1964), for instance. This is why, upon its release, the film provoked such impassioned denunciations from both the right and the left. The Inglewood, California, district of the American Legion, for example, declared in a resolution that "Communist infiltration in motion pictures has accelerated since the last investigation," citing *The Manchurian Candidate* as a vivid example of a cinematic attempt to "undermine congressional committees." The resolution urged a resumption of hearings to "determine once again to what extent this vital information medium (motion pictures) has been recaptured by agents of the Communist conspiracy." (George Axelrod, for his part, found this reading of the film so "hilarious" that he joked about pursuing the movie rights to the story of the American Legion's dissent.) Within weeks, however, the Communist *People's World* had also condemned the film as "the most vicious attempt yet made by the [film] industry to cash in on Soviet–American tensions."[30]

That *The Manchurian Candidate*'s articulations of anticommunism and anti-anticommunism are inseparably conjoined is precisely the point, and speaks eloquently to the convoluted, contradictory textures of Cold War culture; one hesitates to put too much weight to either side of this equation in its delicate equipoise. But because the McCarthyite, public/private dichotomy in the construction of the Iselin character is far subtler than the brash, absurd behavior of the satirized McCarthy, this side of the equation bears emphasis. In its intentional excesses, the film may part ways with McCarthy on the question of the communist peril per se—Frankenheimer is perhaps on solid ground in his contention that *The Manchurian Candidate* was not "anti-Soviet"—but it is right *with* McCarthy in its understanding of public masks and private truths, and thus in the philosophical orientation toward the political "zones of sovereignty" which that worldview implies. Like its unremitting Orientalism, to which we turn next, its tacit endorsement of Hooverism and surveillance suggests that *The Manchurian Candidate* is a text not simply *on* the Cold War, but *of* it, participating subtly but deeply in the fortification of precisely the political edifice it would seem at first glance to demolish.

5

Like Fu Manchu

Mapping Manchuria

I can see that Chinese cat standing there smiling like Fu Manchu.

—*Bennett Marco*

When Ben Marco likens Dr. Yen Lo to an iconic literary and screen villain of the 1920s and 1930s, he is executing a powerful double maneuver. First, he is demonstrating yet again the mass-mediated quality of the organization man's consciousness: that he can apparently see and comprehend Yen Lo only according to the ready-made template provided by pulp novels and Hollywood films speaks volumes about the borrowed quality of Marco's own thought processes. And second, he is further reifying that ready-made image for *us* by insisting on how closely this "real" Chinese figure approximates the Hollywood stereotype. By Marco's vicious and circular logic of race, representation, and reality, the still-looming image of Fu Manchu "explains" the nature of Dr. Yen Lo, even as Yen Lo's presence—and ultimately, his particular brand of evil—"proves" the sociological truth behind the popular Fu Manchu iconography. Frankenheimer and Axelrod may self-consciously call attention to an absurd Hollywood stereotype, but they pass it right along to us nonetheless.

The "Manchurian" of *The Manchurian Candidate* is rich in its sig-
nifications. Even if, as some have argued, the film signals the breakup
of the Cold War consensus rather than expressing the consensus itself,
still it elaborates its thesis in large part through both long-standing
and shorter-term mythologies of "the Orient." Eleanor Iselin may get
us to drop our guard when, in parodic fashion, she ventriloquizes
anti-Asian racism by gruffly addressing Chunjin as "Chu Chin Chow,
or whatever your name is." Here as elsewhere the film has it both
ways: it pokes fun at Eleanor Iselin's garden-variety racism, but finally
the narrative itself is cast in reflexive terms that are no less anti-
Asian than her uncaring address. The Oriental geisha/harem evoked
by the opening brothel scene, Yen Lo's chilly glee in murder, Chunjin's duplicity in his role as faithful servant (both platoon interpreter
and New York houseboy)—all play upon long-established images and
meanings. The free play of such Orientalist representations in the
United States stretches from mid-nineteenth-century commercial culture's "edifying curiosities" (such as Chang and Eng the Siamese
Twins), to the Yellow Peril literature of the early twentieth century,
to the "Mongol-Slav" enemy in the policy discourse of the Truman
and Eisenhower administrations, to—indeed—post-9/11 depictions
of Islam or of Iraqi resistance.[1]

For this reason it is useful to examine the conceptions of Asia and
Asianness in *The Manchurian Candidate* within three distinct hori-
zons of interpretation: first, within the long-range, glacial Orientalist
thinking that has characterized U.S.–Asian relations since the time
that George Washington first outfitted his New York home with opu-
lent "china bowls"; second, within the proximate, period-specific,
and heightened Orientalism that characterized American outlooks in
the years from the 1940s to the 1960s, encompassing the war in the
Pacific, the Korean War, and the beginnings of the war in Vietnam;
and finally, within Hollywood's own history of Orientalist images,
plotlines, and practices—both the celluloid cosmos within which
Dr. Yen Lo and Chunjin were located as all-too-familiar types and
the hiring practices of the Hollywood studio itself, by which these
actors, Khigh Diegh and Henry Silva, were consistently typecast. It is
not just that the film has much to reveal about the geographic and
racial imagination in the United States; it is also the case that the

wider universe of American Orientalism casts some light on the cultural work that the film accomplishes—and how the film gathers its power—both as conscious political satire and as reflexive Cold War ideology.

Before proceeding to Frankenheimer's "Manchuria," it is worth defining "Orientalism" at the outset, as the term has perhaps circulated with more frequency than precision of late. "Orientalism" does not simply mean anti-Asian or anti–Middle Eastern *racism*, although in American political culture, as in British and French, there is a significant degree of overlap between the two. Rather, though "race" may remain one of its most reliable markers, "Orientalism" as first articulated by Edward Said refers to a very particular set of ideas presuming a geotemporal bifurcation of human history—a yawning developmental rift along some imagined divide at the Mediterranean and Black Seas separating the peoples of "the West" from those of "the Orient," a gaping chasm whose depth is thought to render impossible any commonality of interest and understanding from one shore of the breach to the other. "East is East and West is West," as Rudyard Kipling put it in Orientalism's most famous jingle, "and never the twain shall meet."[2] World War II–era depictions of the Japanese enemy as "monkey folk," "apes," or "vermin" were racist, to take an instance; but the domestic project of Japanese-American internment, on the other hand, depended on a racism that was entwined with distinctly *Orientalist* assumptions: according to California Attorney General Earl Warren, "when we deal with the Japanese we are in an entirely different field [in distinction to "Caucasians"] and we cannot form any opinion that we believe to be sound." The Japanese here, Warren is saying, are not simply inferior but are in some sense *unknowable*, which is why, unlike German- or Italian-Americans, they must be interned en masse.[3]

Orientalism takes its name from the emergent nineteenth-century academic discipline that trained its gaze and its interpretive apparatus on "the East," whose practitioners, such as Evelyn Baring Cromer and Edward William Lane, called themselves "Orientalists." Thus, for Edward Said Orientalism represented not simply a template of potent stereotypes, but a deeper epistemological project, a way of knowing the world that both derived from *and contributed to* the grossly uneven power relations between Europe (and America), on the one hand, and the peoples of "the Orient," on the other. The Orientalist's tenets regarding "Oriental" peoples may have rationalized colonial rule, that is, but so were they initially nourished and cultivated within the context of colonial (actually, colonizing) conditions. Such "knowledge" could never be value-neutral, but was and could only be an epistemology of opposition, competition, subjugation, or exploitation—"a Western style for dominating, restructuring, and having authority over the Orient."[4]

The Orientalists' worldview, then, entailed an elaborate set of polar oppositions between East and West whose logic both justified and naturalized Western domination: "from the point of view of governing him," wrote Lord Cromer, "... I content myself with noting the fact that somehow or other the Oriental generally acts, speaks, and thinks in a manner exactly opposite to the European."[5] Where the West is rational, the Orient is irrational; the West active, the Orient passive; the West masculine, the Orient feminine; the West cerebral, the Orient sensual; the West progressive, the Orient decadent and semi- (or fully) barbaric—perhaps outside the stream of history altogether; the West straight-talking and direct, the Orient inscrutable, mysterious; the West scientific and empirical, the Orient superstitious; the West self-governing, the Orient prone to despotism; the West orderly, the Orient chaotic; the West noble and trustworthy, the Orient habitually dishonest—"want of accuracy, which easily degenerates into untruthfulness, is in fact the main characteristic of the Oriental mind," wrote Cromer.[6]

One conclusion widely drawn in the West was that there was no "Oriental" subjectivity capable of articulating itself reliably. The Orient existed solely as an object for Western inspection and apprehension: "only the Orientalist can interpret the Orient, the Orient being radically incapable of interpreting itself."[7] The primary implication for Said, then, was that Orientalists were therefore not *describing* an already-existing, objective "Orient," but were in fact *creating* one, speaking it into existence:

> The relation between Orientalist and Orient was essentially hermeneutical: standing before a distant, barely intelligible civilization or cultural monument, the Orientalist scholar reduced the obscurity by

translating, sympathetically portraying, inwardly grasping the hard-to-reach object. Yet the Orientalist remained outside the Orient, which, however much it was made to appear intelligible, remained beyond the Occident. This cultural, temporal, and geographical distance was expressed in metaphors of depth, secrecy, and sexual promise: phrases like "the veils of an Eastern bride" or "the inscrutable Orient" passed into the common language.[8]

Western practices of inquiry and explication were integral to Western practices of governance and colonial administration. This body of Orientalist thinking—at the intersection of "knowledge" and power—has outlived figures such as Lord Cromer by more than a century and is still very much with us. When Western journalists "cover" Islam today, in Said's view, they still tend to do so in the sense that they are *concealing* it even while "reporting" on it—citing ninth-century Islamic clerics, for instance, to prove some point about modern-day Iran.[9]

By "the Orient" Said, like his nineteenth-century Orientalists themselves, meant primarily that region which we inaccurately call the Middle East, stretching perhaps from Morocco on the far western rim of North Africa, to the Central Asian lands east of the Caspian Sea. But several recent scholars have noted the applicability of Said's framework for understanding the position of East Asia, too, in Euro-Americans' common imaginative geographies, and of East Asians themselves in U.S. political culture. The discourse of Orientalism was a transatlantic discourse from the outset; but from the sailing of the first Asia-bound trading ship, the *China Clipper,* to the earliest arrival of Chinese immigrants on the West Coast, to the Open Door Notes and the Philippine-American War, the United States was generally more concerned with the Far East than the Near East, and Americans adapted the same totalizing and essentializing tropes— "never the twain shall meet"—in discussing China or Japan that Cromer and others had developed in reference to Egypt and Arabia. In his 1950s effort to assemble a composite picture of Americans' perceptions of the Far East, Harold Isaacs's interviews tended to elicit vernacular descriptions cast in precisely the terms of Edward Said's nineteenth-century commentators on Egypt or the Ottoman Empire:

they are heathen; people with other gods, different religious concepts, religiosity; cultural, religious, language differences; customs strange to an American; the idea of the Eastern soul, mind, mentality, morals, different from ours; they are difficult to understand; they are different.[10]

No matter how deep the specific exception, wrote Said of the Middle Eastern character in the Western imagination, "no matter how much a single Oriental can escape the fences placed around him, he is *first* an Oriental, *second* a human being, and *last* again an Oriental."[11] The same was true here. Although in the mid-twentieth century American Orientalism would fix upon the Middle East at last, throughout much of U.S. history the chief object of this kind of thinking has been the Far East and its peoples: the Chinese during the Exclusion era, the Japanese in the era of the Yellow Peril, popular silver-screen villains like Fu Manchu in the 1930s, or, indeed, the inscrutable and duplicitous Koreans and Chinese of *The Manchurian Candidate* during the Cold War.[12]

American Orientalism has a remarkably deep genealogy. As John Kuo Wei Tchen has argued, "The use of Chinese things, ideas, and people in the United States, in various imagined and real forms, has been instrumental in forming this nation's cultural identity" from the revolutionary generation on down. A "passionate coveting of refined Chinese things" was an integral element to the "culture of distinction" by which the new nation articulated its social variegations, having loosed itself from aristocracy's mores of social hierarchy. Tchen captures the significance of such distinctions—and the centrality of the Orient to them—in the hilarious image of General Washington feverishly acquiring "imported creamware dishes, sauceboats, plates, and fluted bowls, including three, more costly, 'china bowls'" for his New York home, even as war rattled the cobbles of the city outside. This revolutionary era's "patrician Orientalism," woven of symbolic attachments to Asian and Asian-style goods and ideas—porcelains, teas, Japan'd tea trays, Chinese silks, tragic plays like *The Orphan of China*—all served to define for the young nation "an independent occidental identity emulating China and drawing upon British patrician culture, but not tied too tightly to either."[13]

One of the hallmarks of Orientalist thought is that "the Orient" can appear in *either* admiring or fully demonizing shades—Orientalism is characterized less by its positive or negative valences than by its totalizing conception of immutable "difference."[14] The admiring, even partially emulative aspect of patrician Orientalism gave way to a much harsher (and more overtly racialized) set of conceptions in mid-nineteenth-century commercial culture. The fiercely negative judgments of the Far East that made their way into the penny press— particularly the reports of American missionaries, merchants, and diplomats, all of whom were thwarted in their designs in one way or another by the stubborn intractability of Chinese habits and will— were matched in the images of rising urban entertainments. The spectacle of "edifying curiosities"—Yan Zoo the Chinese Juggler, Afong Moy the Chinese Lady, Chang and Eng the Siamese Twins, the famous "Ten Thousand Things" of John Peters's Great Chinese Museum, P. T. Barnum's "Chinese Family," Quimbo Appo the "Exemplary Chinaman"—all put China and Chineseness on rather zoological display for Americans in the middle decades of the century. The racialized and ferociously exoticizing images of commercial Orientalism thus created an idiom for anti-Asian political comment long before actual Asian immigrants had arrived in the United States in appreciable numbers.[15]

The era of *political* Orientalism, inaugurated in the anti-Chinese agitation among white workers on the infamous Sand Lot in San Francisco in the 1870s, has persisted in one form or another ever since. Although American Orientalism has occasionally taken some more benign turns—American sentimentality about prerevolutionary China, for instance, as conveyed most famously in Pearl Buck's *The Good Earth;* or the "model minority" mythology of the post-1960s—the picture from the Chinese Exclusion Act (1882) onward has been fairly dark. In the run-up to the Exclusion Act the Forty-fourth Congress estimated that "The Mongolian race seems to have no desire for progress and to have no conception of representative and free institutions."[16] Conjoined notions of racial inferiority and "Oriental" unassimilability run through American political culture fairly continuously from this point on—in the anti-Japanese movement in Western states in the 1890s; in citizenship cases like *Ah Yup, Ozawa,*

and *Thind* between the 1870s and the 1920s; in the rumors of Chinatown's white slavery that swirled around New York and other urban
centers in the early 1900s; in the Asian Barred Zone established by
immigration law in 1924 (effectively extending the Exclusion Act to
the rest of Asia); in Japanese-American internment; in the endan-
gered "perpetual foreigner" status of Vincent Chin, Navorze Mody,
Vandy Phorng, Jim Loo, Hung Trong, and Thien Minh Ly, all of whom
were murdered in anti-Asian incidents in the 1980s and 1990s, some
amid taunts such as "Go home!" and "Get out of my Country!"[17]

The images and conventional narratives of popular culture have
buttressed anti-Asian politics all along, from "Heathen Chinee" dog-
gerels and "John Chinaman" songsters in the nineteenth century, to
the supreme Japanese treachery depicted in Michael Crichton's *Rising
Sun* toward the end of the twentieth. The circulation of Orientalist
imagery accelerated significantly, of course, with the growth of the
movie industry in the 1920s (concurrent, not incidentally, with the
establishment of the Asian Barred Zone). As one of Harold Isaacs's
informants recalled of the films from her girlhood:

> The mystery of Chinatown was suggested by a whole series of visual
> clichés—the ominous shadow of an Oriental figure thrown against a
> wall, secret panels which slide back to reveal an inscrutable Oriental
> face, the huge shadow of a hand with tapering fingers and long pointed
> fingernails poised menacingly, the raised dagger appearing suddenly
> and unexpectedly from between closed curtains.[18]

The greatest and most popular exemplar of the genre appeared in
a cycle of films beginning in 1929, with Boris Karloff in yellowface as
Fu Manchu, who, according to Hollywood's publicity material, had
"menace in every twitch of his finger, a threat in every twitch of his
eyebrow, terror in each split-second of his slanted eyes."[19] This is not
to say that the films in any way *improved* upon the Orientalist images
of evil available in other cultural forms, merely that film accelerated
and expanded their circulation. As Sax Rohmer (Arthur Ward) had
written in his pulp novel *The Insidious Dr. Fu Manchu* (1913):

> Imagine a person tall, lean and feline, high shouldered, with a brow
> like Shakespeare, and a face like Satan, a close shaven skull and long
> magnetic eyes of true cat green. Invest him with all the cruel cunning
> of an entire eastern race, accumulated in one giant intellect, with all

Boris Karloff in yellowface. (John Springer Collection/Corbis)

the resources . . . of a wealthy government . . . Imagine that awful
being, and you have a mental picture of Dr. Fu Manchu, the yellow
peril incarnate in one man.[20]

Here, then, is the antecedent to Condon and Frankenheimer's Dr. Yen
Lo—the satanic concentration of an entire continent's cruel cunning.

Such long-standing narrative and visual conventions in the representation of Asianness in U.S. culture would themselves have been

Warner Oland in *The Mysterious Dr. Fu Manchu* (1929). (John Springer Collection/Corbis)

quite enough to authenticate a villain like Yen Lo for American audiences. But both *The Manchurian Candidate* and the war it presumes to depict were produced during a period of especially heightened Orientalist concern. As Harold Isaacs wrote in the wake of the Korean War and on the eve of Vietnam, "Asia has become important above all because it has become dangerous. For most of those to whom Asia is newly discovered, a strong feeling of uneasiness, apprehension, or immanent peril overhangs all the immensity, complexity, unintelligibility of it."[21] (One might be inclined to flip the argument here, attributing Asia's "danger" to its "importance" rather than vice versa; but the general marriage of import and danger still holds.) Although newsman Eric Sevareid underscored the enduring continuities of the "Oriental" character—"The Chinese Reds did not invent official Chinese indifference to human life . . ."—still such images took on new meanings and achieved a new degree of menace in the years between the war in the Pacific and the Cold War engagements in Korea and Vietnam.[22]

Pearl Harbor, of course, inaugurated neither the brutal anti-Asian imagery nor the brutal military tactics that would characterize U.S. efforts in Japan, Korea, and Vietnam: in America's first land war in Asia, the oft forgotten Philippine-American War (1899–1902), one field general had promised to reduce the entire province of Samar to a "howling wilderness," and he advocated killing as combatants *all Filipinos over the age of ten.* "It is not civilized warfare, but we are not dealing with a civilized people," one Philadelphia paper had explained. "The only thing they know and fear is force, violence, and brutality, and we give it to them."[23] Our brutality is attributable to *them,* in other words; they are nothing like us—never the twain shall meet. Estimates of the Filipino death toll in this forgotten war range upwards of 220,000.

But by the mid-twentieth century, when the United States had become more thoroughly integrated into the global system on the terms of a major economic and military power, analogues would multiply. In Japan, the fire-bombing of Tokyo (in which nearly a hundred thousand civilians in a sixteen-square-mile area were "scorched and boiled and baked to death," in Major General Curtis LeMay's words) and the atomic bombing of Hiroshima and Nagasaki raised the specter of "total war" to levels undreamed of by previous generations.[24] In Korea, where Americans resisted the nuclear temptation, the unleashing of napalm and the intentional bombing of northern dams nonetheless resulted in the remarkable civilian death toll of two million (the civilian-to-soldier kill ratio, which had been 40 percent in

World War II, was 70 percent in Korea).[25] And the Vietnam War—
from systematic U.S. search-and-destroy missions, "Zippo raids," and
carpet bombings, to aberrations such as My Lai—has been famously
summed up in phrases like "We had to destroy the village in order to
save it," or "Then the village, which was no longer a village, was *our*
village." The United States destroyed thousands of villages and ham-
lets, twenty-five million acres of farmland, twelve million acres of
forest, and 1.5 million farm animals. The war also left in its wake
more than 879,000 orphans and one million widows.[26]

The unleashing of astonishing levels of violence in Asia, then, is
one of the consistent features of the period, as the war against fascism—and, ironically, "against racism"—gave way to the first hot
wars in the showdown against communism. Echoing "Hell Roarin'"
Jake Smith's order in the Philippines fifty years earlier, one U.S. officer
said of Korean children, "They're troops. Shoot 'em."[27] Curtis LeMay,
too, reflecting perhaps a distaste for *inefficiency* but also a rather
relaxed attitude toward civilian Korean deaths, later remarked:

> we slipped a note kind of under the door into the Pentagon and said,
> "Look, let's go up there . . . and burn down five of the biggest towns in
> North Korea—and they're not very big—and that ought to stop it."
> Well, the answer to that was four or five screams—"You'll kill a lot
> of non-combatants," and "It's too horrible." Yet over a period of
> three years or so . . . we burned down *every* town in North Korea
> and South Korea too.[28]

All of these mid-century military operations were carried out amid
a pervasive and fairly casual American discourse of Asian treacheries
and shortcomings. The Japanese were "vermin," "lice," "monkey-
men," "cockroaches or mice," "vipers," a "yellow serpent," "a veritable
human beehive or anthill," whose *total* "extermination" or "annihilation" was consistently favored by some 10 to 13 percent of the U.S.
population when polled.[29] The Koreans were "yellow bastards," "apes,"
and "gooks" who "scorn all the rules of civilized warfare." By "occidental standards," according to one military report in 1945, "Koreans
are not ready for independence"; and a CIA personality study of Syng-
man Rhee, the United States' handpicked *ally*, concluded that his
behavior was "irrational and even childish."[30] The Vietnamese, too,

were "little yellow bastards," "gooks," "slopes," and "slants" who did
not "value human life." So racialized were the tactics and the languages
of the Vietnam War that when he spoke out against it in 1967, Martin
Luther King Jr. identified "racism" and "militarism" as two of America's "interrelated flaws."[31] Parsing the public testimony of a former
undersecretary of the air force in 1970, Noam Chomsky wrote:

> Hoopes does not tell us how he knows that the Asian poor do not
> love life or fear pain, or that happiness is probably beyond their emo-
> tional comprehension. But he goes on to explain how "ideologues in
> Asia" make use of these characteristics of the Asian hordes. Their
> strategy is to convert Asia's capacity for endurance in suffering into
> an instrument into exploiting "a basic vulnerability of the Christian
> West." They do this by inviting the West "to carry its strategic logic
> to the final conclusion, which is genocide."[32]

Downright diabolical—very much like the Filipino insurgents whose
own savagery had elicited uncivilized warfare from U.S. soldiers in
Manila and Samar seventy years earlier.

In representing the "Oriental" enemy of the Korean 1950s for an
American audience at the dawn of the Vietnam era, then, *The Manchurian Candidate* could not exactly claim political innocence or detachment. The Orientalist motif in *The Manchurian Candidate* consists of three conceptual elements carried in three distinct characters
or plot points: sexual possession of the Orient, in the opening brothel
scene; Oriental inscrutability—and behind that, treachery—in Chunjin's double cross and his (false) domestication as Raymond's houseboy in New York; and Oriental brutality, embodied primarily in the
Yen Lo character and the brainwashing sequences.

In terms of both its overarching Orientalism and its ideological
work on the Korean War, one of the film's most significant but easily
overlooked scenes is the opening sequence at a Korean brothel. After
the opening legend, "Korea 1952," two soldiers whom we will later
know as Raymond Shaw and Bennett Marco pull up in a military
truck and park in front of a small, poorly lit clapboard building, Miss
Gertrude's. Marco remains in the truck, smoking and reading, while
Shaw gets out and enters the building. Once inside, we hear the blare
of a jazz record and the muffled, inarticulate hubbub of some kind of
party; Shaw makes his way past a disheveled couple who have come

Members of the platoon revel at Miss Gertrude's before being rousted by
Sergeant Raymond Shaw. Like the domesticated interior of the wagon in
Stagecoach (1939), the brothel repositions the Americans as "at home" in
this foreign clime, and therefore as something other than intruders.

into the entry hall from a side room (obviously a bedroom), and now
pause, necking in the hallway, as Shaw passes. He slides open an Oriental screen to reveal a smoky room full of revelers—uniformed (but
partly undressed) American soldiers, and Asian women in various
suggestive states of attire. One woman approaches Shaw and takes
his arm as if to lead him off somewhere, but Shaw, resisting, blows a
whistle to call an end to the festivity. One of the women reacts in
fear, but in voices dripping with sarcasm, various soldiers explain by
turns that this is only "our Raymond," "our lovable Sergeant Shaw,"
"Saint Raymond," as Shaw finally rousts them and leads them out
to the truck. The entire sequence encompasses about a minute and
a half.

As for its narrative work, the scene's most urgent plot point is to
establish Shaw as someone who is decidedly *not* "the kindest, bravest,
warmest, most wonderful human being" in the eyes of his platoon
(and, perhaps, to call into question his relationship to "normal" sexuality—a theme that will come into play later on in the triangulation
between Raymond, his mother, and Jocie). But there is a lot more
going on here besides. For one thing, the scene puts an extraordinarily
benign face on a very difficult set of social realities and social relations.
The Korean War, writes historian Katherine Moon,

with its accompanying poverty, social and political chaos, separation
of families, and millions of young orphans and widows, "mass produced" prostitutes, creating a large supply of girls and women without
homes and livelihoods. Fleeing bombs and gunfire and seeking food,
shelter, and work, camp followers flocked to areas where the UN/U.S.
forces were bivouacked.

By the 1960s, the "golden age" of the *kijich'on* (camptown) R&R infrastructure, the combination of economic transformations within parti-
tioned Korea, wrenching social dislocations, a massive and enduring
U.S. military presence, and deliberate U.S. and South Korean policies had conspired to create a "military-sexual complex" of more
than twenty thousand registered prostitutes "servicing" sixty-two
thousand soldiers. One of these *panjatjip* (houses of boards), Tong-
duch'on, evolved into an R&R "town" of more than seven thousand
prostitutes.[33]

Of course, John Frankenheimer was not the only American who
lacked a vocabulary in 1962 for addressing the politics of military
prostitution. The point is not to pillory him or George Axelrod for
their facile, even cheerful depiction of the brothel. Rather, it is to note
the significance of sexuality to the Orientalist construction of Korea;
and, further, to suggest that the film's more abiding image of Asianness—its villainy—relies quite heavily on this initial image of East–
West sexuality.

Among the structuring dualisms that Edward Said attributed to
Orientalist thinking was that of a masculine West and a feminine
Orient—indeed, this might be said to be the founding dualism of
them all: "the Orient was routinely described as feminine, its riches
as fertile, its main symbols the sensual woman, the harem and the
despotic—but curiously attractive—ruler."[34] The implication of this
sensual notion is profound, and it is twofold. First, East–West economic or geopolitical relations are scripted as an encounter whose
"natural" systems of dominance and submission borrow their authority from the "natural" order of patriarchal sexual relations. East and
West are made for each other, just like the "opposite sexes." The
West has the will to conquer, to possess; the East, no more than a will
to be possessed (or, in the parlance of neocolonialism, to be "pene-
trated"). It is thus inevitable that the male/West will "have" the

female/East, just as it is natural that, for the female/East, such possession will represent fulfillment itself. Second, then, the psychodrama of
sexualized East–West relations is scripted back upon the living, breath-
ing bodies of "Western" and "Oriental" people: the Asian woman (in
this case Korean) *stands for* the submissive East, assuming in fantasy
the image of the hyperfeminine-hypersubmissive-hypersexualized
object—the geisha, the comfort woman, the concubine, the harem
girl. As one contributor wrote in the military magazine *Pacific Stars
and Stripes* as late as 1977:

> Picture having three or four of the loveliest creatures God ever
> created hovering around you, singing, dancing, feeding you, washing
> what they feed you down with rice wine or beer, all saying at once,
> "You are the greatest." This is the Orient you heard about and came
> to find.[35]

Here, as elsewhere, the sexual availability and subservience of the
Asian woman strangely "proves" the availability and subservience of
Asia itself, and vice versa.

This narrative of sexualized East–West encounter, of course, tends
to generate problematic and fraught images of Asian masculinity—
either feminized (as in the case of the Chinese laundryman or the
Korean houseboy) or masculine yet brutish (as in the case of the
World War II–era Japanese soldier, whose only alternative in popular
perception during the war's grimmest moments would seem to have
been some unacceptable version of a virile, militarized masculinity).[36]
Both of these come into play in later scenes of *The Manchurian Candidate* as well.

For the moment, however, we are most interested in the Korean
brothel as *the* site that naturalizes and so justifies the U.S. presence in
East Asia. One of the young women in the brothel is conspicuously
reading an American fan magazine, *Movie Life*, a detail that—like
the jazz record playing in the background—seems to indicate an easy
affinity between East and West. But this also begs the question, *where
did these American cultural trappings come from?* They must be among
the accoutrements of the U.S. mission to the Far East. They may
help to naturalize the U.S. presence in Asia within the symbolic economy of the scene; but, upon reflection, they are not exactly *natural*.

As historian Bruce Cumings has written, one compelling interpretation—never terribly popular in the United States—posits the Korean War not as an East–West conflict characterized by Sino-Soviet "invasion," but fundamentally as an internal *civil* war, in which outside powers from both major Cold War blocs ultimately became involved.[37] Such a reading significantly revises standard American narratives, recasting the United States from home team to visitor, so to say, from "natural" Korean defender to unnaturalized, "foreign" meddler or occupier. This is precisely the reading that *The Manchurian Candidate* precludes, whatever else Frankenheimer wants to say about the politics of the film. The opening sequence establishes the United States as invited, cheerfully entertained, very much belonging and at home—"naturally" (which is to say, *sexually*) matched to Korea. (This is one reason that *North* Korea is entirely outside the consciousness of the film. "Korea" here is exclusively the Korea that desires America and that America desires; with the single exception of Chunjin, "the enemy" is depicted, not as Korean at all, but as Chinese and Soviet.)

In this sense, both the sexuality and the interiority of the brothel scene function for the Korean War very much as the domesticity of the coach had functioned for the Indian wars in westerns like John Ford's *Stagecoach* (1939), to cite but one example: it reverses the historical script of the encounter, casting the intruder as natural resident, the natural resident as invader. *The Manchurian Candidate* belongs, for a moment anyway, to America's longest-standing and popular genre, the captivity narrative. One of the most pressing ideological requirements of this genre—like the ideological imperatives of Harry Truman's 1950 and indeed John Frankenheimer's 1962—is that the captive must be *beset* by invaders, not an invader himself or herself. A later text like both the film and the TV series M*A*S*H (though trading in Orientalist images of its own—the general facelessness of the Asian masses, for instance) still managed, in the political commentary of Hawkeye Pierce, to raise precisely the question of the *unnatural* American presence in Korea that *The Manchurian Candidate* did not. It is the Orientalism of the opening scene, its sexualized logic and imagery, that underpins the film's mute acceptance of this first major U.S. deployment under NSC-68's regime of global commitment.

This Orientalist, sexualized opening gambit not only frames the U.S. presence in East Asia, but it provides the foundation for the film's ensuing renditions of Oriental villainy. It is against the backdrop of the brothel's hospitality that, in the very next scene, we see Chunjin sell out "Cholly Company" and hand them over to the Sino-Soviet plotters. The visual cues of this next sequence are important and familiar—the inscrutable but seemingly trustworthy "native guide" leading the men across unfamiliar terrain; then, after their sacking, his handshake with an enemy officer and an almost leering mid-shot of Chunjin's duplicitous and self-satisfied face. The duplicity here—like the sensuality of the Oriental woman—was ready-made in U.S. culture and already had thousands of well-known precedents, Fu Manchu, the white slaver, and Japanese Emperor Hirohito among them. But so does Frankenheimer's rendering of Chunjin's duplicity both depend on, and flow from, the sociopolitical equation established moments ago in the brothel. If there is any room at all to think of the Korean conflict as a civil war—if we are aware in the least of Koreans fighting Koreans for the soul and future of the nation—then Chunjin's treachery might read as, say, *patriotism*; one person's traitor is another's freedom fighter. But because the Koreans' affinity for, and lusty desires toward, America are already "known" in the film, Chunjin can only be serving Chinese and Soviet, not Korean, interests: he is not only a sellout to his American allies, but a turncoat to his country as well, a pattern of despicable political disloyalties that lie safely hidden behind his inscrutable Oriental eyes.

The Orientalist brief against Chunjin is extended later on, when he turns up in New York to apply for a job as Raymond Shaw's valet. Here he rather uneasily inhabits two contradictory stereotypes of the Asian male. On the one hand, he is the feminized houseboy—"I am tailor and mender, I am cook, I am cleaner and scroo-ber, I fix anything, I take message..." His willing subservience is exaggerated as he simultaneously bows *and* salutes to Shaw. His subservience is also exaggerated—as is his duplicity—when, rudely addressing him as "Chu Chin Chow or whatever your name is," Eleanor Iselin berates

Chunjin's and Marco's martial-arts blowout, after Marco recognizes Shaw's new Korean houseboy as the recording secretary from his own recurring dream. (Bettmann/Corbis)

him over the details of how properly to prepare a steak. He silently submits, demonstrating yet again his capacity for cunning, as we already know that he is in New York not as a cook or a houseboy at all, but as an operative. (Later we recognize that this exchange demonstrates Eleanor Iselin's capacity for duplicity, too: she knows precisely who "Chu Chin Chow" is.)

But if Chunjin is the feminized houseboy, so is he the fierce Asian fighter, an image whose lineage descends from Samurai warriors, to kamikaze pilots, to a later generation's kung fu masters. Upon a visit to Raymond Shaw's New York apartment, when he recognizes the houseboy as the recording secretary of his fevered dreams, Marco attacks Chunjin and the two have a rib- and furniture-cracking karate blowout until the police arrive. In retrospect, it is hard not to read this scene through the comic martial-arts ambushes between Cato and Clouseau in the later *Pink Panther* films. Perhaps the scene was a little bit funny even in 1962. But as a narrative detail, it should be noted, Chunjin's presence in New York is hardly necessary—he has no role to play in the Manchurian plot as it unfolds on this continent. Rather, his presence merely suspends the issue of who Raymond's "American operative" really is, and perhaps it allows Marco another puzzle piece. ("What was Raymond doing with his hands? How did the old ladies turn into Russians? And what were *you* doing there?" he keeps asking, as he and Chunjin go crashing through the tables, lamps, and china closets in Raymond's living room as they fight.) In any case, Chunjin's skill as a fighter, when twinned with his softer, more feminized status as houseboy, serves primarily to underscore his duplicitous nature and in this to underscore the larger theme of Oriental danger.

The third Orientalist element, and easily the heart of *The Manchurian Candidate*'s ideological work in this area, consists of the brainwashing sequences: the dreamy and disorienting scenes at the New Jersey hydrangea seminar, as dredged up from the disjointed memories of Ben Marco and Allen Melvin, and Yen Lo's subsequent visit with Raymond in a Soviet-run sanitarium in Manhattan. It is here that Yen Lo makes his appearance, "smiling like Fu Manchu," as Marco sees him; and indeed, the combination of Yen's diabolical ingenuity and his casual capacity for brutality ("Shoot Bobby, Raymond—through the forehead") makes this an apposite association on Marco's part. American audiences in the early 1960s had a readymade, thoroughly racialized frame for the brainwashing sequence. Although the psychiatric technologies named here have explicitly to do with the legacy of Ivan Petrovich Pavlov and the Soviet Pavlov Institute, the film—like American discourse at the time of the actual brainwashing scare—locates brainwashing as a distinctly "Oriental" practice. It is Yen Lo who has done the "conditioning," and it is he alone who runs the Manchurian brainwashing seminar for this international gathering of commissars.

"The dilemma of the American subjected to 'brainwashing' by an unscrupulous and remorseless foe was only just becoming the subject of governmental, medical, social scientific, and literary inquiry" in the 1950s, writes Harold Isaacs. But the inquiry itself, and its hold on the American imagination, drew from a deep well of Orientalist imagery and suspicion:

it was clear that great power was already attached to the *mystique* which gave the Chinese such extraordinary skill in the use of these weapons of mental and emotional torture. It obviously was going to outstrip by far anything attributed to the Russians . . . For the Chinese there was a whole battery of relevant qualities to draw upon, qualities which had been long attributed to them in some unique measure in the past: their inhuman cruelty, for one thing, and at its service, their inscrutability, their deviousness, their subtlety, and their devilish cleverness.

In the wake of the "revelations" of brainwashing in Korea, Isaacs judged, "the older figure of the 'evil and untrustworthy Oriental'" actually paled before the reality. "The fictionally evil Fu Manchu could hardly compete with a real-life Chinese Communist commissar."[38] As Isaacs dimly recognized, there was a confounding circularity here: borrowing as they did on preexisting presumptions of Oriental "mystique," the Korean brainwashing stories in the popular media carried a strong trace of "fictional evil" themselves, even if every allegation had turned out to be true.

The character of Yen Lo thus draws upon and also feeds into a longer-standing cultural conversation about "the Oriental." The unnerving thing about Yen Lo—the quality that raises him above his Soviet comrades in the metrics of sheer evil—is his calm, even cheerful approach to villainy. Yen Lo laughs a lot, and he talks a lot about laughing. He laughs mischievously when he reports that he has replaced the U.S. soldiers' tobacco with yak dung. "There is nothing like a good laugh to lighten the burdens of the day," he says to Zilkov before asking Raymond nonchalantly, "Do you remember murdering Mavole and Lembeck?" He smiles icily while Raymond recites the story he has been conditioned to recall, and then he laughs a sustained, sinister laugh when he observes that Raymond's brain "has not only been washed, as they say, it has been *dry-cleaned*." When the Soviets insist on a "practical test" to assure that their fabricated assassin is functioning properly, Yen suggests, sweet as you please, "Have him kill one of your own people." But then, with a steely laugh—"With humor, Mr. Zilkov, always with a little humor"—he decides on Raymond's boss, Holborne Gaines, as the best victim in this "test." All of which is to say, Yen Lo is beyond the normal (read: Western) reach of conscience and remorse. If all of his laughter tells

Khigh Dhiegh as Yen Lo (characteristically, in a mirthful state).

us anything, it tells us this: he does not value human life. This sets him apart even from the Soviets.

The Orientalism of the depiction could scarcely be stronger, but this is not the only racialized element of the brainwashing plotline. As Marco is white and Corporal Melvin is black, when these two dream about their Manchurian sojourn we see the same scene through two distinct racial consciousnesses. Frankenheimer's brilliant construction of the Manchurian seminar at once disorients and fascinates: a slow, methodical three-hundred-and-sixty-degree pan around a New Jersey hotel where Mrs. Henry Whittaker is lecturing on the air drainage of hydrangeas turns up a few odd, out-of-place details—one particularly coarse, almost masculine-looking club woman in the audience, for instance, another holding her cigarette the way German officers in World War II movies always do, between thumb and forefinger from underneath. By the time the camera completes its three-hundred-and-sixty-degree pan, the garden club speaker has become Dr. Yen Lo, now flanked by huge posters of Stalin and Mao. He seems not to be talking about hydrangeas anymore; Chunjin, evidently a recording secretary, is taking notes at a small table near the podium. From this point on, the visual details of the scene will shift in uneven, unpredictable fashion between the New Jersey club women and the Communist officers.

Later, when Allen Melvin has the same nightmare, we see a continuation of this scene with the same scrambled visual technique,

The brainwashing sequence, as dredged up in Marco's recurring dream:
a hydrangea seminar before a ladies' garden club in New Jersey eerily fuses
with a meeting of high-powered Chinese and Soviet officials.

but this time all the club women are black. This is not a small thing.
The Manchurian Candidate is among the very first—and it remains
among a very few—"white" Hollywood productions that attempt to
convey a black consciousness or to see the world through African-
American eyes. The Korean War was the first to be fought by America's newly integrated military; and this film not only gives us the
standard Hollywood offering of the multiracial unit, but at least in a
small way attempts to consider the "white" and "black" experiences
as distinct. It is not easy to articulate exactly what is "liberal" about
this sequence; but even more than the low salience and the general

invisibility of anti-Asian stereotypes to most white Americans, it is almost certainly *this*—the Marco/Melvin pairing—that would preclude most white viewers' ever thinking of *The Manchurian Candidate* as a "racist" film, its hideous caricatures of Yen Lo and Chunjin notwithstanding.

And this is no small thing either. If it is difficult to say exactly why this move on Frankenheimer's part might be "liberal" in the conventional sense, it is easier to locate his deployment of Corporal Melvin's blackness in relationship to the larger project of Cold War *liberalism*. The Cold War era, as Martin Luther King Jr.'s Vietnam protest reminds us, represented a tricky moment in racialized discourses of all sorts: the nascent civil rights movement had introduced new standards and a new urgency to the concept of racial evenhandedness in the operations of American democracy, even as racism itself not only persisted, but actively structured American outlooks on the First, Second, and Third Worlds. Although a conspicuous antiracism was needed to win the hearts and minds of the unaligned, decolonizing world, antiracism still bore a bit of the Popular Front taint of discredited leftism. "Of course the fact that a person believes in racial equality doesn't *prove* that he's a Communist," said one loyalty board chairman in the 1950s, "but it certainly does make you look twice, doesn't it?"[39] Various strains of racism, moreover, remained reflexive and deeply embedded in American political culture, not easily to be rooted out. Indeed, as Christina Klein writes, "the global imaginary of containment mapped the world in terms of Otherness and difference," at once borrowing from and paying into racialized languages such as Orientalism. George Kennan's famous "Long Telegram" on Cold War strategy attributed Soviet behavior in part to its "attitude of Oriental secretiveness and conspiracy," for instance; and John Foster Dulles could tell the ambassador from Taiwan, quite unselfconsciously, that "the Oriental mind, particularly that of the Japanese, was always more devious than the Occidental mind."[40]

Antiracism, as Klein argues, thus "occupied an ambiguous position in the ideological landscape of the Cold War": if racism at home was an untenable liability in the Cold War, still race itself held the key to understanding the geopolitical realities that presented the Cold War's most pressing imperatives.[41] This is precisely the ideological instability

that the layered racializations of the brainwashing sequences intro-
duce to *The Manchurian Candidate*. Although the white/black Marco/
Melvin contrast is more likely to attract our racial attentions, in fact
the Melvin/Yen pairing is much more significant: Yen proves the importance of race in deciphering international enmities, while Melvin
demonstrates that America is not racist; the figure of Yen embodies
more than a century's worth of what Isaacs called "fictional evil," while
the sympathetic figure of Melvin "proves"—by endorsing it—that
the image is neither racist nor inaccurate. In the wake of the Black
Power movement, as the "model minority" stereotype of Asian-
Americans was beginning to gain currency, Chinese-American playwright Frank Chin remarked, "Whites love us because we're not
black."[42] In the *pre*–Black Power era, however—against the backdrop
of the "loss" of China, decolonization, and the Korean and early Vietnam Wars, on the one hand, and *Brown v. Board of Education*, the
Montgomery bus boycott, and the lunch-counter sit-ins, on the
other—the black–Asian racial calculus was quite different: back
then, loving *blacks* (or at least seeming to) was an important creden-
tial in the Cold War business of vilifying "Orientals." Paradoxically,
then, the Allen Melvin character (along with the black psychiatrist
who helps Marco to crack the communists' code) is doing some heavy
lifting on behalf of American racism.

Finally, it remains only to point out that Chunjin and Yen Lo
were rather characteristic of an entire gallery of Asian characters in
American popular culture in the Korea/Vietnam era, from Fu Manchu
himself—who, astonishingly, remained very much alive in productions like *The Adventures of Fu Manchu* (TV, 1956), *The Face of Fu
Manchu* (1965), *The Brides of Fu Manchu* (1966), *The Vengeance of
Fu Manchu* (1967), *The Blood of Fu Manchu* (1968), and *The Torture
Chamber of Fu Manchu* (1969)—to Mickey Rooney's hideous yellowface routine as Mr. Yunioshi in *Breakfast at Tiffany's* (1961, screenplay
by George Axelrod), to Harold Sakata's portrayal of Odd Job in
Goldfinger (1964), to Jack Soo and Pat Morita's appearances as "Oriental #1" and "Oriental #2" in *Thoroughly Modern Millie* (1967), a
musical comedy (for crying out loud) about Chinatown's putative
white slavers in the 1920s.

Perhaps nothing says more about the culture industries' conventional handling of Asianness—both its thoroughly constructed quality and its pervasiveness around the margins—than the careers of Khigh Dhiegh (pronounced Ky Dee) and Henry Silva, the two actors who played Yen Lo and Chunjin. Neither was Asian or Asian-American, for one thing, and so the perfection to which each approximated the standard motifs and gestures of the classic "Oriental" bespeaks the perfected power of the cultural stereotype that had been handed down from Boris Karloff. Khigh Dhiegh was born to an Anglo-Egyptian-Sudanese family in New Jersey; his birth name was Kenneth Dickerson. Henry Silva was a Puerto Rican who grew up in Brooklyn. But both made their names in the business by playing the "exotic"—and most often the evil exotic—a screen type that afforded fairly steady work. If Pat Morita (known as "the Hip Nip") was able to move on from his first role in *Thoroughly Modern Millie* to become something of a professional Oriental (Ah Chew in *Sanford and Son*, Arthur Chen in *Kung Fu*, Arnold Takahashi in *Happy Days*, Rear Admiral Kusaka in *Midway*, Kesuke Miyagi in *The Karate Kid*, the Chink in *Even Cowgirls Get the Blues*, the Emperor of China in *Mulan*), the Orientalism industry found these ethnic North African and Puerto Rican actors only slightly less useful.[43]

Khigh Dhiegh played Kang in *Thirteen Frightened Girls* (1963, your typical girls' boardinghouse caper turned Cold War espionage thriller) and King Chou Lai in *The Destructors* (1968, a spy adventure involving "laser rubies"), but he became most famous between 1968 and 1980 as the Red Chinese villain, Wo Fat, on television's *Hawaii Five-O*. The character—described in the original script as "a little Buddha with thick glasses"—actually borrowed his name from a popular Chinese restaurant, Wo Fat's, on Hotel Street in Honolulu.[44] There seems something oddly revealing of the culture in this grafting of a popular restaurant name onto an Anglo-Sudanese-Egyptian body to create a Chinese type; but more revealing still is the extent to which, for a certain generation, the figure of Wo Fat became as memorable and as current as Fu Manchu himself had been at one time. As recently as 2000, for instance, as the federal government's case against accused spy Wen Ho Lee began to unravel, one brilliant Internet

Khigh Dhiegh as Wo Fat in television's *Hawaii Five-O*, with nemesis Steve McGarrett (Jack Lord). (Bettmann/Corbis)

satirist purported to "explain" his impending release by leaking a threatening letter from "The Federation of Evil Oriental Super-villains," over the signature of "steering committee" members, Dr. Fu Manchu, Ming the Merciless (from *Flash Gordon*), and Wo Fat. The popular image of Oriental villainy lives on, as Wo Fat's fans (and Wen Ho Lee himself) can attest.[45]

But much as Pat Morita did in *The Karate Kid*, Khigh Dhiegh was also able to capitalize on the stereotypical Eastern motifs—the "positive" Orientalism—of New Age philosophy and the 1970s popular-ization of Eastern thought. He founded a Taoist institute in North Hollywood; and until his death in 1991 he conducted seminars on the *I Ching* and Eastern ways of knowing, and he wrote several books on Taoism, including *The Eleventh Wing, The Golden Oracle,* and *I Ching: Taoist Book of Days.* This is not to question Khigh Dhiegh's motive in these pursuits, or to denigrate his philosophy or the depth of his belief. Rather, it is to indicate one of the surprising rivulets of American Orientalism in the Vietnam era and after: the (mostly white) counterculture and New Age fascination with Eastern thought represented a kind of cultural secession or refusal, a quest for mean-ing whose cultural crossing over did not *bridge* the Orientalist chasm between East and West, but rather relied on it and even reveled in it. Fu Manchu, Yen Lo, and Wo Fat might be triplets, that is, but their brother—nonidentical, perhaps, but a brother nonetheless—was the newly translated and popularized Lao Tzu.

The counterculture's Orientalist secession—like the popularity of neopaganism and wicca around the same time—also marked a rising American antimodernism, a response to the same social dissatisfac-tions that an earlier generation had summed up in phrases like "rat race," "organization man," "lonely crowd," "air-conditioned night-mare," "cog in the machine," "packaged soul." Allen Ginsberg's in-tellectual trajectory from the "robot apartments," "invisible suburbs," and "skeleton treasuries" of *Howl* to the Eastern teachings of the Naropa Institute in Boulder, Colorado, then, strangely conjoins Khigh Dhiegh's career path from the garden club/brainwashing scene in *The Manchurian Candidate* to his Taoist Sanctuary and *The Golden Oracle.* The more positive valence that American Orientalism could take on in the 1970s was not unrelated to *either* the monstrously negative

Orientalism of the Korea/Vietnam era *or* the stultifying, spiritually impoverished atmosphere suffered by the gray flannel suit crowd in the "affluent society."[46] The intellectual and ideological lines running from Yen Lo and *Howl* to the Taoist Sanctuary and the Naropa Institute chart an important countercurrent within Cold War America.

Henry Silva's career, on the other hand, took a different turn from Khigh Dhiegh's and therefore has something slightly different to suggest about Orientalism and the American "exotic." Ironically, Silva's screen credits constitute a more hybridized list of characters than those of the multiethnic Khigh Dhiegh. Silva broke into film playing a Mexican "peon" in *Viva Zapata!* (1952), and from that point on he made good use of his ethnic indeterminacy in America's visual lexicon: in addition to his Asian role in *The Manchurian Candidate*, he played "Chink" in *The Tall T* (1957, a western), Kua-Ko, an inexplicably Orientalized "native" of the Amazon jungle in *Green Mansions* (1959), and Mr. Moto in *The Return of Mr. Moto* (1965); but he also played Latinos (*The Bravados, A Gathering of Eagles*), Native Americans (*Sergeants 3, The Plainsman*), Italians (*Johnny Cool, Battle of the Godfathers, Cry of a Prostitute, The Boss*), and even one Michael Saxon in the Hong Kong action film *Woo Fook* (1977). Among Silva's greatest successes—and among his relatively few opportunities to play heroes rather than villains—was a series of Italian "spaghetti westerns," beginning with *The Hills Run Red* (*Un fiume di dolari*, 1966), which made him something of a box-office smash in Europe.

Silva's typecasting in American film as the always-dark villain—nicely underscored by his occasional exile to Italy in order to play good guys—helps to reposition U.S. Orientalism within the wider universe of racialized images and meanings. As an intellectual project and an ideological current, Orientalism does have a history of its own—indeed, as Said has argued, it has a very particular epistemology all its own as well. But that history—the history, say, of Orientalist representations like Chunjin, Mr. Moto, and the Chink—intersects and traffics with several other lines of racial thought and with other historically developed social relations: not just the history of those "Orientals" from farther west (critic Jack Shaheen's "reel bad Arabs" in U.S. film and media culture, for instance), but also the Indians and the Mexican bandits of the Cold War western, the

African-American criminals of urban crime drama, the African or South American savages of safari and conquest films, and, to a certain extent, even the swarthy overlords of the Italian underworld in Prohibition and Mafia films.[47] For a society so transfixed by a duochromatic, white/black binary when it comes to matters of racial politics and racial debate, popular culture in the United States has depicted a surprisingly *multichromatic* spectrum of race and races—at least when it comes to the villains—Corporal Melvin's tacit assurances notwithstanding. If Khigh Dhiegh's screen and publishing career encompassed both the very best and the very worst that U.S. Orientalism had to offer, then Henry Silva has proven the perfect screen villain in a culture for whom a free-fire zone in Vietnam might represent "Indian country," and Iraqi soldiers "sand niggers," a nation that has been ceaselessly at war in either Central America, the Caribbean, the Middle East, or Asia for more than a century.

6

The Red Queen

Sexuality, Subversion, and the American Family

You just cannot believe, Ben, how lovable the whole damn thing was. All summer long we were together. I was lovable, Jocie was lovable, the senator was lovable, the days were lovable, the nights were lovable, and everyone was lovable. Except, of course, my mother.

—*Raymond Shaw*

"The queen of diamonds," says Yen Lo, "in so many ways reminiscent of Raymond's dearly loved and hated mother, is the second key that will clear his mechanism for any assignments." The original referent here would seem to be the murderous queen in Lewis Carroll's *Alice in Wonderland*, whose response to every rising circumstance was "Off with their heads!" The association with *Alice* is reinforced when Jocie appears at the Iselins' costume party dressed precisely after the fashion of the playing cards in "The Queen's Croquet-Ground" (and reinforced, too, perhaps, by the absurdist aesthetic of the brainwashing sequences and the white-rabbit loopiness of Marco's first encounter with Rosie). But finally the subversive character and the dominance of Raymond's mother—that is, her "redness" and her "queenness"—

evoke less about life through the looking glass than they say about the Cold War's twinned discourses of communism and gender. Eleanor Iselin's power *as a woman*—her power over both Johnny and Raymond, and her ruthless deployment of power in her dealings with Jordan—is depicted as nothing short of perverse; and this brand of "perversion" is closely aligned with the communists' geopolitical scheme of *sub*version of which she is a chief instrument.

The concurrent sexual and political valences of the Cold War era's privacy discourse begin to indicate, as noted earlier, a profound ideological nexus between political loyalty and the imperatives of U.S. nationalism on the one hand, and enforced gender arrangements and codes of sexuality on the other—the readiness "with which questions of national security turned into questions about normative gender and sexuality," as Deborah Nelson has put it. Michael Rogin's insight on Cold War film and Cold War ideology is apposite here: "Domestic and cold war ideologies not only dissolve the private into the public; they also do the reverse. They depoliticize politics by blaming subversion on personal influence." There is no such thing as privacy, in other words, and not only because of the various ways that the national security apparatus now reaches into those "private spaces" that might afford "sanctuary" to national enemies, but also because the conceptual scheme of countersubversion identifies a spectrum of "private" behaviors running from the aberrant at one end to the normative at the other, whose every point signifies something important about "public" questions of loyalty, allegiance, patriotism, and acceptable Americanism.[1] The figure of Eleanor Iselin, to take a case, operates in a constellation of Cold War images and ideas regarding proper femininity, proper motherhood, and a healthy ("normal") family as the embodiment of "the American way of life"—a constellation of politicized sexual and gendered meanings which in its turn lent both form and portent to notions of proper manhood, "natural" sexual hierarchy, normative heterosexuality, and "deviant" homosexuality. The innermost sanctuaries of private life are where the seeds of a vigorous national life are nourished; and thus national duty is itself refracted through the details of private habits, decisions, and arrangements. "Domesticity," writes historian Elaine Tyler May, "was not so much a retreat from public affairs as an expression of one's citizenship."[2]

The poster boy for the era's conflation of gender imperatives and national imperatives is Philip Wylie, a prolific—and, in his time, quite popular—writer of short stories, novels, and works of social criticism and moral philosophy, now best remembered for his 1942 social tract *Generation of Vipers*. This work most thoroughly laid out the brief against "mom" as a too-powerful, emasculating, finally nation-threatening figure on the American scene—"the taloned, cackling residue of burnt-out puberty in a land that has no use for mature men or women."[3] If Wylie's chapter "Common Women" is primarily a misogynist screed ("I have researched the moms, to the beady brains behind their beady eyes and to the stones at the center of their fat hearts"), still the real pitch of the chapter is a lament for the fate of American manhood in the face of this momist onslaught (204). The pedestaled virtues and powers of American motherhood, and the concomitant "softening" of American masculinity, represent for Wylie an inversion of the natural order and an abdication of proper social authority as potentially catastrophic as the inversions and abdications in Shakespeare's *King Lear*. In his view, "megaloid momworship has got completely out of hand. Our land, subjectively mapped, would have more silver cords and apron strings crisscrossing it than railroads and telephone wires" (198). "Our society is too much an institution built to appease the rapacity of loving mothers. If that condition is an ineluctable experiment of nature, then we are the victims of a failure" (216). Expect "hurricanoes," Lear might say.

Wylie himself did not necessarily see the communist threat as momism's sole province. Indeed, in a postscript for a later edition of *Generation of Vipers* he averred that, "as the news photos abundantly make plain, mom composes the majority of Senator McCarthy's shock troops—paying blind tribute to a blind authoritarianism like her own." McCarthyism, he concluded, "the rule of unreason, is one with momism: a noble end aborted by sick-minded means, a righteous intent—in terrorism fouled and tyranny foundered" (196). But writing in 1942, Wylie had posited a natural alignment between mom's authoritarianism and authoritarianism plain and simple, and so notwithstanding his caveats on McCarthyism, as wartime gave way to the postwar's shifting geopolitical concerns, an interpretation of momism resting upon the Hitler analogy did become easily transposed to the perceptions and imperatives of Cold War anticommunism: in either case, natural lines of social authority had been inverted and befouled in the United States, and American manhood was reduced to a cowering sentimentality that ill became a nation at war, whether hot or cold.

But to focus too intently on Wylie's fantastic vision is to understate the import and the reach of such geosexual ideology. Wylie's may be the clearest and most jaw-dropping rendition of the mid-century's gendered and sexualized nationalism—"the women of America raped the men, not sexually, unfortunately, but morally, since neuters come hard by morals" (200)—but some version of this thinking surfaced over and over in myriad cultural and political venues throughout the postwar years, *The Manchurian Candidate* being merely one instance among many. As (Hearst columnist and Sinatra nemesis) Lee Mortimer and Jack Leit wrote in *USA Confidential* (1952), "America has become a matriarchy. Women own and run it. Under a matriarchy men grow soft and women masculine. The self-sufficient girl who doesn't want to become an incubator or Kitchen slavie for a man is a push-over for a predatory Lesbian... Marxian teachings, the examples of women in high political and social places, and the propagandized knowledge that many of the movie set prefer it that way are contributory."[4] Matriarchy, homosexuality, Marxism—a formulation ratified a thousand times over, from the aproned and ineffectual father in *Rebel without a Cause* to the urbane (read: homosexual) son/spy in *My Son John* to J. Edgar Hoover's contention that communism abets "sexual immorality" and vice versa (even if, as has been supposed, Hoover might have known a bit more about "deviance" than he was letting on).[5]

The genesis of this thinking began well before the Cold War proper, with long-standing Euro-American assumptions about the relationship between citizenship, war, and masculinity. The fused categories represented by the familiar political icon of the "citizen soldier" hint at the ways in which not only has the civic realm been traditionally defined as male, but this masculinist construction has itself been upheld and policed primarily by reference to warfare or the threat of warfare. Activities that are said in the vernacular to "separate the men from the boys" most often accomplish the more portentous cultural work of separating the boys from the girls, and war is unequaled in this respect. As Margaret Higonnet and others have argued, war is a "gendering activity," a grand civic ritual that consolidates and even augments preexisting definitions of gender and systems of gender relations.[6] War accomplishes this gendering ideological work, first, by ritually separating the nation into defenders and defended—as one scholar puts it, into "warriors" on one hand, and "beautiful souls" on the other—and so heightening cultural ideals of "male" valor and "female" vulnerability. The culture of war defines violence as masculine, and exalts the "masculine" capacity for violence as a political virtue.[7] As a writer in *Ladies' Home Journal* wrote during World War I, "the biggest thing about a principle or a battle or an army is a man! And the biggest thing that a war can do is bring out that man." The Allied objective, according to this writer, was "to demonstrate the right kind of manhood."[8]

Which brings us, inevitably, to the right kind—or right *kinds*—of womanhood: the Spartan Mother, who births and rears her sons as vigorous and loyal fighters to be sent off to battle; the nurturing nurse, who selflessly cares for the fallen; the sweetheart, whose purity is the symbol of all that is to be defended in war, and yet whose sexuality is war's very prize. By their peculiar patterns of erasure and revision, moreover, popular conceptions of "front" and "home front" exaggerate these representations of sexual difference and enforce the notion that only male combatants (as distinct from the women who inhabit cities under siege, say) really can and do "experience" the horrors of war. Cynthia Enloe has argued that, just as the "front" is masculinized in popular perception, so is the "home front" feminized in a manner that corresponds more to preconceived assumptions about the sexes than to the facts of a given case.[9] (This has largely continued to be so even in the era of the mixed-sex combat arrangements of the Gulf and Iraq wars, which perhaps explains both the sensation and the ideological work of the captivity-and-rescue narrative of Private Jessica Lynch. It might also explain the depth of Americans' revulsion toward Lynndie England—on the far right, for example, where the perversions of Abu Ghraib prison were interpreted as a by-product of the "perversion" of putting women in uniform in the first place.)

The masculinized citizen soldier and the feminized home front constituted a powerful enough ideological inheritance, particularly

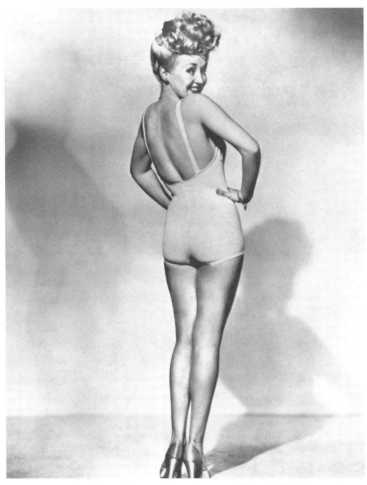

Actress Betty Grable in the most famous pinup of World War II.
(Bettmann/Corbis)

coming off the gendered and gendering national experience of World
War II. But the decade of the 1940s added its own layer of specificity
to these longer-standing cultural inclinations and ideals. "Because of
the thinness of public life" in U.S. political culture, argues Robert
Westbrook, "modern American statesmen and their allies have found
it difficult to call upon their fellow citizens *as citizens* to defend their
nation in time of war." They have "relied heavily on appeals to private

World War II "nose art." Like the pinup, sexualized paintings on military equipment at once articulated the rigidly gendered ideas of "front" and "home front" and provided a highly personal vocabulary for understanding "why we fight." (Guy Motil/Corbis)

(which is not to say selfish) obligations in order to legitimate the sacrifices of war, including the moral commitments believed to exist between men and women."[10] During World War II, American political culture mobilized around a philosophy of political obligation that was couched not in public terms, but private. Representatives of the state and other propagandists "implored Americans as individuals and as families to join the war effort in order to protect the state that protected them." The most prevalent appeal to America's young men was "to go to war to defend *private* interests and discharge *private* obligations."[11] Although rhetorical resort to abstractions such as "liberty" were common enough, private obligations "to families, to children, to parents, to friends, and generally, to an 'American Way of Life' defined as a rich (and richly commodified) private realm of experience—were tirelessly invoked in the campaign to mobilize Americans . . . , and they formed the centerpiece of the propaganda produced by the state and its allies in Hollywood, the War Advertising Council, and elsewhere."[12] If World War II scare posters depicting

Japanese rapists represented but another rendition of the typical gendering work of war, the Betty Grable pinup represented something slightly different: a sexualized icon of soldierly obligation—"why we fight"—for a new, privatized conception of public duty.

In this emergent discourse, in Westbrook's view, "no private obligation outranked the one to the family," a trope of national belonging and political duty reflected across an array of cultural forms, from the familial or parental reference points in Norman Rockwell's *Freedom from Fear* and *Freedom from Want*, to Red Cross or Dixie Cup ads that depicted little girls asking, "Are they coming over here to fight, Daddy?" and "[Daddy] won't let them hurt us, will he, Mommy?"[13] This "thickening" of public commitment in U.S. political culture in the 1940s, then, was a first step toward that fusion of public and private that Michael Rogin and others have identified in the Cold War years. If the family represented the most direct link between the individual and the nation-state during the war, "A 'normal' family and vigilant mother" was to become "the 'front line' of defense" in the tense postwar period, according to family historian Stephanie Coontz: "anticommunists linked deviant family or sexual behavior to sedition."[14]

Interpreting the sexual, patriarchal, and familial imperatives lacing through Cold War political culture, then, is not just a dicey matter of extrapolating principles from Philip Wylie's *Generation of Vipers*: Joseph McCarthy railed against the "Communists and queers" in the State Department, occasionally collapsing the charges into one another, as when he referred to Dean Acheson as "the Red Dean of Fashion"; J. Edgar Hoover outlined American mothers' unique duties in combating "the twin enemies of freedom—crime and communism," and he wrote of communists' "degradation as parents"; *Life* magazine saw a deep significance in the fact that accused spy Gerhard Eisler had abandoned his wife and daughter; and in a report on American communism, Morris Ernst posited a marked and meaningful "tendency" that "in Communist marriages the wife is the more dominant partner." It was broadly asserted, for instance, "that [CPUSA leader] Earl Browder was henpecked"; and Hoover himself relied on a psychological profile of the Rosenbergs that reported, among other things, that "Julius is the slave and his wife, Ethel, the master."[15]

The spectrum of "abnormal" behaviors and arrangements whose significance was presumed to be politically menacing ran from fully "aberrant," "deviant," and "perverted" sexual practices to merely "non-traditional" familial patterns or gender arrangements. But in the political terms of the day, such categories were very closely related. The easiest and least subtle judgment according to this sexual-political logic was the judgment against homosexuality, a notion often cast not in theoretical, but in highly practical terms. "One reason why sex deviates are considered security risks," explained Joseph McCarthy, "is that they are subject to blackmail. It is a known fact that espionage agents often have been successful in extorting information from them by threatening to expose their abnormal habits."[16] Thus McCarthy's concern for "State Department perverts" and the other "Communists and queers" and "striped pants boys" in government. One senator promised to fire the "lavender lads" in the State Department, while another asserted that "You can't . . . separate homosexuals from subversives." Indeed, in 1950, at taxpayers' expense, the federal government generated a report titled *Employment of Homosexuals and Other Sex Perverts in Government*.[17]

Such presumptions, as these latter comments indicate, quickly shaded off from the specific, tightly defined concern for potential blackmail toward a more generalized equation of homosexuality not only with "perversion," but with subversion—the concurrent "politicization of homosexuality" and "homosexualization of left-wing political activity," and the extent to which "the differences between communist activity and homosexual practice tended to commingle" in the popular imagination, as recent scholars have written. It was in this vein, for instance, that a Senate appropriations committee report might worry that "one homosexual can pollute a [whole] Government office."[18] Deborah Nelson disentangles and explicates the Gordian logic at work here:

> defining communists as invisible internal threats, as subversives passing as ordinary Americans, permitted a widespread surveillance of and attack on homosexuals, who were also passing as ordinary Americans, whose subversive "tendencies," a favorite word in the job-testing industry, could also be unmasked by surveillance. From the

early years of the cold war, when, for example, Eisenhower issued an executive order declaring that homosexuality was sufficient grounds for disbarment from federal employment, homosexuality and political deviance were merely different species of the same crime: undermining the "American way of life."[19]

(A similar outlook on such "tendencies" has persisted, of course, into the "don't ask, don't tell" era of U.S. military policy, when the question in some quarters remains as to whether homosexuality represents an inner personal essence to be identified and expunged, or a species of conduct to be proscribed and punished. At stake in either case is unit cohesion, basic trust, and a host of threats to the "normal" functioning of the military unit in the face of "abnormal" tendencies.)[20]

The concurrent politicization and sexualization of "the American way of life"—most readily apparent in the conjoined logics of anti-communism and homophobia—ultimately led outward from questions of compulsory heterosexual coupling, to questions of "proper" familial arrangements, child-rearing practices, parenthood, and especially motherhood. It was not just that communism abets "sexual immorality," as J. Edgar Hoover remarked, and thus that sexual and political "deviance" functioned more or less reliably as symptoms of each other; but in their totalizing conception of "the *communist man*," Hoover and others were led inexorably to examine the family as the seedbed of the subversive character, since "this type of man doesn't just grow; he must be created," "communists are not born; they are made."[21]

Proof was to be found in the functioning of the Communist Party itself: "the Party feels that the basic responsibility of indoctrinating the child lies with the communist parents," wrote Hoover, and in this respect the communist family was not a family at all, but merely another organ in the political apparatus of Moscow. Within the communists' presumed scheme of nurturance and discipline, "loyalty to the Party supersedes all emotions of love and mercy and justice," either within the family or without. "If your marriage is such that you can't work for the Party," one communist official advised, according to Hoover, "…I'd seriously consider divorce."[22] Elsewhere Hoover described the way in which communists prey upon those whose discontents amid the rising postwar order have left them particularly vulnerable to unorthodox pleas:

> the Communist Party is attempting to exploit the rise of materialism, irreligion, and lack of faith in our society. In an era when moral standards have been lowered, when family life has been disrupted, when crime and juvenile delinquency rates are high, communists have tried to set forth a goal . . . that would captivate the longings and hopes of men and women.[23]

This passage is particularly interesting in that communists' "captivating the longings and hopes" of ordinary Americans is quite a different conceptual model for the spread of communism than the one usually posited by Hoover, who more often favored viral metaphors of disease and contagion. Nonetheless, the linkage Hoover establishes here—irreligion or lack of faith, declining morality, disrupted familial relations, juvenile delinquency, crime, and communism—was standard fare between World War II and the 1960s. Strong, patriarchal, "normal" families were at once the nation's best defense against subversive tendencies *and* its most reliable emblem of political health and vitality.

Like Philip Wylie and J. Edgar Hoover, many saw "mom" as the key figure in this equation. The social-scientific literature contributed a great deal to the era's iron framework of normativity on these matters, defining women's seeking fulfillment outside motherhood as "unnatural," or intoning, as one advice manual did, that "the family is the center of your living. If it isn't, you've gone far astray." *Esquire* magazine defined working wives as a "menace"; *Life* saw women's employment as a "disease."[24] In the context of the times, the political valences of words like *unnatural, astray, menace,* and *disease* could hardly be mistaken. As Elaine May observes, "Behind every subversive, it seemed, lurked a woman's misplaced sexuality."[25] Motherhood itself, adds Cynthia Enloe, became "an embattled strategic turf during the Cold War." The militarization of femininity was not fully reversed once the war was over and Rosie the Riveter had been banished from the factory, but was "simply reconstructed upon women's postwar demobilization":

> From 1946 until 1972 femininity was imagined by American government policymakers and nongovernment proponents of Cold War

culture in a fashion that would harmonize with militarized national security goals. Loyal wives of male engineers working for defense contractors, loyal wives of male officials working in intelligence services—all were upholding forms of feminine behavior that sustained the Cold War. Likewise, women teaching elementary school children about the dangers of Communism, mothers who believed they were doing the right thing to support their sons in accepting their draft call-up, women who felt proud doing volunteer work for patriotic organizations such as the Veterans of Foreign Wars—all of them, as well, were fulfilling this Cold War, militarized ideal of American femininity... as the hot war was replaced by the Cold War in American gendered political culture, there was less ideological confusion over, but not necessarily less militarization of, American femininity.[26]

Richard Condon's *The Manchurian Candidate* takes up these sexual themes fairly explicitly. The novel is shot through with sexualized references that link communism and subversion to unorthodox familial and gender arrangements, or perversion: the key players in the fantastic Manchurian plot are all linked in one way or another to homosexuality, "abnormal" sexuality, or incest. When, unlike all the other red-blooded American boys home from Korea, Raymond proves a little shy when it comes to sex, his consort Winona Meighan asks, "What the hell is the matter with you, honey?... Are you queer?" And when his mother seeks to break up the budding romance between Raymond and Jocie—Raymond's one shot at normalcy—she tells the Jordans that her son is "homosexual and in other ways degenerate."[27] Johnny and Eleanor's marriage, meanwhile, has never been consummated, because Iselin "found himself as impotent as a male butterfly atop a female pterodactyl when he tried to have commerce with Raymond's mother" (70).

Iselin's sexual history also includes an extraordinary tale, recapitulated from a 1944 diary entry by one of the men he had served with during the war, of his attempted conquest of an Eskimo woman—any Eskimo woman—in the Arctic. "Johnny Iselin has become possessed by the idea of sex," this character wrote. "To get that interested in sex on top of this ice cap is either suicidal or homosexual, on its surface, but Johnny isn't either. He is a persistent and determined zealot." The fictive diary entry goes on to recount the odd and fairly ugly story of Iselin's acclimatizing himself to "the special smell of the Eskimo women" who "wash their hair in stored urine, ... live sewed up in those musty skins, and ... eat an endless diet of putrescent food like fish heads and whale fat." On one of his treks across the ice to the Eskimo women, Iselin encounters a German officer of similar predilections in the igloo; when he mistakenly makes advances on that officer's Eskimo girlfriend, an arctic fracas ensues in which Iselin ends up getting bitten so fiercely, the wound festering so badly, that he is relieved of duty and reassigned elsewhere (85–86). Although this strange episode functions mainly to establish the distance between public and private truths in Iselin's life (he makes quite a lot of his "war injury" on the campaign trail), nonetheless the constellation of sexual and political ideas at work here—the conflation of perversion and subversion—is symptomatic: his aberrant sexual zealotry puts Iselin in the same category with homosexuals and Nazi officers; it also leads to his discharge from military duty. No ordinary citizen soldier he.

But by far the most significant element in the novel's marriage of perversion and subversion is Eleanor Iselin's own sexual biography, which reaches back to an incestuous relationship with her father:

> She had loved her father with a bond so secret, so deep, and so thrill-
> ing that it surpassed into eternity the drab feelings of other people,
> all other people, particularly the feelings of her brother and her clot
> of a mother. She had had woman's breasts from the time she had
> been ten years old, and she had felt a woman's yearnings as she had
> lain in the high, dark attic of her father's great house, only on rainy
> nights, only when the other slept. She would lie in the darkness and
> hear the rain, then hear her father's soft, soft step rising on the stairs
> after he had slipped the bolt into the lock of the attic door, and she
> would slip out of her long woolen night dress and wait for the warmth
> of him and the wonder of him. (73–74)

"How much you look like Poppa!" she later tells Raymond, indicating that perhaps her son is not only an instrument of her political subversion, but also of her sexual perversion. "You have his beautiful hands and you hold your beautiful head in that same proud, proud way. And when you smile! Smile, my darling."

Raymond smiled, naturally and beautifully, under orders. She caught
her breath in a gasp. "When you smile, Raymond dearest, for that
instant I am a little girl again and the miracle of love begins all over
again. How right that seems to me. Smile for me again, sweetheart.
Yes. Yes. Now kiss me. Really, really kiss me." Her long fingers dug
into his shoulders and pulled him to her on the chaise, and as her left
hand opened the Chinese robe she remembered Poppa and the sound
of rain high in the attic when she had been a little girl, and she found
again the ecstatic peace she had lost so long, long before. (290)

In Frankenheimer's rendering, most of these sexualized strands are
boiled down to one, telling, incestuous kiss between Eleanor and
Raymond. Frankenheimer augmented the sexual/incestuous charge
in this relationship by casting Angela Lansbury as Raymond's mother,
though she was only three years older than Laurence Harvey. Audiences (at least college audiences) invariably "eewww" and squirm
when Eleanor takes Raymond's face in her hands and kisses him
deeply; but in fact the perversity of this relationship is woven into
their exchanges long before the distasteful kiss. The character of
Eleanor Iselin, one might say, is a patchwork creation whose elements
are the very ideological elements of sexualized nationalism—neither
Elaine Tyler May nor Cynthia Enloe could improve the character to
better illustrate the argument about gender, sexuality, the family, and
the politics of citizenship during the Cold War.

Eleanor Iselin occupies the screen for eleven scenes, virtually
every one of them speaking directly to this constellation of gendered,
sexual, and political concerns:

1. At the Washington airfield where she has arranged to turn
Raymond's Congressional Medal of Honor ceremony into a
"disgusting TV circus" on behalf of Iselin's campaign, Eleanor charges through the parade guard, jostling two soldiers
aside, in an effort to secure a photo op for Iselin with Raymond. Then, in the limo with her husband and son, she
chides the latter for his cold reception ("What's the matter
with you, Raymond, we've gone to a lot of trouble . . ."),
before justifying her behavior in language that could have
been scripted by Philip Wylie: "You know I want nothing

for myself. You know that my entire life is devoted to helping you and to helping Johnny. My two boys, my two little boys." (Raymond, meanwhile, holds his palms over his ears; rocking and grimacing, he chants, "Stop, stop, stop.") This fleeting scene establishes Eleanor as crass, crude, smothering, and brash—in a word, as "mom."

2. On board Johnny Iselin's plane, Eleanor continues to denigrate her son: "What's the matter with you, Raymond? You look as though your head were going to come to a point in the next thirteen seconds." Raymond reveals that he does not intend to stay with his family, but instead has taken a job in New York jornalism working for Holborne Gaines—"that communist," "that dreadful old man," in Eleanor's view. Raymond explains his affinity with Gaines: "For one thing, we discovered that we both loathe and despise you and Johnny." This in a nutshell would be that rotted familial pattern that Hoover and others had described, in which a severing of the proper tie between parent and child portends a disease in the body politic.

3. Eleanor watches Iselin on a TV monitor as he confronts the secretary of defense. Then she, he, and a small crowd of inquiring reporters and others (including Marco) move into the adjoining vestibule. Confronted by Marco on the question of how many communists were in defense, Johnny answers only when he is prompted by Eleanor, who first mouths "104" and then "275." It is our first inkling that Mom not only rules the roost at home, but wields an unnatural power in Iselin's political cosmos as well— rather like Hoover's Ethel Rosenberg.

4. Shortly after, Johnny pleads with Eleanor to provide him one consistent number of communists to cite, as his inconsistencies are making him look like an "idiot." "You're going to look like an even bigger idiot if you don't just go out there and do as you're told," she barks. She then explains the brilliance of her chosen method: in the context of Iselin's inconsistencies, no one is asking *if* there are communists in the Defense Department, but

rather *how many*. This scene augments the creeping sense
of Eleanor as a political operative that had been introduced in scene 3.

5. In a flashback sequence (part of Raymond's tale of woe to
Marco), Eleanor and Raymond are alone in her library,
she trying to pry her son's affections away from Jocie
Jordan. "We are at war," she warns. "It's a cold war, but it
will get worse and worse until every man and woman and
child in this country will have to stand up and be counted,
to say whether they are on the side of right and freedom,
or on the side of the Thomas Jordans of this country."
This scene reiterates Eleanor's unnatural powers within
the family, as in scenes 3 and 4 ("She won, of course,"
Raymond tells Marco. "She always does. I couldn't beat
her. I still can't."). But Eleanor's language of "every man
and woman and child" having to stand up and be counted
also firmly hitches the domestic realm to the geopolitical
realm of the Cold War. There is no such thing, exactly,
as a "private citizen" as this war rages; and all kinds of
private concerns—romance, for instance—will finally
come to bear on public questions of "right and freedom."

6. Eleanor and Johnny (with Johnny's entourage present)
now plot to bring Jocie and Raymond back together. It
is here that Eleanor warns, "I keep telling you not to
think . . ." and instructs her husband to "just keep yelling
'point of order' . . . [and] I'll handle the rest." As in scenes
3 and 4, Eleanor's domination of Iselin is the crux (made
all the more unnerving, perhaps, by the frankness of her
discussion in the presence of Iselin's aides). Her control
of Iselin is unabashed and it is total.

7. Eleanor, Raymond, and "Chu Chin Chow or whatever
your name is" (actually, Chunjin) are in Raymond's den
for what Raymond cynically terms his and his mother's
"annual meeting." Eleanor invites Raymond to a party
"in honor" of Jocie Jordan upon her return from Europe, a
conciliatory gesture in view of "the shabby way [Raymond]
treated her." Like scene 5, this exchange annexes the realm

of private romantic desire to Eleanor's political projects. It also ratchets up our understanding of Eleanor's capacity for treachery toward her son: as we know that it was she who disrupted Raymond and Jocie's brief domestic idyll earlier on, her remark about *his* "shabby treatment" of Jocie reveals an astonishing willingness to trample Raymond underfoot, wholly without art, subtlety, or hesitation.

8. The party for Jocie: dressed as L'il Bo Peep, Eleanor demonstrates her virtues as both wife and mother (she yanks her husband around using the crook of her shepherdess's walking stick, for example, and later commands him to "run along, the grown-ups have to talk." She instructs Raymond to get "a drink or a tranquilizer or something," before going on to complain about what a "royal pain" he is). When she leads Raymond into the library, locks the door, and suggests, "Why don't you pass the time by playing a little solitaire," we understand for the first time that she is her brainwashed son's "American operative." The immensity of her ambition becomes clear when she sounds out Thomas Jordan on the prospect of securing for Johnny the party's vice presidential nomination. Mommy is a commie.

9. In Eleanor's library, Raymond has come to confront her after seeing Iselin on TV slandering Thomas Jordan. "Darling," she says, "something very important has come up. There's something you have to do." She reaches for a deck of cards. This, of course, is where (offscreen) she will issue the order to assassinate Senator Jordan. This scene skitters past in a mere thirteen seconds, but in some ways it is the most powerful of all in conveying Eleanor's power over her son and her ensnarement with wider geopolitical conspiracies.

10. Raymond and Eleanor are in her library as she gives him his final instructions for the assassination at the convention site. It is here that Raymond's mother speaks of amassing "powers that will make martial law look like anarchy." Her roles as red queen and mother become

Raymond Shaw and his mother. "Our land, subjectively mapped," wrote Philip Wylie, "would have more silver cords and apron strings crisscrossing it than railroads and telephone wires."

thoroughly entwined here, as she first pleads with Raymond, "You must believe that I did not know [the Soviets' handpicked assassin] would be you." She then vows revenge: "When I take power they will be pulled down and ground into dirt for what they did to you, and for what they did in so contemptuously underestimating me." In a pale but still quite powerful replication of the novel's incest motif, she takes Raymond's face in her hands and kisses him three times—on the forehead (almost maternally), on the cheek (somewhat too intimately), and on the mouth (far too deeply). This is the only scene in the film where the "merely" aberrant merges into the fully perverse; but the skein of entangled sexual-political themes is tight: momism, poisonous familial relations, inverted domestic lines of authority, political subversion, espionage, and sexual deviance. The private *is* public, as commentators like Hoover suggested, because sexuality and the domestic arrangements of the family will invariably radiate outward to affect those spheres more typically identified as "public" or "civic."

11. Eleanor Iselin's final scene depicts her on the dais at the nominating convention, first alive and then dead. Her

The kiss—the most clearly "perverse" moment in the Iselin/Shaw family's private dealings. The perversion of Eleanor's iron matriarchal rule and the rotted bonds between mother and son have offered clues to her subversive intentions throughout the film.

stranglehold has been broken, though Raymond cannot live without her.

Perhaps more thoroughly than any other text in the era, then, *The Manchurian Candidate* articulates the complicated linkages between the private and the public, the familial and the national, the sexual and the political in Cold War ideology. Like its reflexive Orientalism and its stealthy McCarthyism, this subtle commitment to politicized sexuality—or sexualized politics, if one prefers—suggests that, however intelligent, as an artifact of the period the film perhaps has as much to tell us by its preconscious impulses as it does by its highly self-conscious and stylized narrative declarations.

The "anticommunist story" may have indeed been in "tatters" by 1962, as Thomas Engelhardt has it, and certain elements of *The Manchurian Candidate* may indeed capture the unraveling.[28] But, on the other hand, a figure such as Jude Wanniski (later an archconservative economic adviser to Ronald Reagan) still remembers the straight anticommunist punch that the film held for him as a young man. Working as a reporter for the Las Vegas *Review-Journal*, Wanniski had voted "for JFK over the hated Richard Nixon" in 1960, but began to experience some "disillusionment with 'liberals.'" "Then along came *The Manchurian Candidate*," he writes, "...about how the COM-

MUNISTS were able to scheme in ways that could actually capture the American presidency. The movie hit me at a vulnerable moment and may have helped push me toward an eventual vote for Nixon in 1968."[29] How many Jude Wanniskis there were among Frankenheimer's 1962 audience we cannot know. But that there were any at all indicates that the film cannot be read simply as wry commentary on a waning political consensus. Rather, the kind of cinematic power described by Wanniski could only derive from the film's having imbibed and recapitulated some of the period's deepest—if subtlest—predispositions. *The Manchurian Candidate* may lampoon many of the sexual, patriarchal, and political beliefs peddled by Hoover, McCarthy, and others, but so does it rearticulate them and, in doing so, uphold them.

7

Strangers on a Train
The Perils of Cold War Courtship

Go away, Ben. Find yourself a girl, lie in the sun.

—*Colonel Milt to Bennett Marco*

The Manchurian Candidate, more than four decades after its release, remains a disturbing film, its litany of obscenities—Raymond Shaw's strangling of Ed Mavole, his point-blank execution of Bobby Lembeck, his murder of Senator Jordan and of his beloved Jocie, the revelation of his mother's incestuous love for him, his killing of her, and, finally, his own violent death—constituting a relentless, near-unbearable assault on the viewer. And yet, for many, it is the secondary story line, the romance between Marco and Rosie, that lingers as a troubling preoccupation after the last frame. Who is Rosie, and what does she *really* want?

The most common reading of the relationship is that Rosie is somehow involved in the conspiracy, is herself a communist agent. Describing Marco's first encounter with her aboard the New York–bound train, Greil Marcus observes:

When in the vestibule of the train [Leigh's] Rosie tells Sinatra's Marco, "I was one of the original Chinese workmen who laid the track on this straight [sic] . . ." You almost wonder why she doesn't look Chinese—or the second or third time through the picture, if the word "Chinese" is a clue. "Maryland is a beautiful state," she says again, as if "Maryland" is the key to the lock. "So is Ohio for that matter," she says; maybe *that's* it.[1]

While accurately capturing the sense of unease the relationship—and the train scene in particular—produces in the viewer, Marcus resists passing judgment on Rosie; to him, her inscrutability is enough. She *could* be a communist agent. Movie critic Roger Ebert pushes the interpretive envelope further: "What's going on [in the train scene]?" he inquires, before attempting to answer the question. "My notion is that Sinatra's character is a Manchurian killer, too—one allowed to remember details of [Laurence] Harvey's brainwashing because that would make him more credible. And Leigh? She's Sinatra's controller."[2]

Leigh may be Sinatra's "controller," but not in the way Marcus implies or Ebert believes. The train scene (and the relationship that ensues) derives its power, its ability to disrupt, not from some hidden meaning, some component of the conspiracy that remains shrouded from the viewer, but from the manner in which it simultaneously exploits Cold War cultural anxieties regarding gender roles and calls attention to the authoring of such cultural anxieties—the manner in which it borrows from cinematic antecedents to simultaneously construct and deconstruct the paranoia of the Cold War. In this respect, it may be the scene in *The Manchurian Candidate* that most powerfully articulates the logic of the film as a whole. As such, it is worth considering on its own.

To fully understand how the scene functions ideologically, one must place it in the context of other Cold War encounters aboard trains—specifically, those in two Alfred Hitchcock classics from the period, *Strangers on a Train* (1951) and *North by Northwest* (1959), two films that, consciously or unconsciously, Frankenheimer is both taking from and working against.

The plot of *Strangers on a Train*, as the title implies, is built entirely around a chance, and homoerotically charged, encounter between two men on a train, playboy Bruno Anthony (Robert Walker) and tennis pro Guy Haines (Farley Granger). In the opening scene, they are shown arriving simultaneously at the train station, each in a different

Guy (Farley Granger) is all smiles as Bruno (Robert Walker) lights up in Alfred Hitchcock's *Strangers on a Train* (1951).

taxi. Bruno, conspicuously dressed in pin-striped suit and saddle shoes, emerges from his cab first. Guy exits his cab wearing dark trousers and wing-tip shoes. Hitchcock utilizes parallel editing to show one man, then the other, making his way toward the station. In both cases, he fixes the camera on their legs and feet, striding purposefully. Bruno walks from right to left; Guy from left to right—a foreshadowing (one of many) not only of how their paths will soon cross, but of how their destinies will become inextricably linked.

Inside the train's club car, Guy accidentally nudges Bruno's foot with his own when he sits directly across from him. Bruno recognizes him instantly: "I beg your pardon. Aren't you Guy Haines?" Before Guy can answer, Bruno does it for him: "Aw, sure, I saw you blast Farraday right off the court in South Orange last season." Practically lunging across the table, Bruno grabs Guy's hand and shakes it, introducing himself by showing off his novelty tie, which bears his name ("Bruno") written in script above a depiction of a lobster. "I suppose you think it's corny but my mother gave it to me, so I have to wear it to please her," he explains with some embarrassment, before offering Guy a cigarette.

As Guy will soon discover, Bruno knows quite a bit about him, all from the newspapers (as in Condon's novel and Frankenheimer's film, life is lived through the media): his unhappy marriage, his love affair with a U.S. senator's daughter. Bruno apologizes for bringing these things up, but he doesn't really mean it. He invites Guy back to his compartment for lunch, but Guy refuses—until he discovers he can't get a table in the dining room for another twenty minutes.

Inside the suite, Bruno, reclining in his seat, smoking a cigarette, spills his heart out about how his father "hates" him: "With all the money he's got, he thinks that I oughtta catch the . . . bus every morning and work my way up selling paint or something . . . I get so sore at him sometimes, I . . . I want to kill him." Eventually, he will unveil his idea for how the two men can solve each other's problem; that is, a way for Guy to rid himself of his wife and Bruno of his father. "Listen, it's so simple . . . [two strangers] *swap* murders. Each fellow does the other fellow's murder, then there's nothing to connect them . . . You do my murder, I do yours."

Bruno's plan is motivated not by his old man's millions, but, the film has already implicitly established, by his unresolved Oedipal complex, his emotional overdependence on his mother, and his attraction to Haines. As Robert Corber has pointed out, in his choice of wardrobe and his demeanor, Bruno "adheres to the [mid-century] stereotype of the effeminate gay man."[3] Certainly, the language of his proposition—"you do mine, I do yours"—is laced with sexual innuendo.

But if Bruno threatens Guy's (presumptive) heterosexuality, it is also true that, in the Cold War context, he threatens much more—the nation itself. As Corber has written, "following the publication of the Kinsey reports [the first in 1948, three years before *Strangers on a Train;* the second in 1953], homosexuals and lesbians were thought to threaten national security not only because they were emotionally unstable and susceptible to blackmail but also because they might convert heterosexuals to their 'perverted' practices by seducing them."[4] This ideological leap, which *My Son John* would later trade on (with the same actor in the title role) is here made by Hitchcock, who transplanted the story from New York and Connecticut (where the Patricia Highsmith novel unfolds) to Washington, D.C. Guy's girlfriend herself undergoes a significant transformation in the adaptation; in the novel, she was the daughter of a socialite.

Thus it is that Bruno—murderous, magnetic, and man-loving— emerges as one of the earliest, and most ideologically disruptive mama's boys of the Cold War cinema. The cultural roots of the type, of course, lay in Philip Wylie's vitriolic tome *Generation of Vipers*. Momism was concern enough in the pre–Cold War 1940s. In the 1950s, where the personal, as we have seen, was not only political but potentially subversive ("Are you now or have you ever been . . ."), momism, and the subsequent "confusion" it produced, became one more problem for the state (and the movies) to resolve.

The connection between sexual deviance and the threat to the state is rendered much more overtly in *North by Northwest* (1959), a film Hitchcock made eight years later, in which there is a similar encounter on a train between strangers. Roger Thornhill (Cary Grant) is a middle-aged, New York advertising man with an identity problem; more than one, actually: first, he identifies too closely with his mother, and second, enemy agents confuse him for a CIA operative. On the run from the police for a murder he did not commit—the foreign agents framed him—he encounters the mysterious lady Eve (Eva Marie Saint) aboard the *Twentieth Century Limited*, en route to Chicago.

Their first meeting comes in the narrow hallway of a sleeper car, when Thornhill, having just boarded the train and being chased by a pair of uniformed officers, ducks into an empty compartment. Eve, for reasons that will not be made apparent until later in the film, covers for him, telling the officers that the man they're looking for "went that way . . . I think he got off." Thornhill, emerging from the compartment, deadpans: "Thank you . . . seven parking tickets."

As with Bruno and Guy, however, their first real exchange will come in the dining car of the train, when Thornhill is seated at Eve's table. "Well, here we are again," he says. "Yes," she purrs back, fixing her stare on him. "I know, I look vaguely familiar . . . you feel you've seen me somewhere before," he offers. "It's something about my face." She jumps at the line: "It's a *nice* face."

Rising to the promise of the repartee, Thornhill confesses to Eve that honest women put him at a disadvantage, because "the moment

Roger Thornhill (Cary Grant) encounters the lady Eve (Eva Marie Saint) aboard the *Twentieth Century Limited* in Hitchcock's *North by Northwest* (1959).

I meet an attractive woman, I have to start pretending I have no desire to make love to her...she might find the idea objectionable." She matches him: "Then again, she might not." Smiling like the cat with at least one eye on the canary, Thornhill replies, "Think how lucky I am to have been seated here." Eve informs him that luck had nothing to do with it—"I tipped the steward five dollars to seat you here if you should come in." He is amused by her forthrightness and asks her if she is propositioning him. "I never discuss love on an empty stomach," she declares.

The sexual tryst seemingly secure, he moves on to the social niceties, asking her name and introducing himself as Jack Phillips, western sales manager for an electronics firm. "No, you're not," she replies. "You're Roger Thornhill of Madison Avenue and you're wanted for murder on every front page in America...Don't worry. I won't say a word...It's going to be a long night...and I don't particularly like the book I've started. You know what I mean?" He nods. "Yes, I know exactly what you mean." Their meal almost over, she invites him back to her compartment, "Drawing room E, car 3901," she instructs him. "Such a nice number...3901," he says in return,

before they hurry from the dining car to avoid being seen by detec-
tives boarding the train at a rural stop.

The two scenes share structural similarities. In both cases, there is
a protagonist who possesses key information about the stranger they
have encountered: Bruno knows Guy's complicated home life; Eve
knows Thornhill's dilemma. In both cases, the information facilitates
the sexual liaison (whether actual or symbolic). This is not, of course,
to draw *direct* correlations between the characters in the two scenes.
If Thornhill can be said to be reminiscent of Guy (for all of his witty
banter, it is Eve who is driving the action; as the viewer will soon discover, she planned to bed Thornhill all along), he also owes much to
Bruno, the arrested male personality.

Indeed, as Corber has observed, within the logic of the film, it is
Thornhill's lack of a fixed, stable (psychological) identity and his
overdependence on his mother that gets him into trouble in the first
place:

> His devotion to [his mother] is indirectly responsible for his kidnap-
> ping, for it is when he tries to send her a telegram reminding her of
> their theater engagement that he is mistaken [by the enemy agents]
> for [the CIA operative] Kaplan. Thus his kidnapping . . . serves as
> punishment for his continuing dependence. Because he has failed to
> internalize the Law of the Father, his identity remains unsutured and
> he is susceptible to manipulation by Communist agents.[5]

The point is driven home most explicitly during the train scene,
when Eve reaches for a cigarette and Thornhill offers her a light from
a matchbook bearing the initials R.O.T. "That's my trademark,"
he tells her, pronouncing it "rot" and explaining that it stands for
"Roger O. Thornhill." She inquires what the "O" is for. "Nothing,"
he shrugs. Like his made-up middle initial, Thornhill is hollow in the
middle; with no identity to call his own, he is symbolically "rotting"
from the inside out. (Thornhill, remember, is an advertising man; what
industry is more emblematic of the peer-driven, "other-directed" personality that David Riesman argued was the modern American character?) Ultimately, the personal and the political plotlines will turn
out to be one and the same, and will be firmly resolved on the side of
the state: Thornhill will escape the threat of momism, be delivered

Major Bennett Marco (Frank Sinatra), on his way to New York and, it would appear, a nervous breakdown.

into heterosexual love, and, in the process, foil a plot to deliver government secrets to America's enemies. (Likewise, the resolution of *Strangers on a Train* falls decidedly on the side of normative masculinity: Bruno, after murdering Guy's wife—thereby freeing him to marry the senator's daughter—is himself killed, ending whatever sexual "threat" he might have posed to Guy.)

The train scene in *The Manchurian Candidate*, while clearly referencing both *Strangers on a Train* and *North by Northwest*, ideologically speaking offers a much bumpier ride. It is, of course, the later scene in *North by Northwest* that Frankenheimer's train scene most resembles, at least in its iconography—both portray a pickup in which an attractive blonde woman acts as the sexual aggressor. The scene in *The Manchurian Candidate* opens with a medium shot of Marco sitting in the club car of a New York–bound train, looking very much like a man on the verge, if not in the throes, of a nervous breakdown. His right eye twitches. With trembling hands he reaches for a cigarette. He barely succeeds in bringing it to his mouth. When he reaches into his pocket for a light, the cigarette falls into his drink. Embarrassed, he looks around to see if anyone has noticed. Frankenheimer cuts to a medium shot of Rosie, sitting to Marco's left, staring at him sympathetically. The camera cuts back to Marco, who manages to get another cigarette to his mouth, but, with his case of the

Rosie (Janet Leigh) eyes Marco.

shakes, he can't quite steer the match to meet it. Frustrated, he extinguishes the light, again looking around to see who might have been watching.

This time, he realizes Rosie is staring at him and attempts to camouflage his condition as an outbreak of good manners: "Do you mind if I smoke?" he asks her. "Not at all. Please do," she replies. But, of course, he can't. Attempting one more time to light up, Marco's hands shake so much that the flame is extinguished before he can get it anywhere near the cigarette in his mouth. Slamming the book of matches down, he abruptly stands up, knocking over the table in front of him, and staggers out to the car's observation deck. Taking in the fresh air as if he had just emerged from a prolonged stay underwater, Marco closes his eyes and rests his head on the car wall. Then Rosie steps through the door onto the platform. She lights a cigarette, taps Marco on the shoulder to get his attention, and hands it to him. He accepts it. The exchange that follows—as odd a stretch of dialogue as one is likely to encounter in a Hollywood film—is worth considering in its entirety:

ROSIE: Maryland is a beautiful state.

MARCO: This is Delaware.

ROSIE: I know. I was one of the original Chinese workmen who laid the track on this stretch. But, um, nonetheless, Maryland is a beautiful state. So is Ohio, for that matter.

MARCO: I guess so . . . Columbus is a tremendous football town. *(Pause)* You in the railroad business?

ROSIE: Not anymore. However, if you'll permit me to point out, when you ask that question you really should say, "Are you in the railroad line?" *(Pause)* Where's your home?

MARCO: I'm in the army. I'm a major. I've been in the army most of my life. We move a good deal. *(Sigh)* I was born in New Hampshire.

ROSIE: I went to a girls' camp once in Lake Francis.

MARCO: That's pretty far north. *(Pause)* What's your name?

ROSIE: Eugénie.

MARCO: Pardon?

ROSIE: No kidding, I really mean it . . . crazy French pronunciation and all.

MARCO: It's pretty.

ROSIE: Thank you.

MARCO: I guess your friends call you Jenny.

ROSIE: Not yet they haven't, for which I'm deeply grateful. But you may call me Jenny.

MARCO: What do your friends call you?

ROSIE: Rosie.

MARCO: Why?

ROSIE: My full name is Eugénie Rose. Of the two names, I've always favored Rosie, because it smells of brown soap and beer. Eugénie is somehow more fragile.

MARCO: Still, when I asked you what your name was, you said it was Eugénie.

ROSIE: It's quite possible I was feeling more or less fragile at that instant.

MARCO: I could never figure out what that phrase meant . . . more or less. *(Pause)* You Arabic?

ROSIE: No.

MARCO: My name is Ben. It's really Bennett. I was named after Arnold Bennett.

ROSIE: The writer?

MARCO: No, a lieutenant colonel. He was my father's commanding officer at the time.

ROSIE: What's your last name?

MARCO: Marco.

ROSIE: "Major Marco." *(Pause)* Are you Arabic?

MARCO: No.

ROSIE: Let me put it another way: Are you married?

MARCO: No . . . you?

ROSIE: No.

MARCO: What's your last name?

ROSIE: Cheyney. I'm production assistant for a man named Justin, who had two hits last season. I live on 54th Street, a few doors from the Modern Museum of Art, of which I'm a tea privileges member, no cream. I live at 53 West 54th Street, apartment 3B. Can you remember that?

MARCO: Yes.

ROSIE: El Dorado 5-9970 . . . can you remember that?

MARCO: Yes.

ROSIE: Are you stationed in New York . . . or is "stationed' the right word?

MARCO: I'm not exactly stationed in New York. I was stationed in Washington, but I got sick and now I'm on leave and I'm going to spend it in New York.

ROSIE: El Dorado 5-9970.

MARCO: I'm gonna look up an old friend of mine who's a newspaperman. We were in Korea together.

The scene is lifted almost word for word from Condon's novel.[6] But it is most reminiscent of Hitchcock, and not only his *North by North-west* and *Strangers on a Train*. (In *The Lady Vanishes* [1938], mysterious goings-on aboard a European train are ultimately linked to matters of state and foreign intrigue on the eve of World War II.)

Certainly, the casting of Janet Leigh—whatever its motivation—gives the scene a certain Hitchcockian feel. It isn't simply that Leigh, by 1962, had gained the status of "Hitchcock blonde"—so had Kim Novak (*Vertigo*) and Grace Kelly (*Dial M for Murder*, *Rear Window*, *It Takes a Thief*), although she was no longer making films. It's the timing of Leigh's appearance that so intrigues (timing in terms both of where Leigh was in her career and of where her first appearance in

Between train cars, an odd exchange.

The Manchurian Candidate comes). Leigh's previous screen role—with
the exception of a brief cameo (as herself) in the all-star ensemble
Pepe—had been as ill-fated Marion Crane in the Hitchcock masterpiece *Psycho* (1960). Having famously exited that film early, she steps
into *The Manchurian Candidate* conspicuously late, at least by Hollywood standards (the train scene comes approximately forty minutes
into the film). It isn't simply a case, then, of Frankenheimer "borrowing" one of the director's most famous (and, for that matter, his most
recent) blonde, but of introducing her in a way that recalls *and* inverts
Hitchcock's oeuvre.

Indeed—Greil Marcus's characterization of *The Manchurian Candidate* as "made up of bits and pieces of Hitchcock and Orson Welles"
notwithstanding—if one compares Frankenheimer's train scene to
the one in *North by Northwest,* it becomes clear that he is not so much
borrowing from or citing Hitchcock's work as purposely *misquoting*
the earlier film. William Rothman, in *Hitchcock: The Murderous Gaze,*
argues that Hitchcock is one of the few directors who successfully
conveys to the audience that his films are "authored," that he is the
auteur.[7] In marked contrast, Frankenheimer appears to be attempting
to convey to the audience that he is a plagiarist. The scene simultaneously courts recognition and misrecognition, constructs *and* deconstructs the Cold War cultural anxieties surrounding masculinity
previously mined by Hitchcock in *North by Northwest* (and, by extension, in *Strangers on a Train*).

Where Roger Thornhill is quite capable of sparring with Eve, advancing the flirtation, and, eventually, sealing the sexual deal, Marco remains a disturbingly passive and confused subject, or, rather, *object*. Marco, when the scene begins, is not pursuing Rosie. Indeed, he doesn't even notice her until he realizes *she* is staring at him, realizes that he is the object of *her* gaze. By positioning Rosie as the voyeur (and there is no more accurate term, given the painfully private moment Marco is having), Frankenheimer is not only constructing her as the sexual aggressor—long before she follows Marco out to the observation deck—but reversing traditional gender roles as defined by the classical Hollywood cinema. As film theorist Laura Mulvey observed in her foundational essay "Visual Pleasure and Narrative Cinema," in the classical Hollywood paradigm, a woman performs within the narrative, while the gaze of the spectator and the male characters in the film is linked. The effect of this, according to Mulvey, is that "as the spectator identifies with the main male protagonist . . . the power of the male protagonist as he controls events coincides with the active power of the erotic look, both giving a satisfying sense of omnipotence."[8] The scopophilia, or pleasure derived from looking, observed by Mulvey may not occur in every classical film, but it is a staple of Hitchcock's 1950s films, once again suggesting that it is Hitchcock with whom Frankenheimer is symbolically sparring.[9]

Sitting there, sweating, shaking, twitching, unable to consummate the meeting of match and cigarette, Marco signifies anything but omnipotence; he is, instead, the embodiment of masculinity in crisis. Indeed, his breakdown has been coded as a crisis of sexuality since the beginning of the film. What kind of man, after all, dreams night after night that he is attending a meeting of a ladies' garden club? Little wonder that his commanding officer should suggest to Marco a hetero rest cure, recommend that he "find a girl and lie in the sun."

Unlike Thornhill, who, in the high Hollywood tradition, lights Eve's cigarette, Marco is incapable of even lighting his own, and must rely on Rosie to do it for him. And while it is Rosie who is mistaken about their location ("Maryland is a beautiful state"), the exchange really serves to underscore Marco's psychological disorientation, his "state" of confusion. In a shrewd use of mise-en-scène, his condition is visually communicated by the constantly shifting landscape out-side the window.

The exchange between them also serves to raise our suspicions of her motives, but not for the reason most commonly cited. While the remark about being one of the original Chinese workmen begs to be ascribed evil intent, the disruptive quality of the line can better be attributed to the sexual innuendo contained therein. Rosie claims to be, after all, "one of the original Chinese workmen *who laid the track* on this stretch." The double entendre, which further establishes Rosie as the sexual aggressor, coupled with Marco's indifference to it, only serves to emphasize his deepening (male) identity crisis.

Unlike the scene in *North by Northwest,* the scene in *The Man-churian Candidate* frustrates all attempts at instant gratification (Rosie's and the viewer's). Unlike Roger, who knows "exactly what Eve means," Marco has no idea what Rosie is talking about. Or, seem-ingly, what she's after. When, for example, she tells him that her name is Eugénie, Marco presumes, wrongly, that "her friends call her Jenny." When she explains that she introduced herself as Eugénie only because she was feeling "more or less fragile at that instant," he misses the import of her answer, instead becoming distracted by the tossed-off qualifier. "I could never figure out what that phrase meant . . . more or less." Perhaps because he staves off sleep every night by absorbing an eclectic and seemingly infinite assortment of books (including one titled *Ethnic Choices of the Arabs*), he inquires, some-what vacantly, if she is Arabic. When she volleys the question back at him—playfully, as a part of her come-on—he is more embarrassed than aroused.

The inverted relationship between the two scenes is most evident at the moment each woman offers her address to the male protago-nist. "Such a nice number," remarks Roger, when Eve directs him to her drawing room aboard the *Twentieth Century*. Marco, on the other hand, acts like a chastened schoolboy being forced to recite the Golden Rule when Rosie asks him if he can remember her street and phone number. It is this last exchange that, perhaps, is most respon-sible for conspiracy theories among film critics and viewers. But Rosie isn't a spy; there is, in fact, nothing in the film to suggest such a thing. She is, however, dangerous—not only because she wants a sexual liaison with Marco, but because she wants to mother him, too. Indeed, what else could possibly be the source of her attraction to this broken-down career army man in the gray flannel suit?

In this respect, Rosie serves as doppelgänger to Raymond Shaw's "dearly loved and hated mother," who, as the viewer, of course, will discover, *is* a communist agent and Raymond's American operator. Consider that the iconography of the train scene is repeated later in the film, in the scene in which Raymond's mother gives him his instructions for assassinating the party's presidential nominee, a killing that will result in Iselin being handed the nomination. Standing over the entranced, deathly passive Raymond, forcing him to commit the nominee's speech (or, if one will, *address*) to memory, just as Rosie forced Marco to commit *her* address to memory, Raymond's mother—tall, blonde, and controlling—suggests an older version of Rosie, the incestuous kiss on her son's lips linking her symbolic rape of Raymond with Rosie's sexual pursuit of Marco. (Consider, as well, the similarity in name between Marco's "Rosie" and Shaw's "Jocie"—*The Manchurian Candidate* is a film that takes its doubling seriously.)

In *North by Northwest*, national security and Thornhill's heterosexuality are both ensured by the ending; indeed, as Robert Corber has shown, they are established as mutually reinforcing principles.[10] Eve *does* turn out to be an agent in the employ of foreign powers (she is also an agent for the American government), but Thornhill rescues both his country and Eve from danger by romancing her, by literally and figuratively turning her into an honest woman. The film closes with Mr. and Mrs. Thornhill back on the train, in a state of newlywed bliss. (The question of who is the dominant partner is answered cinematically when Thornhill pulls Eve into the upper berth.)

The Manchurian Candidate's evolution (and resolution) of the relationship, again, is more problematic. After the train scene, Rosie appears in only four more scenes in the film. The first scene, following their meeting, in many ways is a duplicate of the train scene and cements the dynamics of the relationship as earlier established.

Following his fight with Chunjin, Marco, his face bloody, sits in a Manhattan police precinct. As in the train scene, he is in the foreground, staring off into space. Rosie can be seen entering in the background. The viewer is again aligned with her; both she and the viewer are looking at Marco. He doesn't realize she has arrived. He's apologetic for having dragged her down to the station, but he had no one else to call. As Marco and Rosie exit, a Puerto Rican police detective is heard speaking on the phone (in Spanish). Trying to make a love connection of his own, he is leaving a message for "María," letting her know that he'll be by later. Remarkably, it is the only time a foreign language is spoken in the film, and its effect is unsettling—standing in for the Chinese and Russian that are never heard, it introduces a vague sense of "the other" into the scene. The exchange between the lovelorn cop (María is, apparently, out on the town) and the person on the other end of the line is ultimately of no consequence to the plot, but, in a film that has trained us to be wary of foreign influences, it nevertheless manages to disrupt.

In the taxi on the way home, Rosie (replicating the gesture from the train scene) lights a cigarette and places it in Marco's mouth. As on the train, the landscape (this time, Manhattan) is a blur outside the window—again, perhaps, a comment on Marco's continuing state of disorientation. Rosie dabs at his bruises with a kerchief and informs him that she has just broken off her engagement (the fiancé had never come up), before—in a manner that recalls the nonsensical conversation aboard the train—making a joke about how "Washington" had vouched for Marco: "I figured if they were willing to go to all the trouble to get a comment on you out of George Washington, well, you must be someone very important, indeed. And I must say it was rather sweet of the general, with you only a major. I didn't even know you knew him." Then, softer: "If they were the tiniest bit puzzled about you, they could have asked me . . . Oh, yes indeed, my darling Ben, they could have asked me, and I would have told them." They kiss and, once again, she is the sexual aggressor sealing the deal.

Rosie's third appearance in the film is in a domestic scene, she and Marco at home. He sits at a table, shuffling the "forced deck" of red queens he's going to use to deprogram Raymond, while she sets the table for dinner. Then, abruptly, he proposes: "Rosie, let's get married." Her response is indirect, almost evasive: "Certainly are in good spirits tonight, aren't we?" she says, wheeling toward the kitchen. Marco follows her, pressing the issue. He senses her detachment: "Why don't you pay attention to me when I speak to you?" Finally, she gives him his answer (sort of): "Oh, Bennie, I want to marry you more than I want go on eating Italian food" (a line Sinatra must have loved).

If the scene has so far suggested Rosie's disproportionate power in the relationship—Marco has to follow her into the kitchen to get an answer, and even then, the viewer knows the two will get married only when, and if, Rosie decides—the exchange that follows confirms it. Marco wants to know when they can "get with it," start making plans, sending out the invitations. Only then, apparently, does he discover that Rosie's parents are deceased. "I used to be convinced that, as a baby, I was the sole survivor of a spaceship that overshot Mars," she tells him. He, it would seem, knows almost nothing about her. She knows almost everything about him, including what happened in Korea. The scene, like the one on the train, is troubling not only because things would appear to be moving too quickly, almost artificially so (are these two people who should be considering matrimony?), but because, again, Rosie is the dominant figure.

Rosie's fourth appearance is a brief one. Marco, having learned that Senator Jordan and Jocie are dead, staggers into Rosie's apartment carrying a copy of that day's *New York Post*, the sad news splattered on the front page. The frame is tilted throughout the scene to heighten the sense of anguish Marco feels. It is, like so much in the film, an excessive gesture ("over the top," as Frankenheimer once said, referring to other, similarly extravagant shots), but it works, in part, because of Rosie and Marco, because their relationship itself has seemed so off-kilter all along; the angle of the shot, like the blurred landscape outside the train window, functions as an articulation of the characters' interior states.[11]

Rosie's fifth and final appearance comes at the film's conclusion. Following Raymond's murder-suicide, Marco reads to Rosie from a book listing the heroic deeds of former Medal of Honor winners. Closing the book solemnly, he authors an entry for Raymond Shaw, whom he ultimately could not save. Holding back tears, his words catching in his throat, he slams the book on the table, uttering a defeated "Hell...hell..." Rosie, as she has from the beginning, watches him.

Even without the final snippet of dialogue contained in the script (but never heard in the film)—"It's all right, Ben! It's all right! A man is allowed to cry...for a friend..."[12]—Marco, at film's end, remains an impotent figure, as susceptible as ever not necessarily to communist infiltration, but to the "threat" posed by Rosie, or, more accurately, what she represents—the continued influence of the strong-willed woman and the symbolic castration of the male.

If, as Michael Rogin has written, *The Manchurian Candidate* does feel like "the last cold war movie," it is not simply "because the assassination to which it pointed [the Kennedy assassination] brought the cold war consensus to an end."[13] It feels like the last Cold War movie because, as the relationship between Marco and Rosie demonstrates perhaps most acutely, the film so ingeniously lays bare the cultural underwritings of American anticommunism and deconstructs the cultural Cold War to reveal its dependence on overly restrictive models (of citizenship, sexuality, and domesticity). The mystery in question— Is she or isn't she part of the conspiracy?—has little to do with Rosie's secret desires, and everything to do with our own.

8

Cold War Redux

From Kennedy to Reagan's America and Beyond

I've been driven nearly out of my mind by this same
recurring dream.

—*Bennett Marco*

"If you come in five minutes after this picture begins, you won't know
what it's all about!" promised the movie poster for *The Manchurian
Candidate*. "When you've seen it all, you'll swear there's never been
anything like it!"

When the film opened in the fall of 1962, most reviewers agreed
that it was quite novel. Whether that was a good thing or not, however, was open to debate. *The New York Times*'s Bosley Crowther,
acknowledging Frankenheimer's debt to the Master of Suspense, called
it "as wild a piece of fiction as anything Hitchcock might present,"
adding that "it could serve to scare some viewers half to death." This
warning, though, came with a caveat—it would so scare viewers only
if they "should be dupes enough to believe [the film's premise]." And,
for his part, Crowther did not: "The nature of the plot and its key
figure here in this country, when finally revealed, are so fantastic that
one is suspicious of the author's sincerity." It was, for Crowther, finally,
a triumph of style over substance. Although he couldn't recommend

Movie poster for *The Manchurian Candidate* (1962). (MGM/Corbis)

its story line, he had no choice but to admit that "the film is so artfully contrived, the direction is so exciting...that the fascination of it is strong."[1]

Writing in the *Saturday Review*, Arthur Knight came to a similar opinion, if by a different route. Calling the film "enormously effective," Knight nevertheless detected in it telling traces of the Saturday afternoon matinee. Describing his reaction to Yen Lo's visit to the New York hospital (the "rest home for wealthy alcoholics"), the scene in which Yen Lo "smilingly orders Harvey to another purposeless killing," Knight writes: "The image snapped into place. This was not Yen Lo, the Red superman, but our old childhood friend, the insidious Dr. Fu Manchu. And if this was epicene, inscrutable, dangerous Dr. Fu, with his incessant, devious schemes for world domination, then the reliable Dr. Petrie and the redoubtable Nailand Smyth must also be close at hand. And sure enough, they were—in the persons of Sinatra, [Shaw's] commanding officer, and an Army psychiatrist."[2]

No great leap of insight—the film self-consciously traded on such stereotypes, Marco himself describing Yen Lo as "that Chinese cat, standing there smiling like Fu Manchu"—Knight's observation nevertheless proved reassuring to him, because in a way it served to contain the implications of the story. "It is always disturbing when melodrama plays fast and loose with serious, even incendiary material," he explained. "Indeed, the more effectively it is presented, the greater the cause for alarm." To Knight, Yen Lo's resemblance to the stock stereotype kept the film from being *too* effective. A good thing, he concluded, because "without question, [The Manchurian Candidate] is the best-told story of the year [and] without question, it is also the most irresponsible."[3]

Other reviews were, at best, mixed. *Time* panned it altogether: "As translated into cinema by director John Frankenheimer...the story is notable chiefly for a systematic error it makes. It tries so hard to be different that it fails to be itself."[4] Stanley Kauffmann, writing in the *New Republic*, saw it as inflated and fatally derivative: "The picture features the supposedly sharp, sexy dialogue of George Axelrod, hard as rusty nails; and it has been directed by John Frankenheimer with an eagerness to distinguish himself that is matched only by his memory of Hitchcock films."[5] Even the *New Yorker*, which declared it "a thriller guaranteed to raise all but the limpest hair," acknowledged that, in the cold light of day, far from the seductive darkness of the movie house, it might add up to little more than "glittering hokum."[6]

Given such reviews, one might be tempted to group *The Manchurian Candidate* with any number of films that were initially dismissed, only to be later embraced as cinematic classics. But to do so would be to ignore the fact that, from the moment of its inception—certainly from the time Sinatra went to John F. Kennedy to secure his blessings—the project seemed tied to the larger world, to its cultural and sociopolitical moment, in quite exceptional ways. Its moment of release would be no different.

If one detects in these reviews—Kauffmann's, especially—a certain tension, a pull between embracing the film as a cinematic product and somehow containing (in the truest sense of that loaded term) the implied threat in its story line, it might have something to do with events playing out not in the entertainment sections, but on the front pages and covers of American newspapers and magazines: Frankenheimer's Cold War nightmare was unleashed on the culture the week of October 21, at the exact moment that the Cuban missile crisis was reaching its climax.

Having confirmed the presence of Soviet missiles in Cuba the preceding week, Kennedy addressed the nation on Monday, October 22, telling viewers that a number of measures would be immediately adopted, including "a strict quarantine on all offensive military equipment under shipment to Cuba." Kennedy closed his speech on what undoubtedly must have seemed an ominous note: "Let no one doubt that this is a difficult and dangerous effort on which we have set out. No one can see precisely what course it will take or what costs or casualties will be incurred. Many months of sacrifice and self-discipline lie ahead—months in which our patience and our will will be tested—months in which many threats and denunciations will keep us aware of our dangers."[7]

Two days later, on October 24, "with the air full of international tension" (as Crowther wrote in his review), *The Manchurian Candidate* opened in New York City. The Cuban missile crisis would last another four days, culminating in Nikita Khrushchev's announcement on Radio Moscow on Sunday, October 28, that the Soviet Union would dismantle the weapons. (The film's association with the missile crisis, symbolic and otherwise, would appear to have had a longer life than even this chronology suggests. According to film critic and historian J. Hoberman, Kennedy screened *The Manchurian Candidate* at the White House on August 29, the same day that a U-2 spy plane reported that Soviet missile installations in Cuba were only weeks away from being completed.)[8]

Populated by Kennedyesque heroes (and his friend, Sinatra), *The Manchurian Candidate*, Michael Rogin argues, like the administration, "warned against both right-wing hysteria and bureaucratic complacency... [and] aimed to breathe new life into the cold war."[9] That the film shared Kennedy's strenuous Cold War liberalism there can be little doubt. But who could have predicted that, in its narrative and emotional logic, it would mirror the missile crisis so completely? "No one can see precisely what course it will take or what costs or casualties will be incurred," Kennedy had told the nation, though he just as easily could have been describing Frankenheimer's film. Both in the streets and on the screen, it was a week of unlikely plot twists, unspeakable possibilities, and "happy" endings that left one feeling more disturbed than comforted.

Ultimately, of course, the film's strongest link to Kennedy and the historical moment would come not from the timeliness of its release, but from its presaging of the events of November 22, 1963. "Was 'Manchurian' Film a Prophet?" wondered the *Hollywood Citizen-News* in the wake of the Kennedy assassination.[10] Richard Condon, writing in the *Nation* that December, answered those who would seek to make a connection between the cinematic adaptation of his book and the events in Dallas. "When a reporter from a South African press association... [asked] if I felt responsible for the President's killing...," explained Condon, by then living in Paris, "I told the reporter that, with all Americans, I had contributed to form the attitudes of the assassin; and that the assassin, and Americans like him, had contributed to the attitudes which had caused me to write the novel."[11]

Citing the continued sale of cigarettes, even when there were known to be "suicide weapons," the proliferation of violent images in popular culture (Condon mentioned newspapers, television, music, and, not at all ironically, "$5 novels which soon become 50-cent paperbacks"), the grip of organized crime, and the existence of the "most gigantically complex overcommunications system ever developed," Condon ridiculed the cultivated-at-all-costs naïveté of his onetime countrymen, throwing in a well-placed critique of American apartheid in the process: "We can feign surprise, as we did with the murder of President Kennedy, but none of us seemed either surprised or moved by the murder of Medgar Evers, who was also a brave leader of his people, also a man who had a young wife and children, and whose assassin most certainly matched the basic, American psychological pattern of the killer of our President."[12] No, Condon concluded, to point the finger at him (or Frankenheimer) would be to miss the point: "We are violent and unstable because we have been so conditioned to these responses that civilized, thoughtful conduct has become impossible for us. It is a hell of a spot for a country to be in. Who, the least brainwashed among us, will cast the first redemptive thought?"[13]

Although the Warren Commission the following year would give voice in the extreme to the contrary opinion—the term "lone gunman" implying not simply that Lee Harvey Oswald acted alone, but that he was an aberration—one mystery would remain. What, exactly, happened to *The Manchurian Candidate* after the assassination? Condon, in his article (written only five weeks after the events in Dallas) mentions that the film "had just been 'frozen' in the United States because it was felt that the assassin might have seen it and been influenced by it." Film critic Roger Ebert claimed, upon the film's rediscovery in the late 1980s, that it had never turned up on TV.[14] Greil Marcus rejects both accounts: "*The Manchurian Candidate* was taken out of circulation [but] . . . not that quickly, not right after the assassination . . . while Frankenheimer refused to allow a second theatrical run, the film played on television. Then it went missing."[15] The truth would appear to be slightly less dramatic than these conspiracy-tinged accounts, though, in a way, no less intriguing. *The Manchurian*

Candidate, in fact, was shown on television for more than a decade after the Kennedy assassination; as late as April 1974, it was featured on *NBC Saturday Night at the Movies.*[16] At the same time, it is true that it was eventually pulled from circulation, but not because of its explosive story line or any role it might have played in the assassination of the president. The motive, according to both Frankenheimer and Axelrod, was money. As Aljean Harmetz wrote in the *New York Times* in 1988: "According to Mr. Frankenheimer, the movie [the original release] was listed on the studio's books at such a loss that any sales would profit the studio but not Mr. Sinatra, Mr. Axelrod and Mr. Frankenheimer, who were partners in the film." Or, as Axelrod put it, "There was no reason to enrich the coffers of UA [by authorizing its rerelease]." The studio, smelling the potential income from video sales, wiped its books clean, thereby facilitating the film's redistribution.[17]

The Manchurian Candidate would make a remarkable cultural (and financial) comeback.[18] If, in the moment of its conception, it had been—as both Rogin and Marcus have described it—the classic Kennedy administration film, it returned, in many ways, as the quintessential film of the Reagan era, providing a matching bookend (by doubling itself) to the Cold War. "Are we now being ruled by the fantasies of a 1940s countersubversive B movie?" Rogin asked during the 1980s, a reference to Ronald Reagan's earlier career in Hollywood, and the manner in which it had resulted in "a psychological shift from an embodied self to its simulacrum on film."[19] The president, Rogin argued, had discovered his identity through the movie roles he had taken over the years, a process that confused fantasy with reality. Rogin dubbed the end product of this confusion—which also became the image of Reagan in the public consciousness—"*Ronald Reagan, the movie.*"

Certainly, the president's penchant for taking scenarios, dialogue, and lessons from the movies—without necessarily crediting his sources, or even being aware of what he was doing—was well documented at the time. As Rogin recounts:

> CBS' *Sixty Minutes* has traced the process by which Reagan first credited the line "Where do we find such men?" [about the American D-Day dead] to the movie admiral in *Bridges at Toko-Ri,* then assigned

that line to a real admiral, and finally quoted it as if he had thought
of it himself . . . He has told a mass audience about the captain of a
bomber who chose to go down with his plane rather than abandon a
wounded crew member—"Congressional Medal of Honor, posthu-
mous," concluded Reagan with tears in his eyes—only to have it
revealed . . . that the episode was taken from Dana Andrews' *A Wing
and a Prayer*.[20]

As Rogin and, most recently, Anthony Lane have shown, Reagan's own filmography exerted an especially powerful hold over him.
"Even Reagan's nickname, the Gipper," writes Lane, "was a reference
not to the original George Gipp, the hard-drinking Notre Dame football
hero who died at twenty-five, but to Reagan's blameless incarnation
of him in *Knute Rockne—All-American* (1940) and to the death-
bed scene in which Rockne's team is urged to 'win just one for the
Gipper.'"[21]

It was into this celluloid republic that *The Manchurian Candidate*
was (re)introduced in 1987. It's reemergence at the tail end of the
Reagan years was coincidental, yet it appeared the perfect postscript
to the era, the film that most completely mapped the particular
obsessions of the 1980s—both Reagan's and our own (with him). As
we will see, the film's adherence to anticommunist ideology (not an
unproblematized adherence, but adherence nevertheless), its similarities to the prevailing 1980s genre of the Vietnam POW film, and,
finally, Sinatra's embrace of another sitting president, conspired to
make *The Manchurian Candidate*, in a manner that defied chronology
(but not history), seem as much a document of the Reagan presidency as of the era in which it was first conceived.

The Manchurian Candidate's brand of Cold War paranoia, its cultural cues, might have seemed sadly outdated in the 1970s climate of
détente, but, by 1987, Reagan had sufficiently (and, to hear his political opponents tell it, almost single-handedly) revitalized the once-
dominant paradigms. Just over a year into his first term, he made
what came to be known simply as the "evil empire" speech. Addressing the British House of Commons on June 8, 1982, Reagan pushed
aside the nuances of geopolitics in the nuclear age to produce a black-
and-white picture (hadn't his best Hollywood performances always
been in black and white?) of the international scene:

We see totalitarian forces in the world who seek subversion and
conflict around the globe to further their barbarous assault on the
human spirit. What, then, is our course?...Must freedom wither in
a quiet, deadening accommodation with totalitarian evil?[22]

It was the type of speech that would have worked well as a voice-
over at the beginning of Casablanca, a film Reagan reportedly had
been up for as a young actor (not really a coincidence given that, as
Rogin puts it, communism was "substituted" for Nazism in the political unconscious in the postwar period; and it was anticommunism that
supplied Reagan, in Rogin's words, with both "an explanation for
and an alternative to his declining Hollywood career").[23]

If The Manchurian Candidate had traded in both black humor and
melodrama, didn't Reagan (and, for that matter, Ronald Reagan) do
the same, albeit often unintentionally? "Reagan didn't just hate Communism," Lane has written, recalling one of the president's best post-
Hollywood performances. "He sought concrete expression for his
hatred by flying to Europe, standing next to the concrete in question,
and exclaiming 'Tear down this wall!'"[24]

Three years earlier, in a moment Axelrod might have scripted for
Johnny Iselin (with scotch and water in hand), Reagan, during a radio
broadcast, thinking the microphones were off, jokingly informed his
audience, "My fellow Americans, I'm pleased to tell you today that
I've signed legislation that will outlaw Russia forever. We begin bombing in five minutes."[25] It was not as self-conscious a pronouncement
on the power of the mass media as either Condon's novel or Frankenheimer's film had been, but then, it wasn't all that different in kind,
either.

And, like The Manchurian Candidate, Ronald Reagan drew freely
from the cultural vocabulary of the early Cold War period, most
directly from the films Hollywood produced in the 1950s. One movie
in particular would appear to have prefigured the other two "films" in
significant ways. In 1954, near the end of his Hollywood career, Reagan starred in Prisoner of War, a documentary-style drama about
brainwashing in North Korean prison camps. Reagan played Web
Sloane, an army intelligence officer who allows himself to be captured
so that he can expose the torture of American POWs. "He pretends
to cooperate with the Communists to gather evidence against them,"

Rogin writes. "Although the movie audience is in on the secret (that Web is a loyal American), it nevertheless watches other Americans starved and hideously tortured while Web grows fat. Extended masochistic scenes establish the Americans as victims, but Web is not one of them" (39).

The film, no doubt inspired by the same Korean War accounts as Condon's novel, resonates with *The Manchurian Candidate* in significant ways. Not only does Reagan's character appear to be an amalgam of Shaw and Marco—like Marco, he is an army intelligence officer and, like Shaw, a kind of spy—but the dynamics themselves anticipate the later film. If Sloane isn't made to kill any of his countrymen (as Shaw was), his "participation" in their torture is not altogether inconsequential, either in the film or for the audience who watched it. As Rogin documents, Reagan often portrayed characters who infiltrated criminal or subversive organizations, but, in the case of *Prisoner of War*, "the disturbing images of torture and identity confusion [unsettled] Reagan's aura of innocence more than the film intended" (ibid.).

By imagining a scenario in which an American could be made to appear complicit in the torture of other Americans, *Prisoner of War* served as symbolic midwife to *The Manchurian Candidate*. The latter film was no doubt more knowing—overtly acknowledging what *Prisoner of War* only incidentally hinted at; namely, that the difference between America and its Cold War enemies was largely one of construction. "Cold war ideology," Rogin writes, "required America simultaneously to imitate practices attributed to the enemy and to demonize the subversive in order to defend against the resulting breakdown of difference" (ibid.). *The Manchurian Candidate*, through its excesses, may have laid this cultural maneuver bare, but, as we have shown, it remained very much a document of the Cold War. If, as one of his aides once put it, Reagan believed that "cinema heightens reality instead of lessening it," *The Manchurian Candidate* must have confirmed every (reactionary) fear he'd ever had (7).

But if *The Manchurian Candidate* touched a nerve upon its rerelease, it was not because the U.S. commander in chief had once made a film dealing with the same subject matter (in popular recitations of Reagan's résumé, *Prisoner of War* rarely, if ever, came up; *Knute Rockne*,

King's Row, and even *Bedtime for Bonzo* were usually invoked as barometers of the president's Hollywood career). Whatever resonance *The Manchurian Candidate* may have had for Reagan personally, its enthusiastic rediscovery no doubt was more indebted to the popularity of a new film genre: the POW rescue adventure.

As historian H. Bruce Franklin has written, "Essential to [the] process of remilitarization [begun by the Carter administration and accelerated under Reagan] was a rewriting and reimaging of the history of the Vietnam War, which would restore the discredited vision of idealistic, courageous Americans heroically battling hordes of sadistic Oriental Communists."[26] On the pop culture front, this desire to rewrite history manifested itself in a series of films that followed a basic formula: A group of American soldiers (or, in some cases, a one-man killing machine) is secretly sent by the military brass to Southeast Asia (Vietnam, Laos, what's the difference?) to rescue American POWs held captive since the war, a mission that just as often puts them/him at odds with the U.S. government (which, for political reasons, has chosen to ignore the matter of POWs) as with the hordes of Asian soldiers with which he will eventually dispense.

In *Uncommon Valor* (1983)—in many ways, the progenitor of the genre—retired marine colonel Gene Hackman organizes an excursion into Laos to search for his son, reported missing in action during the war. *Uncommon Valor* was followed by, among others, the Chuck Norris *Missing in Action* trilogy, in which Norris, in quick succession, rescues American POWs from Vietnam (1984), himself escapes from a Vietnamese POW camp (1985), and, finally, returns to Vietnam to search for his Vietnamese wife (1988). The plot outline of the first *Missing in Action* film, as described by Franklin, is a sufficient summary of how these films played out:

> Vietnamese bodies pile up faster and faster as Braddock's [Norris's] exploits become ever more implausible. The Vietnamese have conveniently situated the POW camp eight kilometers from the coast, easily accessible from Braddock's bulletproof assault boat; after vowing to complete the entire mission in fourteen hours, he single-handedly wipes out an entire POW camp; a helicopter he had charted in Bangkok arrives with seconds to spare so that he can escape with his freed POWs and fly them back to Saigon; thus, just as the U.S. delegation is nodding to the evil Vietnamese official's declaration "In

conclusion, we categorically deny that there are any living MIAs in the People's Republic of Vietnam," Braddock bursts into their splendiferous meeting room, with ragged and emaciated POWs in tow. (150)

But, without doubt, the defining entry in the cycle of POW films was *Rambo: First Blood Part II* (1985), in which disaffected Vietnam vet John Rambo (played by Sylvester Stallone) is sent to Cambodia to rescue American POWs, jointly held by Russian and Vietnamese captors. The action—and the story line of governmental betrayal—was, if anything, more exaggerated than it had been in previous efforts. Perhaps because of that, the film and its modern-day superhero became cultural icons of the highest magnitude. "The nation," writes Franklin, "was flooded with Rambo 'action dolls,' watches, walkie-talkies, water guns, bubble gum, pinball machines, sportswear for all ages, TV cartoons, and even 'Rambo-Grams,' messages delivered by headbanded musclemen sporting bandoleers across their bare chests. A *Rambo* cartoon serial . . . began its extended run in 1986. And for 'adult' audiences there were the pornographic video spin-offs such as *Ramb-Ohh!* (1986) and *Bimbo: Hot Blood Part I!* (1985) and *Bimbo: The Homecoming!* (1986)" (ibid.).

No surprise that this Hollywood production would find its way into Reagan's discourse: "Boy, I saw *Rambo* last night," the president declared, during another of those unintentional/intentional microphone checks prior to a national address, this one concerning the release of American hostages from Beirut. "Now I know what to do" (ibid.). Or, for that matter, that *The Manchurian Candidate* was so warmly received upon its rerelease. Although by no means in the spirit of films like *Rambo* and the *Missing in Action* series, *The Manchurian Candidate* did share a number of characteristics with those 1980s offerings, the most obvious being that it is a POW film, very much about the awful things that can happen to American GIs at the hands of enemy agents (*The Manchurian Candidate*'s Chinese–Soviet "axis of evil" approximates the Vietnamese and Soviet villains in *Rambo*).

Then, too, there is the hero's betrayal by the government. In the case of Marco, the betrayal is twofold. First, there is the army's reluctance to give any credence to his accounts of what really happened during the patrol's absence, an element accompanied, it should be noted, by the same skepticism of the government's ability to act that is the hallmark of the 1980s POW films: "You couldn't have stopped them, the army couldn't have stopped them, so I had to," Shaw tells Marco when the major confronts him, following his killing of Iselin and his mother.

Second, there is the larger betrayal of the nation. If the *Rambo* and *Missing in Action* films depicted an American government made up of ineffectual leaders being led around by the nose by the Vietnamese and Soviets, *The Manchurian Candidate* did them one better (and these are tough films to outdo on any front), portraying a leading "patriot" as an enemy agent. (On the other hand, poor Senator Jordan, the bleeding heart ultimately victimized by the conspiracy he can hardly imagine, could have stepped out of *The Manchurian Candidate* and into *Rambo* without missing a beat.)

Beyond the generic similarities, there are the symbolic resonances, the way *The Manchurian Candidate* might have been understood as a subversive imagining of the Reagan presidency itself, and of the relationships between the president and *The Manchurian Candidate*'s star, Frank Sinatra. Certainly, there was a persistent sense that, like Raymond Shaw, Reagan was always being guided, or given instruction. "He simply looks to someone to tell him what to do," his former campaign manager, John Sears, once said (Rogin, *Ronald Reagan, The Movie,* 31). Reagan, as Rogin has pointed out, did not disagree with that opinion: "When press spokesman Larry Speakes stepped in front of him to ward off a reporter's question about the reappointment of Anne Burford, the president quipped, 'My guardian says I can't talk'" (ibid.).

The point is not necessarily that Reagan was manipulated by the people around him, but that so often that was the perception—particularly when it came to his wife. "Reagan did not relinquish the need for care [when he left Hollywood for politics]," Rogin argues. "[He found] caretakers he could trust. The president was silent in response to a reporter's question on arms control until he repeated aloud his wife's whisper, 'Doing all we can.' Reagan has realized the dream of the American male, to be taken care of in the name of independence, to be supported while playing the man in charge" (34).

This last observation, and particularly the anecdote that accompanies it, a well-publicized incident captured by the television

Nancy Reagan makes sure her husband looks the part for *Prisoner of War* (1954). (Bettman/Corbis)

cameras, recalls the relationship between Eleanor and John Iselin. Whether supplying him with the number of communists in the Defense Department or engineering Raymond's reunion with Jocie, Eleanor is eerily reminiscent of Nancy Reagan, or at least the public's view of the first lady. Likewise, Eleanor's repeated references to Iselin in the diminutive ("Johnny"), and her obsessive mothering of him, bring to mind not only Nancy Reagan's overprotectiveness of her

own husband, but her nickname for him, expressed so often in public: "Ronnie."

Indeed, given the synchronicity of Nancy Davis's entrance into
Ronald Reagan's life and his turn toward conservative politics in the
early 1950s, one might be tempted to wonder if they didn't fall in
love over a game of cards. Reagan had been, as he once put it, "a
near-hemophiliac liberal. I bled for 'causes': I had voted Democratic,
following my father, in every election." Then, as Rogin notes, a symbolic (and yet not merely symbolic) shift occurred: "[Ronald Reagan]
left behind [his father] Jack Reagan's politics when he married Loyal
Davis's daughter, and he adopted the punitive, right-wing politics of
[his father-in-law]" (33).

If Reagan's mind, politically speaking, appears to have been washed,
one could make the case that Sinatra's, by the 1980s, had been dry-
cleaned (to borrow a line from Yen Lo). Well into the 1960s, the
singer remained an unredeemed New Dealer, espousing liberal sentiments, particularly on matters of race: "Remember that leering, cursing
lynch mob in Little Rock reviling a meek, innocent little 12-year-old
Negro girl as she tried to enroll in public school?" he asked *Playboy*
interviewer Joe Hyams in 1963, setting himself up to make a point not
only about racism but about religious hypocrisy. "Weren't they—or
most of them—devout churchgoers? I detest the two-faced who pre-
tend liberality but are practiced bigots in their own mean little
spheres."[27]

He had, of course, supported Kennedy in 1960 and, as late as 1968,
campaigned for Democratic presidential nominee Hubert Humphrey.
In May 1968, at a fund-raising concert at the Oakland Coliseum,
Sinatra slightly altered the lyrics of the Rodgers and Hart standard
"The Lady Is a Tramp" to express his contempt for the state's Republican governor: "She hates California," Sinatra sang, referring to the
lady of the title. "It's *Reagan* and damp / That's why the lady is a
tramp." (The lyric called for "It's cold and it's damp.") To compound
the insult, Sinatra pronounced Reagan's name "ree-gan," the way the
future president had himself pronounced it when he had been a strug-
gling B movie player.[28]

By 1972, however, Sinatra was solidly in the Republican camp,
campaigning on behalf of incumbent President Richard Nixon and

hanging out with Vice President Spiro Agnew, whom he considered a friend. In many ways, Sinatra had simply followed the same path as many white ethnics, former Democrats now members of Nixon's "Silent Majority," but Michael Nelson offers another possible motivation: "Loyalty was the supreme virtue in Sinatra's code of morality... Republicans, it seemed to Sinatra, understood loyalty in the same way that he did, and the Democrats did not."[29]

President Kennedy had begun, by 1962—the year of *The Manchurian Candidate*'s original release—to distance himself from Sinatra, having been advised by friends, colleagues, and even brother Bobby that the singer's swingin' lifestyle and questionable associations (most obviously, Sam Giancana, the Chicago Mob boss) were not exactly the image he should seek to cultivate. It was in March of that year that the personal relationship between the two men was irrevocably damaged. It had been made public that Kennedy would spend a few days at Sinatra's Palm Springs estate. Just before the scheduled trip, however, the plans were altered—the president would stay at Republican (and onetime Sinatra singing rival) Bing Crosby's home. Sinatra, humiliated, apparently never forgave the Kennedys or Peter Lawford, who, by virtue of his relationship to both men (he was married to one of the president's sisters and had become a member of Sinatra's showbiz Rat Pack), was chosen to deliver the bad news.[30]

Eventually, Sinatra embraced even Reagan, serving as cochair of Democrats for Reagan in 1970 (in support of the California governor's reelection bid), hosting fund-raisers for Reagan's unsuccessful run at the 1976 Republican nomination for president, and campaigning hard for him in 1980, when he secured the nomination and succeeded in becoming president.[31] It was Sinatra who organized Reagan's inaugural gala, just as he had organized John Kennedy's twenty years earlier. In 1985, he was tapped to reprise the role.

By the mid-1980s, Sinatra seemed like an extended member of the First Family, a status he had aspired to, but had never achieved, in the Kennedy White House. "[Sinatra] ardently defended Nancy Reagan against press criticisms of her extravagance in clothes and china," Nelson recounts. "He... arranged [White House] concerts by artists ranging from Zubin Mehta to Mel Tillis. In 1984, Sinatra raised money for the Reagan campaign at a series of cocktail parties and accompanied

President Ronald Reagan awards Frank Sinatra the Medal of Freedom,
1985. (Bettman/Corbis)

the president on a frenzied campaign visit to the festival of St. Ann
in Hoboken [Sinatra's hometown]."[32] The following year, Reagan re-
paid Sinatra's efforts, and cemented their association, by presenting
him with the Presidential Medal of Freedom.

Could anyone have blamed viewers watching *The Manchurian
Candidate*'s rerelease in 1987 (it premiered at the New York Film Festival) if, seeing the current president's most visible Hollywood supporter
starring in a fevered Cold War drama about POWs held by Chinese
and Soviet communists, they experienced not a feeling of déjà vu
(which would have been expected), but the opposite—a feeling that
they were watching something completely new, yet eerily familiar?
Indeed, he consciously may have only been speaking of the film's
visual and narrative qualities, but critic Roger Ebert would appear to
have expressed the collective political unconscious in a review of
the rerelease. "Here is a movie that was made in 1962," Ebert began,
"and it feels as if it were made yesterday."[33]

Postscript

She told me . . . that when she and Johnny got into the White
House, she was going to start and finish a holy war, without ten
minutes' warning, that would wipe them off the face of the earth,
and that then we—I do not mean this country, I mean Mother
and whoever she decides to use—will run this country and we'll
run the whole world.

—*Raymond Shaw to Bennett Marco*
(from Richard Condon's novel, 1959)

In 2004, director Jonathan Demme's remake of *The Manchurian Candi-*
date was released. The film retained the basic contours of the original
story, with some significant changes: Bennett Marco (Denzel Washington), Raymond Shaw (Liev Schreiber), and their platoon are taken
captive, not in Korea, but during Operation Desert Storm in 1991. A
few years later, war hero Shaw is a U.S. congressman. His controlling
mother (as in the original, the term will be exploited to its fullest
potential) is the U.S. senator from New York. Manchuria, in this case,
is not a place, but a multinational corporation specializing in defense
contracts: Manchurian Global. Conspiring with his mother, Manchurian Global abducts Shaw in Kuwait, and subsequently installs

Congressman Raymond Shaw (Liev Schreiber) plays to a national television audience in Jonathan Demme's *The Manchurian Candidate* (2004).

a microchip in his brain. Shaw returns to the United States a war
hero—as in the original, the cover story is that he saved his platoon—and is elected to the House of Representatives. In this version, Eleanor Shaw (Meryl Streep) secures her party's vice presidential nomination not for her husband (she is a widow), but for her son.
Marco, once again an army intelligence officer trying to solve the
riddle of his recurring nightmare, is tapped to do the dirty work (he
too has been programmed) of murdering the presidential nominee so
that Shaw may rise to the top of the ticket.

Although certain elements may seem a necessary "updating" of
the story—recognizing the increased visibility of women in politics
by making Eleanor Shaw herself a senator (and not simply the wife of
one), for example—Demme's film also points, symbolically, to a disquieting shift in the culture since the release of the original. In
Frankenheimer's version, Marco is the consummate organization man,
linked to the army and, by extension, the nation, by common purpose. If he must, at times, skirt the army bureaucracy and assert his
individualism (as when he travels to New York against orders), it is
also true that his service to the army is ultimately rewarded: the army

(along with the CIA and the FBI) helps Marco uncover the truth about Shaw. The army, in Frankenheimer's version, is like the democracy it defends: flawed, but, in the end, responsible. "Ben, the army has got a lot of things wrong with it," his friend, the colonel, tells him, "but it does take care of its own people."

The organization in Demme's version that "takes care of its own" is not the army; in the remake, Marco is largely on his own, and this distinctly post-Vietnam rendition of Al Melvin as the discarded vet vividly recalls H. Bruce Franklin's observation that *maybe* some hippie chick somewhere once spit in the face of a returning soldier, as legend allows, but the Veterans' Administration did for sure.[1] But for Demme, by the new millennium, "the organization" is chiefly the corporation. It is Manchurian Global that rewards its friends with high office and riches in exchange for loyalty and political favor, an arrangement that has little to do with defending the republic. In this respect at least, it would appear that Demme outdid Frankenheimer (and Condon), by pressing Major Marco into a different kind of "service"—that of the conspiracy. Indeed, Demme, unlike Axelrod, Frankenheimer, or even the hypercynical Condon, seems incapable of imagining a world in which anyone is clean. Consider just a few of the plot details: this time around, Rosie (Kimberly Elise), whom Marco (once again) meets on a train to New York, is in reality a federal agent, assigned to keep tabs on the troubled soldier; the rifle that Marco will use to shoot the nominee is placed inside the convention building, not through some elaborate masquerade (as in the original, when Shaw, disguised as a priest, smuggled it in), but by a member of Shaw's Secret Service detail; after Marco, deviating from the script, shoots and kills both Raymond and Eleanor Shaw at the convention, the directors of Manchurian Global are implicated in the conspiracy only after the government "frames" them by altering security-video footage to place one of the company's operatives at the scene. Frankenheimer's "organization man" has been supplanted by Demme's "multinational man." In Demme's film, to paraphrase Walt Kelly, we meet the enemy and they are us.

In many ways, then, this latest version of *The Manchurian Candidate* is not so much a remake as a reimagining, taking in not only its original source material—Condon's novel—and Frankenheimer's adaptation of it, but another of Frankenheimer's films, *Seconds* (1966). Released almost four years after *The Manchurian Candidate*, *Seconds* told the story of Arthur Hamilton (John Randolph), a middle-aged executive who, finding his staid suburban home life empty to the point of asphyxiation, is unexpectedly given the chance to trade it in for something much more to his liking. Contacted one day by a friend he had long thought dead, Hamilton is introduced to a secret corporation that specializes in identity makeovers. The corporation fakes the deaths of its well-heeled clients (by providing suitably mutilated corpses in their place), transforms their appearances through plastic surgery, and then, after ascertaining their secret desires through hypnosis, sets them up in a "new" life. Hamilton emerges from this process as Tony Wilson, a younger, movie-star handsome (literally; he's played by Rock Hudson) painter whose address is a California beach house. At first, Arthur/Tony has trouble adjusting to his new life, but soon meets a woman named Emily—herself a marked "improvement" over Arthur's "widow"—and things seemingly begin to fall into place. To celebrate his rebirth, Tony throws a party with his personal assistant, John, providing the guest list. However, during the course of the evening, as Tony continues to drink, he begins to give himself away, by reverting to his old self. His guests are shocked, with good reason— they work for the organization. When Tony discovers that Emily and John are also "employees," he realizes that his new existence is at least as empty as his former one, if not more so. When he reconciles himself to the fact that he can't go back to being Arthur Hamilton—how would one do that, exactly?—he asks the company for one more chance, a second "operation." They agree, but on the condition that Tony, like his friend before him, send them a new client, more fodder for the corporate machinery. When Tony refuses, his fate is sealed—he will instead serve as the corpse for the next customer. Strapped down to a gurney, his mouth gagged, he is led away.

There is much in *Seconds* that both echoes Frankenheimer's previous film and anticipates Demme's—the casting of Khigh Dheigh as one of the corporation's officers, for example, or the use of a cranial drill by Arthur Hamilton's/Raymond Shaw's respective "programmers"—but it is in its expansion of the "organization" that the film most clearly bridges the gap between the first and second versions of

The Manchurian Candidate. In *Seconds*, as in Demme's film, the corporation is not just a collectivity, it is an all-consuming, totalizing environment, even if Khigh Dheigh's character has sold this corporation's product as the *antidote* to the gray flannel existence of the postwar businessman. After this makeover, he promises Hamilton, "You are alone in the world, absolved of all responsibility except your own interests. *Isn't that marvelous?*" If you are an organization man quietly dying an organization man's death, it is indeed.

Demme's dystopic vision is, perhaps, a predictable shift in an era in which private interests have become synonymous with the national agenda. The idea was new enough in 1960 that President Dwight Eisenhower, in his farewell address, could still warn against the unchecked growth of the "military-industrial complex."[2] By 2004, it was commonplace for congressional and cabinet offices to be connected to corporate boardrooms by a revolving door, Vice President Dick Cheney's relationship to Halliburton, a major energy company and government contractor, being the most obvious example, but certainly not the only one.

If Frankenheimer's film stands as the quintessential imagining of both the Kennedy and Reagan administrations, Demme's remake evokes nothing so much as Dick Cheney's America, or rather, Cheney's corporate-sponsored version of the American Dream. After all, it was Cheney who served as President George H. W. Bush's secretary of defense during the first Gulf war, the conflict that opens Demme's film. After stepping down from his post in 1993, Cheney went to work for Halliburton, becoming the company's CEO in 1995, a position he held until running for vice president on the Republican ticket in 2000. The vice presidential nominee's ties to corporate America were no secret when he ran. A *USA Today* piece, titled "Cheney as VP Faces a Serious Cut in Pay," outlined the candidate's recent earnings from Halliburton: "$26.4 million compensation package [in 1999] . . . [including] $1.3 million in pay, $5.6 million in stock, and stock options valued at up to $18.9 million."[3] The paper needn't have worried about Cheney's impending retirement from the company; he received a $20 million separation package in 2000.[4]

By the time Demme's film was released, Cheney was firmly ensconced as George W. Bush's vice president and Halliburton was enjoying multibillion-dollar government contracts (awarded on a no-bid basis) to rebuild Iraq, a country many believed had been invaded in 2003 not because it was involved in the terrorist attacks of September 11, 2001 (no connection between Iraq and Al Qaeda was ever substantiated), or posed a threat to the United States (as of this writing, "weapons of mass destruction" have yet to materialize), but for the strategic location of U.S. military bases, for its oil reserves, and for the lucrative business opportunities such an invasion would present. (Cheney's long-standing association with Halliburton produced one of the 2004 election season's more memorable episodes. Upset that Senator Patrick Leahy, a Democrat from Vermont, had openly criticized Halliburton's government contracts in Iraq, Cheney confronted the senator during the Senate's class photo, an exchange that ended with Cheney reportedly telling Leahy, "Go fuck yourself.")[5]

Halliburton's seemingly privileged place within the administration was hardly unique. Kenneth Lay, the disgraced former CEO of Enron, a Texas-based energy company that went bankrupt in 2001 after artificially inflating its stock prices and bilking consumers for services (most famously in California), was a longtime friend and supporter of the president. "Kenny Boy," as Bush called him, had been one of the president's biggest contributors and fund-raisers. Once Bush was elected, he sought Lay's expertise in developing a national energy policy, one that had the effect of directly benefiting Enron and other large energy providers.[6] It would be difficult to imagine a presidential administration more completely associated, from its inception, with private interests. "A new power plant every week for 20 years, new nukes, drilling in the Arctic Wildlife Refuge—is this an energy policy, or a payback for President Bush's big campaign contributors?" asked a BBC report only months after Bush and Cheney took office in 2001.[7]

Demme's version took in all of this recent history, and the dominant perceptions that went with it. Audiences must have registered little surprise when they learned that Manchurian Global's scheme to take over the government ran, not through the presidential candidate, but through his running mate (and not because this plot detail was borrowed from the original). George W. Bush, who took office with little experience in government (less than six years as governor

Senator Shaw (Meryl Streep) introduces her son to some of his
corporate backers.

of Texas) and who was never pegged as the best or brightest of the
Bush bunch (the family supposedly had its money on brother Jeb to
become the heir to the father), is believed by many to be little more
than window dressing for the real brains of the outfit. What other
vice president–elect, after all, has ever been asked if he would function
as a "shadow president," as Cheney was by CNN interviewer Larry
King in 2001?[8]

Demme's *Manchurian Candidate*, coproduced by Sinatra's youngest
child, Tina, was released at the height of the 2004 political season,
on July 30, two days after the close of the Democratic convention in
Boston. The timing of its release, and the contemporary nature of its
story line ("The idea that corporations may be subverting the democratic process is plausible in the age of Enron," intoned Ebert, review-
ing the film for the *Chicago Sun-Times*), inspired mostly literal readings.[9] Was Meryl Streep's Eleanor Shaw "channeling Hillary Clinton,"
as *Variety* put it?[10] Or was she, as another reviewer offered (in a characterization that would suggest that the film Demme remade is the
1980s, and not the 1960s, "version" of *The Manchurian Candidate*), "a
cross between Clint Eastwood and Nancy Reagan?"[11]

Demme, dismissing the notion that he had purposely attempted to depict contemporary figures ("We worked very hard to not try to be on the money about individuals that are actually calling the shots today"), nevertheless admitted that his *Manchurian Candidate*—like the original (twice before)—was firmly rooted in the moment. "I was watching [the finished film]," Demme told an interviewer shortly before the release, "and Jon Voight [Senator Jordan] says [to Raymond], 'Yes, and they want you to be the first fully owned and operated vice-president of the United States,' and that reminded me of Dick Cheney. So don't we have that already?"[12]

The obvious move for Demme in the remake would have been to recast the Cold War as the War on Terror, much as Bush and Patriot Act architect John Ashcroft did. Following the crumbling of the Berlin Wall and the collapse of the Soviet Union, what had seemed an iron epoch called the Cold War rolled over astonishingly easily into the so-called War on Terror. The continuities are disturbing, in both policy and cultural terms: not only did the United States retain its seven hundred–plus foreign military bases and its twelve-digit defense budget, though generations had been taught to think of these as unfortunate necessities in the face of the Soviet threat, but in its first two engagements in the new war the nation faced two enemies who were among the "allies" once gathered and built up in fighting the old—Osama bin Laden for his utility in driving the Soviet Union out of Afghanistan, and Saddam Hussein for his effectiveness in opposing the Islamic fundamentalist and anti-American regime in Iran, and thus providing the secular presence required by U.S. interests. On the morning of 9/11, key members of the U.S. government found themselves in underground Washington bunkers that had originally been designed to protect them from incoming Soviet ICBMs; and as of this writing Osama bin Laden may still be hiding in an Afghan cave whose construction was financed as a U.S. foreign-policy asset in the waning years of the Cold War. Indeed, as the *New York Times* reported in 2005, the methods of torture employed at Abu Ghraib and elsewhere were initially developed by the U.S. government as part of a Cold War–era *counter*torture program, "to recreate the brutal conditions American prisoners of war experienced in Korea and Vietnam, where Communist interrogators forced false confessions from some detainees, and broke the spirits of many more, through Pavlovian and other conditioning."[13]

It is altogether fitting, then, that someone should decide to update and remake *The Manchurian Candidate* for this new era. But Demme rather shunted aside the obvious parallels between the Cold War and the War on Terror, focusing instead on the deeper and less obvious question of corporate power in what is beginning to look like a post-national epoch. Since the Reagan era, and certainly since 9/11, the culture has "built" us to see Islamic extremism as the new communism, to be sure. But more important, since the unleashing of private corporate interest during the Reagan years, what the culture has built us to do especially well is to look at the spreading tentacles of Halliburton or McDonald's or Wal-Mart (or Manchurian Global) and to see the genius of "the free market," a vast improvement on *either* communist or Islamist dreams. The cynicism of post-Vietnam, post-Watergate American culture has perhaps outfitted us with a healthy suspicion that "the national interest" is not really "national" at all, but this suspicion itself has been rendered mostly useless. Post–Cold War American culture has evidently built us to peaceably accept a "common good" that is increasingly defined by multinational corporate marauders and their willing servants in government. Once the Berlin Wall came down and the Soviet Union broke apart, all brakes were removed from the operations of "the free market." We reap this whirlwind in the form of the world's many runaway Manchurian Globals.

As such, *The Manchurian Candidate*—not just Demme's version or Frankenheimer's, but the two taken together, in their three incarnations—might very well represent the repressed history of modern America. Prefiguring the assassination of John Kennedy, reemerging as an almost perfect postscript to the Reagan era, and, most recently, serving as a commentary on the reign of Dick Cheney and George W. Bush, *The Manchurian Candidate* feels less like a vision of the Cold War than a waking, recurring dream.

Acknowledgments

This book began as one of those chance conversations around the water cooler, when a few casual comments, gradually layering atop one another, suddenly took on a life of their own and began to seem like something big and full of possibility. We have had one another all along the way, so we cannot make the usual heroic claims about the deadly isolation of the historian's craft. This has been kind of a gas, actually. Nonetheless, it turns out that a coauthor is really no replacement for the kindness of all sorts of other friends and strangers, and we do find ourselves with the normal raft of debts.

The debt we hold in common begins with those who aided in assembling materials: Barbara Hall and Kristine Krueger at the Margaret Herrick Library at the Academy of Motion Picture Arts and Sciences in Los Angeles; Charles Whittaker, in the Interlibrary Loan Office of the Miami–Dade Public Library—Main Branch; and Christina Lane of the Motion Picture Program at the University of Miami, who (bless her) read everything, offered her insights, and helped with the technical work of securing images. Megan Glick was an energetic and dauntless research assistant, carrying out the most obscure assignments with lightning speed and precision. Not least, she resisted to the end what had to have been a powerful impulse to ask, "And why the hell do you need *that* by tomorrow?"

The anonymous readers for the University of Minnesota Press who critiqued our initial research design offered many useful caveats, criticisms, ideas, and pieces of advice. Paul Buhle, who read a completed draft of the manuscript and was kind enough to sign his review, gave the work a pretty tough reading but was also extremely generous with his encouragement and practical advice. This is no doubt a much better book for his intervention. We are deeply indebted to our editor, Richard Morrison, who not only saw this effort through to completion but, from the beginning, had faith in the concept that two writers, working 1,200 miles apart, could produce something of value.

As we have, in fact, inhabited different latitudes, social circles, and institutional niches, we have each incurred our own individual debts as well.

This project began to take shape during my time as a lecturer at Yale University, and I'd like to express my gratitude to the undergraduates in Cold War Film and Culture (spring 2000) whose enthusiasm for the material first suggested to me that a book on *The Manchurian Candidate* and its historical significance would find an eager audience even among readers who had little, if any, personal recollection of the Cold War. Thanks to Michael Denning, Jean-Christophe Agnew, and Charles Musser for guidance and support during my time as a graduate student (and, later, as their faculty colleague) in the American Studies program. Special thanks to my collaborator (and another former colleague at Yale), Matt Jacobson, who uttered the words that eventually set this book in motion: "You know, I'd been thinking the same thing..." Working with him has been immensely rewarding and just plain fun. Let's do it again sometime.

I made many friends in the American Studies program, as well as through my involvement in the Graduate Employees and Students Organization (GESO)—and I am indebted to all of them—but in particular I would like to recognize five people, without whose love, encouragement, and intellectual support very little would have been possible (and here I speak not exclusively of this book): Joseph Entin, Scott Saul, John Utz, Brendan Walsh, and Cynthia Young. I group them only because I could never hope to convey in these few lines the depth of my affection or what, individually, they have meant to me. Their brilliance, integrity, and commitment to social justice are inspiring. I am proud to know them and grateful to have shared so much.

While the impetus for this book may be traced back to my tenure at Yale, my interest in the subject of the Cold War goes back much further, to conversations I remember adults having around the dinner table and at weddings, funerals, and parties in Miami. My parents, Hilda and Gaspar, were Cuban exiles; they were not overtly "political," nor were they trained historians, but they were Cold War experts nevertheless. Indeed, I don't know of two people whose lives were shaped to a greater degree by the absurd and bitter ironies of that era, or who faced their trials with more courage and dignity. They were my first and my finest teachers.

Finally, for their enduring friendship, for coming through for me in the pinch (and life is nothing if not a series of pinches), and for occasionally remembering to ask how that "Manchurian" book was coming along (thereby helping to keep me at the keyboard), let me thank Steve Satterwhite, Jake Bernstein, John Lantigua, Mercedes Flores, Brett O'Bourke, Victor G. Katz, Pablo Quintana, Julie Quintana, Sophie Bell, Rachel Sulkes, Helen Lennon, Lorraine Paterson, Hugo Viera, Molly Monet-Viera, Carlo Rotella, and Patrick Rivers.

—G. G.

We said that this project started as a casual conversation by the water cooler—surely it is significant that the water cooler was located in Vicki Shepard's office in the American Studies program at Yale University. My life at Yale has been invigorated and enriched by my daily conversations with Vicki (who manages unblinking clarity *and* undying humor when it comes to some pretty grim topics, like the Cold War, George W. Bush, or the Boston Red Sox), but after ten years I'm still amazed every single day by the talent and generosity of the people who drift in and out of that office as a matter of course. Thanks to all of my colleagues, especially (in the context of this project) Jean-Christophe Agnew, Alicia Schmidt Camacho, Hazel Carby, Michael Denning, Seth Fein, Glenda Gilmore, Mary Lui, Sanda Lwin, Steve

Pitti, and Laura Wexler. Their influence on me has been immense. My deep thanks, too, to many friends and colleagues outside of Yale, whose intellectual example has been crucial to my understanding of this era: Bob Lee, Elaine May, Melani McAlister, Nikhil Singh, Judy Smith, Penny Von Eschen.

Without my even knowing it at the time, my part in this book originated in a series of graduate seminars at SUNY Stony Brook in 1993 and 1994. My enduring thanks to those spirited groups, especially to Victoria Allison, Amy Bass, Carrie Clarke, Carlo Corea, Seth Forman, Mandy Frisken, Donna Giordano, and Katy Stewart. This started to assume the form of an actual "project" in American Studies 191 at Yale, "The Formation of Modern American Culture"; some vexed lecture for this course was no doubt my reason for talking about *The Manchurian Candidate* at the water cooler that day in the first place. I have been grateful over the years that students have been such willing guinea pigs when it comes to my ideas on a text like this, and they have ponied up quite a bit in their own right, too. Most of all, thanks to the many teaching assistants I have worked with over the years. They have been pushing and prodding and refashioning and refining and sometimes outright rejecting my intellectual trial balloons since 1995, and I have learned more from them than from even my best teachers. I can trace certain ideas in this book to fruitful conversations with Andrea Becksvoort, Elspeth Brown, Jayna Brown, Megan Glick, Jennifer Greeson, Jeff Hardwick, Brian Herrera, Mandi Jackson, Leah Mancina Khaghani, Mark Krasovic, Ben Looker, Lisa McGill, Kathy Newman, Leah Perry, Besenia Rodriguez, and Heather Williams. I dedicate this work to them, and also to the memory of Shafali Lal, one of the very best among them.

Working with Gaspar has been an education and a kick. If I had known that collaboration could be this painless and this fun, there's no question I would have tried it much sooner.

My family, as ever, has been an inspiration on the one hand and an antidote to the writing life on the other. We have "movie night" every Friday at our house, and much of my desire to wade around in American film has to do with my seeing it reflected back as laughter and pleasure in the eyes of our children, Nick and Tess. They watch too few movies quite as good as *The Manchurian Candidate*, if you ask me; but while I was writing this I never strayed too far from the thought that maybe someday they'll like a good Cold War thriller as much as I do, and maybe—who knows—they'll think that my questions are questions worth asking. My wife, Francesca Schwartz, remains my best critic and my very favorite moviegoer. Enjoy the show.

—M. F. J.

Notes

Introduction

1. Stuart Hall, "Subjects in History: Making Diasporic Identities," in Wahneema Lubiano, ed., *The House That Race Built* (New York: Vintage, 1998), 291. The most influential work along these lines includes Antonio Gramsci, *Selections from the Prison Notebooks* (New York: International Publishers, 1971); Stuart Hall et al., *Culture, Media, Language: Working Papers in Cultural Studies* (London: Routledge, 1991); Edward Said, *Culture and Imperialism* (New York: Knopf, 1993); Edward Said, *Covering Islam: How the Media and the Experts Determine How We See the Rest of the World* (New York: Pantheon Books, 1981); Joan Scott, *Gender and the Politics of History* (New York: Columbia University Press, 1999); Judith Butler, *Gender Trouble* [1989] (London: Routledge, Tenth Anniversary Edition, 1999); Louis Althusser, *For Marx* (London: Allen Lane, 1969); Michel Foucault, *The Foucault Reader* (New York: Pantheon Books, 1984).

1. Backstory

1. Greil Marcus, *The Manchurian Candidate* (London: BFI, 2002), 41.
2. Ibid., 35.
3. Ibid., 33.

4. William Bradford Huie, *The Execution of Private Slovik* [1954] (New York: Dell Publishing Company, 1970), 55.

5. Pete Hamill, *Why Sinatra Matters* (Boston: Little, Brown and Company, 1998), 96.

6. Some even found accolades; in 1956, Trumbo, writing under the pseudonym Robert Rich, was awarded the Academy Award for Best Screenplay (for *The Brave One*). It would go unclaimed until 1975.

7. For a detailed discussion of Dolly Sinatra's role in Hudson County politics, see Hamill, *Why Sinatra Matters*, 72–81.

8. J. Randy Taraborrelli, *Sinatra: Behind the Legend* (Secaucus, N.J.: Birch Lane Press, 1997), 224.

9. Arnold Shaw, *Sinatra: Twentieth-Century Romantic* [1968] (New York: Pocket Books, 1969), 77.

10. Ibid.

11. Frank Sinatra, "People Are Human Beings," in Arnold Herrick and Herbert Askwith, eds., *This Way to Unity: For the Promotion of Good Will and Teamwork among Racial, Religious, and National Groups* (New York: Oxford Book Company, 1945), 181.

12. Ronald Brownstein, *The Power and the Glitter: The Hollywood–Washington Connection* (New York: Pantheon Books, 1990), chapter 4.

13. Shaw, *Sinatra*, 114.

14. Ibid., 84.

15. Jon Wiener, *Professors, Politics and Pop* (New York: Verso, 1991), 263.

16. Michael Nelson, "Ol' Red, White, and Blue Eyes: Frank Sinatra and the American Presidency," *Popular Music and Society* (winter 2000): 84.

17. Lee Mortimer, "Frank Sinatra Confidential: Gangsters in the Night Clubs," *New American Mercury*, August 1951; available at http://www.sinatraarchive.com/tis/gangsters.html.

18. From the album *No One Cares* (Capitol Records, 1959).

19. "Senator Calls It Shocking," *Los Angeles Examiner*, March 22, 1960.

20. "Maltz Toed Red Line on Art," *Los Angeles Examiner*, March 24, 1960.

21. "Sinatra Explains Hiring of Maltz," *Los Angeles Examiner*, March 26, 1960.

22. Ibid.

23. Shawn Levy, *Rat Pack Confidential: Frank, Dean, Sammy, Peter, Joey and the Last Great Showbiz Party* (New York: Doubleday, 1998), 158.

24. Shaw, *Sinatra*, 261.

25. "Note to Sinatra," *Los Angeles Examiner*, March 28, 1960.

26. "Frankly Speaking to Frank," *Los Angeles Times*, April 8, 1960.

27. "Sinatra Accepts Public Protest, Dumps Maltz," *Los Angeles Times*, April 9, 1960.

28. Shaw, *Sinatra*, 263.

29. Ibid., 354.

30. *The Execution of Private Slovik* would not be adapted for the screen until 1974, when it was produced as a made-for-television movie. Directed by Lamont Johnson, it starred Martin Sheen in the title role.

31. Louis Menand, "Brainwashed," *New Yorker*, September 15, 2003, 90.

32. Condon would go on to enjoy a long career as a novelist. After *The Manchurian Candidate*—his second novel—he is, perhaps, best known for his *Prizzi* series: *Prizzi's Honor* (1982), *Prizzi's Family* (1986), *Prizzi's Glory* (1988), and *Prizzi's Money* (1994). Condon died in 1996.

33. Menand, "Brainwashed," 88.

34. Richard Condon, *The Manchurian Candidate* (New York: McGraw-Hill, 1959), 290. Subsequent references are given in the text.

35. John Frankenheimer, voice-over commentary, *The Manchurian Candidate* [DVD], MGM Home Entertainment, 1998.

36. Tise Vahimagi, "Frankenheimer Live," *Film Comment* (November/December 2002): 48.

37. Frankenheimer, voice-over commentary, *The Manchurian Candidate*, 1998.

38. Gerald Pratley, *The Cinema of John Frankenheimer* (London: A. Zwemmer Limited, 1969), 100.

39. Frankenheimer, voice-over commentary, *The Manchurian Candidate*, 1998.

40. "Sinatra to Film 'Manchurian' and 'The New Yorkers,'" *Variety*, March 29, 1961.

41. "Sinatra Not 'Candidate' Now; New Deal," *Variety*, April 10, 1961.

42. "Harvey and Sinatra to Do 'Manchurian' for UA Release," *Variety*, September 7, 1961.

43. "Exclusive Interview with Frank Sinatra, John Frankenheimer, and George Axelrod," *The Manchurian Candidate* [VHS], MGM/UA Home Video, 1988.

44. Levy, *Rat Pack Confidential*, 213.

45. Letter from Geoffrey M. Shurlock to Howard Koch, September 19, 1961. Courtesy of The Margaret Herrick Library, Academy of Motion Picture Arts and Sciences, Beverly Hills, California.

46. Ibid.

47. The cues are not subtle: Upon entering Miss Gertrude's, Shaw encounters one of his men stumbling out from behind the curtain door of a side room with a young Asian woman in tow. When he arrives in the establishment's main room, Shaw himself is set upon by another eager young woman, who slides her arm under his. When Shaw resists her advances and orders his men out, the soldier he had previously encountered in the hallway

offers that "I'm afraid our Saint Raymond, he don't approve." As if to settle all doubt regarding the subject in question, Bobby Lembeck counters, "Well, maybe [Shaw's] got a girl back home, or something."

48. The line made it into the film; it's what Mrs. Iselin whispers to Johnny just before the presidential nominee begins his address at the convention.

49. The finished film—despite the inclusion of a number of plot elements labeled objectionable by the board—gained PCA approval on April 20, 1962, according to the "Analysis of Film Content" form for the film in PCA files. Courtesy of The Margaret Herrick Library, Academy of Motion Picture Arts and Sciences, Beverly Hills, California.

50. "Harvey and Sinatra to Do 'Manchurian' for UA Release," *Variety*, September 7, 1961.

51. "Janet Leigh Joins UA's 'Candidate' Cast," *Variety*, November 29, 1961.

52. Frankenheimer, voice-over commentary, *The Manchurian Candidate*, 1998.

53. Ibid.

54. Ibid.

55. "'Manchurian Candidate' Location Troupe to NY," *Variety*, February 5, 1962.

56. "Spotlight on Garden Main Event," *New York Times*, February 17, 1962.

57. Philip K. Scheuer, "Director Shakes Off Influence of Stars; Frankenheimer Also Critical of Supervision by Studios," *Los Angeles Times*, June 22, 1962.

58. "Exclusive Interview with Frank Sinatra, John Frankenheimer, and George Axelrod, *The Manchurian Candidate* [VHS], MGM/UA Home Video, 1988.

2. A Culture of Contradiction

1. Walter LaFeber, *America, Russia, and the Cold War, 1945–2002*, 9th ed. (New York: McGraw-Hill, 2002); Thomas Patterson, *On Every Front: The Making and Unmaking of the Cold War* (New York: W. W. Norton, 1992); Melvin Leffler, *The Specter of Communism: The United States and the Origins of the Cold War, 1917–1953* (New York: Hill and Wang, 1994); Michael Sherry, *In the Shadow of War: The United States since the 1930s* (New Haven: Yale University Press, 1995).

2. John Lewis Gaddis, *Strategies of Containment: A Critical Appraisal of Postwar American National Security Policy* (New York: Oxford University Press, 1982), 91.

3. Ibid., 92.

4. Ibid., 110. See Micheal Hogan, *A Cross of Iron: Harry S. Truman and the Origins of the National Security State, 1945–1954* (Cambridge: Cambridge University Press, 1998), esp. chapters 7 and 8.

5. Ron Robin, *The Making of the Cold War Enemy: Culture and Politics in the Military-Intellectual Complex* (Princeton, N.J.: Princeton University Press, 2001), 41, 105.

6. Defense budget cited in Gaddis, *Strategies of Containment*, 113. On the United States' very early (pre-Korean) involvement in Vietnam, see Marilyn Young, *Vietnam Wars, 1945–1990* (New York: Perennial, 1991).

7. Serge Guilbaut, *How New York Stole the Idea of Modern Art: Abstract Expressionism, Freedom, and the Cold War* (Chicago: University of Chicago Press, 1983), 168.

8. Richard Freeland, *The Truman Doctrine and the Origins of McCarthyism: Foreign Policy, Domestic Politics, and Internal Security, 1946–1948* (New York: New York University Press, 1985), 85–86.

9. Ibid., 123, 209; Tom Engelhardt, *The End of Victory Culture: Cold War America and the Disillusioning of a Generation* (Amherst: University of Massachusetts Press, 1995), 119. See also Richard Fried, *Nightmare in Red: The McCarthy Era in Perspective* (New York: Oxford University Press, 1990), 59–86.

10. Vance Packard, *The Status Seekers* [1959] (New York: Pocket Books, 1961), 316.

11. Sloan Wilson, *The Man in the Gray Flannel Suit* (New York: Simon and Schuster, 1955), 185, 186.

12. William H. Whyte Jr., *The Organization Man* [1956] (Philadelphia: University of Pennsylvania Press, 2002), 3–4.

13. Ibid., 201.

14. Arthur Schlesinger Jr., *The Vital Center: The Politics of Freedom* [1949] (New Brunswick, N.J.: Transaction, 1998), 26, 9; Mills in Lee Bernstein, "Unlucky Luciano: Fear of Crime during the Cold War," in Nancy Lusignon Schultz, ed., *Fear Itself: Enemies Real and Imagined in American Culture* (West Lafayette, Ind.: Purdue University Press, 1999), 260–61.

15. David Riesman, Nathan Glazer, and Revel Denney, *The Lonely Crowd* [1961] (New Haven: Yale University Press, 1989); Herbert Marcuse, *One-Dimensional Man* [1964] (Boston: Beacon, 1991), 1.

16. Quoted in Michael Smith, "Selling the Moon: The U.S. Manned Space Program and the Triumph of Commodity Scientism," in Richard Wightman Fox and T. J. Jackson Lears, eds., *The Culture of Consumption: Critical Essays in American History, 1880–1980* (New York: Pantheon Books, 1983), 188.

17. Vance Packard, *The Hidden Persuaders* [1957] (New York: Pocket Books, 1975), 200; Schlesinger, *The Vital Center*, 243, 248, 252; Daniel Horowitz, *The Anxieties of Affluence: Critiques of American Consumer Culture, 1939–1979* (Boston: University of Massachusetts Press, 2004).

18. Alan Brinkley, "The Illusion of Unity in Cold War Culture," in Peter Kutznick and James Gilbert, eds., *Rethinking Cold War Culture* (Washington, D.C.: Smithsonian, 2001), 71.

19. John Kenneth Galbraith, *The Affluent Society* [1958] (Boston: Houghton Mifflin, 1998), 187–88.

20. James Morone, *Hellfire Nation: The Politics of Sin in American History* (New Haven: Yale University Press, 2003), 379, 387.

21. Elaine Tyler May, *Homeward Bound: American Families in the Cold War Era* (New York: Basic Books, 1988), 160.

22. Philip Wylie, *Generation of Vipers* [1942] (Normal, Ill.: Dalkey Archive, 1996).

23. Lizabeth Cohen, *A Consumers' Republic: The Politics of Mass Consumption in Postwar America* (New York: Knopf, 2003), 125; Murrow quoted in Peter Kutznick and James Gilbert, "U.S. Culture and the Cold War," in Kutznick and Gilbert, *Rethinking Cold War Culture*, 2.

24. Galbraith, *The Affluent Society*, 4, 257.

25. Quoted in Guilbaut, *How New York Stole the Idea of Modern Art*, 108.

26. On the so-called kitchen debate, see Karal Ann Marling, "Nixon in Moscow," in *As Seen on TV: The Visual Culture of Everyday Life in the 1950s* (Cambridge: Harvard University Press, 1994), 243–83; Cohen, *A Consumers' Republic*, 126; May, *Homeward Bound*, 16–18.

27. Schlesinger, *The Vital Center*, 52.

28. Ibid., 204.

29. Lisle Rose, *After Yalta: America and the Origins of the Cold War* (New York: Scribner's, 1973), 181–82.

30. On the antistatism that characterizes U.S. political culture and that perhaps tempered the Cold War era's mania for security, see Aaron Friedberg, *In the Shadow of the Garrison State: America's Anti-Statism and Its Cold War Grand Strategy* (Princeton, N.J.: Princeton University Press, 2000).

31. Guilbaut, *How New York Stole the Idea of Modern Art*, 88.

32. Ibid., 108, 156.

33. Erika Doss, "The Art of Cultural Politics: From Regionalism to Abstract Expressionism," in Lary May, ed., *Recasting America: Culture and Politics in the Age of Cold War* (Chicago: University of Chicago Press, 1989), 214–16.

34. Schlesinger, *The Vital Center*, 57.

35. Douglas Dreishpoon, *Between Transcendence and Brutality: American Sculptural Drawings from the 1940s and 1950s: Louise Bourgeois, Dorothy Dehner, Herbert Ferber, Seymour Lipton, Isamu Noguchi, Theodore Roszak, David Smith* (Tampa: Tampa Museum of Art, 1994); Marling, *As Seen on TV*, 252.

36. Engelhardt, *The End of Victory Culture*, 59; Bruce Cummings, *Korea's Place in the Sun: A Modern History* (New York: W. W. Norton, 1997), 272.

37. Richard Condon, *The Manchurian Candidate* [1959] (Halpenden, U.K.: No Exit, 2003), 45, 74.

38. Louis Menand, "Introduction," in Condon, *The Manchurian Candidate*, xi–xii; Robin, *The Making of the Cold War Enemy*, 167–70.

39. Packard, *The Hidden Persuaders*, 2, 31, 155.

40. Engelhardt, *The End of Victory Culture*, 184.

41. "Exclusive Interview with Frank Sinatra, John Frankenheimer, and George Axelrod," *The Manchurian Candidate* [VHS], MGM/UA Home Video, 1988.

42. Schlesinger, *The Vital Center*, 10.

43. Ibid., 243.

3. Five from the Fifties

1. Greil Marcus, *The Manchurian Candidate* (London: BFI, 2002), 48.

2. Frankenheimer confesses to having relied on Hitchcock for at least one narrative trick. At the end, when Marco has to figure out where Shaw might be hiding, Frankenheimer and Axelrod came up with the idea of leaving the light on in the booth when the rest of Madison Square Garden goes dark for the national anthem. In a crucial scene in Hitchcock's *Foreign Correspondent* (1940), a windmill rotating in the opposite direction from the others around it gives away the hiding place. See John Frankenheimer, voice-over commentary, *The Manchurian Candidate* [DVD], MGM Home Entertainment, 1998.

3. Kirsten Ostherr, "Contagion and the Boundaries of the Visible: The Cinema of World Health," *Camera Obscura* 17:2 (2002): 2.

4. As quoted in Thomas Engelhardt, *The End of Victory Culture: Cold War America and the Disillusionment of a Generation* (Amherst: University of Massachusetts Press, 1995), 93; emphasis added.

5. Only a few years later, in 1952, Democratic presidential candidate Adlai Stevenson would avail himself of a similar rhetoric to describe the dangers of communism. The ideology, according to Stevenson, was "a disease which may have killed more people in this world than cancer, tuberculosis, and heart disease combined." See Nora Sayre, *Running Time: Films of the Cold War* (New York: Dial Press, 1982), 201.

6. Presidential news conference, April 7, 1954; as quoted in Robert J. McMahon, ed., *Major Problems in the History of the Vietnam War* (Lexington, Mass.: D. C. Heath and Company, 1990), 121.

7. Engelhardt, *The End of Victory Culture*, 93–94.

8. Sayre, *Running Time*, 94.

9. The comparison to Walker's character in *Strangers on a Train* is especially relevant. Walker died before *My Son John* could be completed; footage from the Hitchcock film was used to supplement *My Son John*.

10. Sayre, *Running Time*, 98.

11. Although, admittedly, political opponents would never accuse McCarey of not knowing how to sing: In 1947, he cooperated with HUAC. Three years later, along with Cecil B. DeMille, he urged the members of the Screen Directors Guild to take a loyalty oath. See ibid., 94. Informing had its

professional rewards: incredibly, McCarey's story for *My Son John* was nominated for an Academy Award.

12. Michael Rogin, *Ronald Reagan, The Movie: And Other Episodes in Political Demonology* (Berkeley: University of California Press, 1987), 238.

13. Ibid., 237.

14. John Frankenheimer, voice-over commentary, *The Manchurian Candidate*, 1998.

15. Richard Condon, *The Manchurian Candidate* (New York: McGraw-Hill, 1959), 258.

16. Rogin, *Ronald Reagan, The Movie*, 247.

17. Marcus, *The Manchurian Candidate*, 198.

18. S. T. Joshi, *The Weird Tale* (Austin: University of Texas Press, 1990), 6.

19. J. P. Telotte, "The Fantastic Realism of Film Noir: *Kiss Me Deadly*," in *Wide Angle* 14:1 (1992): 6.

20. Ibid., 8.

21. Ibid., 11.

22. In the original U.S. release, Hammer and Velda are never shown emerging from the beach house, leading the viewer to reasonably assume that they perished there. The restored version has Hammer and Velda stumbling through the surf. Noted film noir scholar Alan Silver offered the following explanation for the discrepancy: "In discussing it with those persons at MGM/UA who finally restored it, the best that anyone could determine was that the U.S. negative was accidentally damaged sometime after the original release. The 'overseas' negative which was stored in London was the one used for the restored version." From http://www.noirfilm.com/BC_Alain_Silver.htm.

23. Telotte, "The Fantastic Realism of Film Noir," 13.

24. Greil Marcus, "A Dream of the Cold War: On *The Manchurian Candidate*," in *The Dustbin of History* (Cambridge: Harvard University Press, 1997), 203.

25. Axelrod's arithmetic is slightly off—Harvey was actually three years younger than Lansbury—but the point remains the same. "Exclusive Interview with Frank Sinatra, John Frankenheimer, and George Axelrod," *The Manchurian Candidate* [VHS], MGM/UA Home Video, 1988.

26. Frankenheimer, voice-over commentary, *The Manchurian Candidate*, 1998.

27. Peter Biskind, *Seeing Is Believing: How Hollywood Taught Us to Stop Worrying and Love the Fifties* (1983; New York: Henry Holt and Company, 2000), 141. Katrina Mann also sees the film as functioning to reinforce dominant postwar social and economic relations, albeit much more broadly than Biskind: "The threats to Santa Mira's traditional hegemony in *Invasion of the Body Snatchers* can be tied to distinct postwar concerns about the elevated empowerment of women, minorities, and sexual deviants... Yet it is pre-

cisely through the [collective] presentation of this . . . assault that the film's hegemonic message was bolstered. By soliciting partial identification with [Bennell] in any one of his three empowered domains—white, male, or heterosexual privileged—the film encouraged diverse cultural participation in xenophobic tropes that serviced postwar America's current hegemonic constructs" ("'You're Next!': Postwar Hegemony Besieged in *Invasion of the Body Snatchers*," *Cinema Journal* 44:1 (fall 2004): 64–65.

28. Biskind, *Seeing Is Believing*, 140.

4. Bullwhip and Smear

1. Richard Rovere, *Senator Joe McCarthy* (New York: Meridian, 1960), 5–6.

2. Michael Paul Rogin, *The Intellectuals and McCarthy: The Radical Specter* (Cambridge: MIT Press, 1967), 224.

3. Ellen Schrecker, *Many Are the Crimes: McCarthyism in America* (Princeton, N.J.: Princeton University Press, 1998), xii–xiii, 243, 203.

4. Ted Morgan, *Reds: McCarthy in Twentieth-Century America* (New York: Random House, 2003), 374.

5. Walter Bernstein, *Inside Out: A Memoir of the Blacklist* [1996] (New York: Da Capo, 2000), 201.

6. Richard Fried, *Nightmare in Red: The McCarthy Era in Perspective* (New York: Oxford University Press, 1990), 132.

7. Arthur Miller, *The Crucible* (New York: Viking, 1953); Arthur Miller, *A View from the Bridge: Two One-Act Plays* (New York: Viking, 1955). Bentley quoted in Brenda Murphy, *Congressional Theatre: Dramatizing McCarthyism on Stage, Screen, and Television* (Cambridge: Cambridge University Press, 1999), 154. On Miller, see 133–61.

8. Murphy, *Congressional Theatre*, 158–59.

9. Edwin Bayley, *Joe McCarthy and the Press* (New York: Pantheon Books, 1981), 176.

10. Ibid., 200–201.

11. Fried, *Nightmare in Red*, 138.

12. On the *See It Now* cycle, see esp. Thomas Rosteck, *See It Now Confronts McCarthyism: Television Documentary and the Politics of Representation* (Tuscaloosa: University of Alabama Press, 1994), 125.

13. Bayley, *Joe McCarthy and the Press*, 193; Rosteck, *See It Now Confronts McCarthyism*, 132–33.

14. Bayley, *Joe McCarthy and the Press*, 200–201.

15. Rosteck, *See It Now Confronts McCarthyism*, 123.

16. Murphy, *Congressional Theatre*, 71.

17. John Adams, *Without Precedent: The Story of the Death of McCarthyism* (New York: W. W. Norton, 1983), 227–29.

18. Bayley, *Joe McCarthy and the Press*, 208.

19. Ibid., 209.

20. *Major Speeches and Debates of Senator Joe McCarthy Delivered in the United States Senate, 1950–1951: Reprinted from the Congressional Record* (New York: Gordon, 1975), 7, 12, 42, 63.

21. Deborah Nelson, *Pursuing Privacy in Cold War America* (New York: Columbia University Press, 2002), 9.

22. Ibid., 11.

23. Ibid., 9.

24. Morris Ernst and Alan Schwartz, *Privacy: The Right to Be Let Alone* (New York: Macmillan, 1962); Myron Brenton, *The Privacy Invaders* (New York: Coward-McGann, 1964); Vance Packard, *The Naked Society* (New York: David McKay, 1964); Allen Westin, *Privacy and Freedom* (New York: Atheneum, 1967).

25. Nelson, *Pursuing Privacy in Cold War America*, 9.

26. Rogin quoted in ibid., 14.

27. Ibid.

28. Ring Lardner Jr., *I'd Hate Myself in the Morning* (New York: Thunder's Mouth Press, 2000), 196.

29. Morgan, *Reds*, 402.

30. "Legion Flays Film, Urges Solons' Probe," *Los Angeles Herald-Examiner*, November 23, 1962; "Axelrod Finds A. Legion Post's 'Candidate' Blast 'Hilarious,'" *Variety*, November 27, 1962; "Commie Sheet Joins Am. Legion Attack on Sinatra Film," *Variety*, December 18, 1962.

5. Like Fu Manchu

1. John Kuo Wei Tchen, *New York before Chinatown: Orientalism and the Shaping of American Culture, 1776–1882* (Baltimore: Johns Hopkins University Press, 1999), 106–23; Robert Lee, *Orientals: Asian Americans in Popular Culture* (Philadelphia: Temple University Press, 1999), 106–44; Bruce Cumings, *Parallax Visions: Making Sense of American–East Asian Relations* (Durham, N.C.: Duke University Press, 2002); Bruce Cumings, *Korea's Place in the Sun: A Modern History* (New York: W. W. Norton, 1997), 272; Douglas Little, *American Orientalism: The United States and the Middle East since 1945* [2002] (Chapel Hill: University of North Carolina Press, 2004), 307–28; Robert Fisk, "Victims of Our Own High-Flown Morality: The 'Good Guys' Who Can Do No Wrong," www.counterpunch.com, weekend edition, May 1–3, 2004.

2. Rudyard Kipling, "The Ballad of East and West," in *Rudyard Kipling: Complete Verse* (New York: Anchor, 1988), 233.

3. John Dower, *War without Mercy: Race and Power in the Pacific War* (New York: Pantheon Books, 1986), 77–93, 182–89; Michi Weglyn, *Years of*

Infamy: The Untold Story of America's Concentration Camps (New York: Morrow Quill, 1976), 38.

4. Edward Said, *Orientalism* (New York: Vintage, 1978), 3.

5. Ibid., 39.

6. Cromer, *Modern Egypt*, quoted in ibid., 38.

7. Said, *Orientalism*, 289.

8. Ibid., 222.

9. Ibid., 284–328; Edward Said, *Covering Islam* (New York: Pantheon Books, 1981); Melani McAlister, *Epic Encounters: Culture, Media, and U.S. Interests in the Middle East, 1945–2000* (Berkeley: University of California Press, 2001); Little, *American Orientalism*.

10. Harold Isaacs, *Scratches on Our Minds: American Views of China and India* [1958] (Armonk, N.Y: M. E. Sharpe, 1980), 45.

11. Said, *Orientalism*, 102.

12. Robert Lee, *Orientals: Asian Americans in Popular Culture* (Philadelphia: Temple University Press, 1999); Tchen, *New York before Chinatown*; Mari Yoshihara, *Embracing the East: White Women and American Orientalism* (Ithaca, N.Y.: Cornell University Press, 2003); Erika Lee, *At America's Gates: Chinese Immigration during the Exclusion Era, 1882–1943* (Chapel Hill: University of North Carolina Press, 2003); Darrell Hamamoto, *Monitored Peril: Asian Americans and the Politics of TV Representation* (Minneapolis: University of Minnesota Press, 1994); Jun Xing, *Asian America through the Lens: History, Representations, and Identity* (Walnut Creek, Calif.: Alta Mira, 1998).

13. Tchen, *New York before Chinatown*, xv, 3–4, 22, 40.

14. On "positive" Orientalism, see esp. Yoshihara, *Embracing the East*.

15. Tchen, *New York before Chinatown*, 97–163. On missionaries, merchants, and diplomats, see Stuart Creighton Miller, *The Unwelcome Immigrant: The American Image of the Chinese, 1785–1882* (Berkeley: University of California Press, 1969).

16. Matthew Frye Jacobson, *Whiteness of a Different Color: European Immigrants and the Alchemy of Race* (Cambridge: Harvard University Press, 1998), 159.

17. Helen Zia, *Asian American Dreams: The Emergence of an American People* (New York: Farrar, Straus and Giroux, 2000), 58–81; Robert Chang, *Disoriented: Asian Americans, Law, and the Nation-State* (New York: New York University Press, 1999), 21–26; Yen Le Espiritu, *Asian American Panethnicity: Bridging Institutions and Identities* (Philadelphia: Temple University Press, 1992), 141–60; Sheng-Mae Ma, *The Deathly Embrace: Orientalism and Asian American Identity* (Minneapolis: University of Minnesota Press, 2001), 76–92; Amitava Kumar, *Passport Photos* (Berkeley: University of California Press, 2000), 18–19; Lee, *Orientals*, 217.

18. Isaacs, *Scratches on Our Minds*, 116.

19. Ibid., 116.

20. Quoted in Lee, *Orientals*, 113–14.

21. Isaacs, *Scratches on Our Minds*, 55.

22. Ibid., 105.

23. Matthew Frye Jacobson, *Barbarian Virtues: The United States Encounters Foreign Peoples at Home and Abroad, 1876–1917* (New York: Hill and Wang, 2000), 243, 244, 242–47; Stuart Creighton Miller, *Benevolent Assimilation: The American Conquest of the Philippines, 1899–1903* (New Haven: Yale University Press, 1982), 220, 230.

24. Dower, *War without Mercy*, 40–41.

25. Cumings, *Korea's Place in the Sun*, 289–90; Cumings, *Parallax Visions*, 64.

26. Marilyn Young, *The Vietnam Wars, 1945–1990* (New York: Harper, 1991), 301–2; Gabriel Kolko, *Anatomy of War: Vietnam, the United States, and the Modern Historical Experience* (New York: Pantheon Books, 1985), 200.

27. Cumings, *Korea's Place in the Sun*, 271.

28. Ibid., 298.

29. Dower, *War without Mercy*, 53–54, 78, 80, 83, 161, 182, 185.

30. Cumings, *Korea's Place in the Sun*, 271, 287, 198, 215.

31. Martin Luther King Jr., "Time to Break the Silence" [1967], in James Melvin, ed., *Testament of Hope: The Essential Writings of Martin Luther King, Jr.* (New York: Harper and Row, 1986).

32. Chomsky, "On War Crimes" [1970], quoted in Donald Pease, "Hiroshima, the Vietnam Veterans War Memorial, and the Gulf War," in Amy Kaplan and Donald Pease, eds., *Cultures of United States Imperialism* (Durham, N.C.: Duke University Press, 1993), 571.

33. Katherine H. S. Moon, *Sex among Allies: Military Prostitution in U.S.–Korea Relations* (New York: Columbia University Press, 1997), 28, 30; Ji-Yeon Yuh, *Beyond the Shadow of Camptown: Korean Military Brides in America* (New York: New York University Press, 2002), 19–41.

34. Quoted in Matthew Bernstein, "Introduction," in Matthew Bernstein and Gaylyn Studlar, eds., *Visions of the East: Orientalism in Film* (New Brunswick, N.J.: Rutgers University Press, 1997), 3.

35. Moon, *Sex among Allies*, 33.

36. Lee, *Orientals*, 89, 104–5; Dower, *War without Mercy*, 187, 189.

37. Cumings, *Korea's Place in the Sun*, 262–64.

38. Isaacs, *Scratches on Our Minds*, 218.

39. Christina Klein, *Cold War Orientalism: Asia in the Middlebrow Imagination, 1945–1961* (Berkeley: University of California Press, 2003), 41.

40. Ibid., 34; Thomas Borstelmann, *The Cold War and the Color Line: American Race Relations in the Global Arena* (Cambridge: Harvard University Press, 2001), 50, 51.

41. Klein, *Cold War Orientalism*, 41.

42. Lee, *Orientals*, 145.

43. Biographical information and filmographies for Khigh Dhiegh, Henry Silva, and Pat Morita are from the Internet Movie Database (imdb.com). Scattered information on Khigh Dhiegh's off-camera career can be found by googling "Khigh Dhiegh Taoism."

44. Bill Koenig, "Blood Feud: McGarrett vs. Wo Fat," hmss.com/otherspies/mcgarrett.

45. "Earth Threatened, Wen Ho Lee Released: What Is Really behind the Sudden Release of the Diabolical Dr. Lee?" unquietmind.com/wenholee .html. For a sense of Wo Fat's enduring fan base, try googling "Wo Fat Hawaii Five-O."

46. On mid- and late-twentieth-century American antimodernism, see Matthew Frye Jacobson, *Roots Too: White Ethnic Revival in Post-Civil Rights America* (Cambridge: Harvard University Press, 2005), esp. chapter 1.

47. Jack Shaheen, *Reel Bad Arabs: How Hollywood Vilifies a People* (New York: Olive Branch, 2001); Melani McCalister, *Epic Encounters: Culture, Media, and U.S. Interests in the Middle East, 1945–2000* (Berkeley: University of California Press, 2001); Richard Slotkin, *Gun Fighter Nation: The Myth of the Frontier in Twentieth-Century America* (New York: Atheneum, 1992); Clara Rodriguez, ed., *Latin Looks: Images of Latinas and Latinos in U.S. Media* (Boulder, Colo: Westview Press, 1997).

6. The Red Queen

1. Michael Rogin quoted in Deborah Nelson, *Pursuing Privacy in Cold War America* (New York: Columbia University Press, 2002), 14.

2. Elaine Tyler May, *Homeward Bound: American Families in the Cold War Era* (New York: Basic Books, 1988), 160.

3. Philip Wylie, *Generation of Vipers* [1942] (Normal, Ill.: Dalkey Archive, 1996), 197. Subsequent references are given in the text.

4. Quoted in Peter Biskind, *Seeing Is Believing: How Hollywood Taught Us to Stop Worrying and Love the Fifties* [1983] (New York: Henry Holt, 2000), 274.

5. J. Edgar Hoover, *Masters of Deceit: The Story of Communism in America and How to Fight It* (New York: Pocket Books, 1958), 269. On Hoover's own sexuality, see Anthony Summers, *Official and Confidential: The Secret Life of J. Edgar Hoover* (New York: G. P. Putnam's Sons, 1993), and David Johnson, *The Lavender Scare: The Cold War Persecution of Gays and Lesbians in the Federal Government* (Chicago: University of Chicago Press, 2004), 11–13.

6. Margaret Randolph Higgonet, Jean Jensen, Sonya Michel, and Margaret Collins Weitz, eds., *Behind the Lines: Gender and the Two World Wars*

(New Haven: Yale University Press, 1987), 4; George Mosse, *Nationalism and Sexuality: Respectability and Abnormal Sexuality in Modern Europe* (New York: Howard Fertig, 1985), 114.

7. Jean Bethke Elshtain, *Women and War* (New York: Basic Books, 1987); Cynthia Enloe, *Does Khaki Become You? The Militarization of Women's Lives* (London: Pandora, 1983), xxxiii, 6–17; Peter Gabriel Filene, *Him/Her/Self: Sex Roles in Modern America* (New York: New American Library, 1974), 94–115; Susan Gubar, "'This Is My Rifle, This Is My Gun': World War II and the Blitz on Women," in Higgonet et al., *Behind the Lines*, 227–59; Mosse, *Nationalism and Sexuality*, 23–47, 90–114; Catherine Lutz, *Homefront: A Military City and the American Twentieth Century* (Boston: Beacon, 2001), 59–64.

8. Filene, *Him/Her/Self*, 96.

9. Enloe, *Does Khaki Become You?*, 7; Lutz, *Homefront*, 219–20, 228–30.

10. Robert Westbrook, "'I Want a Girl Just like the Girl That Married Harry James': American Women and the Problem of Political Obligation in World War II," *American Quarterly* 42:4 (December 1990): 607, 611.

11. Ibid., 588.

12. Robert Westbrook, *Why We Fought: Forging American Obligations in World War II* (Washington, D.C.: Smithsonian, 2004), 44.

13. Ibid., 40, 46, 49, 52, 53.

14. Stephanie Coontz, *The Way We Never Were: American Families and the Nostalgia Trap* [1992] (New York: Basic Books, 2000), 33.

15. Ellen Schrecker, *Many Are the Crimes: McCarthyism in America* (Princeton, N.J.: Princeton University Press, 1998), 146, 147, 148; May, *Homeward Bound*, 137.

16. Thomas Doherty, *Cold War, Cool Medium: Television, McCarthyism, and American Culture* (New York: Columbia University Press, 2003), 222, 223.

17. Schrecker, *Many Are the Crimes*, 148; Doherty, *Cold War, Cool Medium*, 223; Peter Filene, "'Cold War Culture' Doesn't Say It All," in Peter Kuznick and James Gilbert, eds., *Rethinking Cold War Culture* (Washington, D.C.: Smithsonian, 2001), 161; May, *Homeward Bound*, 95. Johnson, *The Lavender Scare*, develops this theme most fully.

18. Robert Corber, *Homosexuality in Cold War America: Resistance and the Crisis of Masculinity* (Durham, N.C.: Duke University Press, 1997), 3; Doherty, *Cold War, Cool Medium*, 222; Robert Corber, *In the Name of National Security: Hitchcock, Homophobia, and the Political Construction of Gender in Postwar America* (Durham, N.C.: Duke University Press, 1993), 64.

19. Nelson, *Pursuing Privacy in Cold War America*, 13.

20. See esp. Janet Halley, *Don't: A Reader's Guide to the Military's Anti-Gay Policy* (Durham, N.C.: Duke University Press, 1999), 27–33.

21. Hoover, *Masters of Deceit*, 269, 149, 150, 78.

22. Ibid., 159, 171, 79.

23. Ibid., 107–8.

24. Coontz, *The Way We Never Were*, 25, 32.

25. May, *Homeward Bound*, 96.

26. Cynthia Enloe, *The Morning After: Sexual Politics and the End of the Cold War* (Berkeley: University of California Press, 1993), 206–7.

27. Richard Condon, *The Manchurian Candidate* [1959] (London: No Exit, 2003), 111, 104. Subsequent references are given in the text.

28. Thomas Engelhardt, *The End of Victory Culture: Cold War America and the Disillusioning of a Generation* (Amherst: University of Massachusetts Press, 1995), 184.

29. Jude Wanniski, "Memo to website browsers, fans and clients—*The Manchurian Candidate* (1962)," http://reviews.imdb.com/Reviews/128/12856.

7. Strangers on a Train

1. Greil Marcus, *The Manchurian Candidate* (London: BFI, 2002), 38.

2. Roger Ebert, review of *The Manchurian Candidate*, *Chicago Sun-Times*, March 11, 1988; available at http://rogerebert.suntimes.com/apps/pbcs.dll/article?AID=/19880311/REVIEWS/803110301/1023&template=printart.

3. Robert Corber, *In the Name of National Security: Hitchcock, Homophobia, and the Political Construction of Gender in Postwar America* (Durham, N.C.: Duke University Press, 1993), 71.

4. Ibid., 9.

5. Ibid., 195.

6. Richard Condon, *The Manchurian Candidate* (New York: McGraw-Hill, 1959), 166–70.

7. See William Rothman, *Hitchcock: The Murderous Gaze* (Cambridge: Harvard University Press, 1982).

8. Laura Mulvey, "Visual Pleasure and Narrative Cinema," in Bill Nichols, ed., *Movies and Methods, Volume II* (Berkeley: University of California Press, 1985), 310.

9. Mulvey's analysis is based, in part, on her readings of *Rear Window* (1954) and *Vertigo* (1958).

10. Corber, *In the Name of National Security*, 193–218.

11. John Frankenheimer, voice-over commentary, *The Manchurian Candidate* [DVD], MGM Home Entertainment, 1998.

12. Gerald Pratley, *The Cinema of John Frankenheimer* (London: A. Zwemmer, 1969), 96.

13. Michael Rogin, *Ronald Reagan, The Movie: And Other Episodes in Political Demonology* (Berkeley: University of California Press, 1987), 254.

8. Cold War Redux

1. Bosley Crowther, review of *The Manchurian Candidate*, *New York Times*, October 25, 1962, 48.

2. Arthur Knight, "The Fu Manchurian Candidate," *Saturday Review*, October 27, 1962, 65.

3. Ibid.

4. "Down South in North Korea," *Time*, November 2, 1962, 101.

5. Stanley Kauffmann, review of *The Manchurian Candidate*, *New Republic*, December 1, 1962, 62.

6. Brendan Gill, "Bad Men and Good," *New Yorker*, November 3, 1962, 115.

7. President John F. Kennedy, "Radio and Television Report to the American People on the Soviet Arms Buildup in Cuba." Courtesy of the John F. Kennedy Library and Museum. The transcript may be viewed at http://www.jfklibrary.org/j102262.htm.

8. J. Hoberman, "A Co-Production of Sinatra and J.F.K.," *New York Times*, September 14, 2003.

9. Michael Rogin, *Ronald Reagan, The Movie: And Other Episodes in Political Demonology* (Berkeley: University of California Press, 1987), 253.

10. Hazel Flynn, "Was 'Manchurian' Film a Prophet," *Hollywood Citizen-News*, November 28, 1963.

11. Richard Condon, "*Manchurian Candidate* in Dallas," *Nation*, December 28, 1963, 449.

12. Ibid., 450.

13. Ibid., 451.

14. Roger Ebert, review of *The Manchurian Candidate*, *Chicago Sun-Times*, March 11, 1988; available at http://rogerebert.suntimes.com/apps/pbcs.dll/article?AID=/19880311/REVIEWS/803110301/1023&template=printart.

15. Greil Marcus, *The Manchurian Candidate* (London: BFI, 2002), 61.

16. NBC Television Network memo publicizing the April 27, 1974, showing of *The Manchurian Candidate*. Authors' file.

17. Aljean Harmetz, "'Manchurian Candidate,' Old Failure, Is Now a Hit," *New York Times*, February 24, 1988.

18. The film, which cost $2.5 million to make in 1962, had, by early 1989, grossed $2.72 million in its limited theatrical reissue and an additional $2.5 million in video sales, as reported in the *Los Angeles Times*, February 26, 1989.

19. Rogin, *Ronald Reagan, The Movie*, 3.

20. Ibid., 7–8.

21. Anthony Lane, "The Method President," *New Yorker*, October 18, 2004, 190.

22. http://www.pbs.org/wgbh/amex/reagan/filmmore/reference/primary/evil.html.

23. Rogin, *Ronald Reagan, The Movie*, 32. Subsequent references are given in the text.

24. Lane, "The Method President," 190. The reference is to the speech Reagan delivered at the Brandenburg Gate in West Berlin, June 12, 1987: "General Secretary Gorbachev, if you seek peace, if you seek prosperity for the Soviet Union and Eastern Europe, if you seek liberalization: Come here to this gate! Mr. Gorbachev, open this gate! Mr. Gorbachev, tear down this wall!" For the full text, go to http://www.reaganfoundation.org/reagan/speeches/wall.asp.

25. http://news.bbc.co.uk/2/hi/americas/3780871.stm.

26. H. Bruce Franklin, *M.I.A. or Mythmaking in America: How and Why Belief in Live POWs Has Possessed a Nation* (New Brunswick, N.J.: Rutgers University Press, 1992), 133. Subsequent references are given in the text.

27. "Interview with Frank Sinatra," *Playboy*, February 1963. Available at http://www.sinatraarchive.com/tis/play-interview.html.

28. Live recording of Frank Sinatra performing at the Oakland Coliseum, May 22, 1968. Unreleased. Authors' collection.

29. Michael Nelson, "Frank Sinatra and Presidential Politics," in Stanislao Pugliese, ed., *Frank Sinatra: History, Identity, and Italian American Culture* (New York: Palgrave Macmillan, 2004), 65–66.

30. For more on this episode, see Shawn Levy, *Rat Pack Confidential: Frank, Dean, Sammy, Peter, Joey and the Last Great Showbiz Party* (New York: Doubleday, 1998), 212–17.

31. Nelson, "Frank Sinatra and Presidential Politics," 68.

32. Ibid., 69.

33. Ebert, review of *The Manchurian Candidate*, *Chicago Sun-Times*, March 11, 1988.

Postscript

1. See H. Bruce Franklin, *M.I.A. or Mythmaking in America: How and Why Belief in Live POWs Has Possessed a Nation* (New Brunswick, N.J.: Rutgers University Press, 1992), and *Vietnam and Other American Fantasies* (Boston: University of Massachusetts Press, 2000).

2. Dwight D. Eisenhower, "The Military-Industrial Complex," in William H. Chafe and Harvard Sitkoff, eds., *A History of Our Time* (New York: Oxford University Press, 1987), 98–101.

3. Gary Strauss, "Cheney as VP Faces a Serious Cut in Pay," *USA Today*, July 26, 2000; available at http://www.usatoday.com/news/opinion/e2415.htm.

4. Anne Rittman, "A Halliburton Primer," *Washington Post*, July 11, 2002; available at http://www.washingtonpost.com/wp-srv/onpolitics/articles/halliburtonprimer.html.

5. "Sources: Cheney Curses Leahy over Halliburton Criticisms," CNN, June 25, 2004; available at http://www.cnn.com/2004/ALLPOLITICS/06/24/cheney.leahy/.

6. Mike Allen, "GAO Cites Corporate Shaping of Energy Plan," *Washington Post*, August 26, 2003, A01.

7. Greg Palast, "Bush Energy Plan: Policy or Payback?" May 18, 2001, BBC; available at http://news.bbc.co.uk/1/hi/world/americas/1336960.stm.

8. "Cheney to King: Bush Is Captain," January 19, 2001, CNN; available at http://archives.cnn.com/2001/ALLPOLITICS/stories/01/19/cheney.video.toss/.

9. Roger Ebert, review of *The Manchurian Candidate*, *Chicago Sun-Times*, July 30, 2004.

10. Review of *The Manchurian Candidate*, *Variety*, July 17, 2004.

11. Bruce Newman, "New *Candidate* Falls Short: *Manchurian* Remake's Acting Is Great but Plot Isn't," *San Jose Mercury News*, July 30, 2004.

12. "Jonathan Demme, exclusive interview by Daniel Robert Epstein," http://www.ugo.com/channels/filmtv/features/themanchuriancandidate/jonathan.asp.

13. *New York Times*, November 14, 2005. On the latter point, it was this tendency of the Bush administration to hand Al Qaeda so many propaganda victories that prompted columnist Paul Krugman to dub Bush "the Arabian candidate" (*New York Times*, July 20, 2004).

Index

Abstract Expressionism, 42
Abu Ghraib prison, 134, 192
Academy Awards, 4, 11, 17, 21, 55, 63
Acheson, Dean, 137
Advertising, 136, 137
Affluent Society, The, 36, 39
Afghanistan, 192
Africa, 55; North, 104
African-Americans and African-
    Americanness, 24, 76, 121, 122–23,
    182; and communism, 89; conscious-
    ness of, 122; criminality of, 129. *See
    also* Race; Racism
Alamo, The, 21
Aldrich, Robert, 53, 72
Alice in Wonderland, 130
Alienation, 44, 48, 53, 69
Aliens, 40; and alien pods, 43, 53, 78–
    80; illegal, 59, 85; invasion of, 53; as
    mutants, 78
All Fall Down, 22
Allegiance, xv, 45, 131
Allen, Lewis, 7, 53, 67
Al Qaeda, xiv, 190
America First party, 7

"American Century," 32
American Civil Liberties Union
    (ACLU), 45, 89
American dream, 36, 38, 189, 189
American exceptionalism, 34
American family. *See* Nuclear family
Americanism, 40, 131
American Legion, 18, 60, 61, 99
American-style "liberty," xi, xv, 34, 39,
    40, 41–42
"American way of life," xiii, 33, 34, 39,
    131, 139
American Youth for a Free World, 6
Amram, David, 2, 76
Andrews, Dana, 175
Anglo-Saxons, 46–47
"Annie Lee Moss before the McCarthy
    Commission," 89
Anticommunism. *See* Communism
Antiracism, 123
Anxiety, 39, 40, 43, 44, 48
Apocalyptic visions, 74
Arabia, 104
Arabs, 128, 159, 160, 163
Arendt, Hannah, 97

"Argument in Indianapolis, An," 89
Army-McCarthy hearings, 87, 91, 92, 96
Ashcroft, John, 192
Asia, xiii, 101–4
Asian Barred Zone, 107
Asians, xiii, 59, 101, 178; and citizen-
    ship, 107; "conspiracy" of, 83; immi-
    gration of, 106–7; racism towards,
    101, 102, 106, 123; and U.S. culture,
    125; U.S. violence against, 107,
    110–11. See also Chinese; Japanese;
    Korean War; Orientalism; Viet-
    namese War
Asian women, 113–15, 203n.47
Atlantic Monthly, 40
Atomic bomb(s), 38–39, 70, 74; age of,
    xii, 3, 53, 175; explosion of, 74, 77;
    and Hiroshima and Nagasaki, 110;
    and nuclear warfare, 16, 110; radia-
    tion from, 78; and Soviets, 31, 176
Authoritarianism, 44; and momism,
    132–33. See also Totalitarianism
Authority, 41, 45, 47; state, 55, 56, 64–
    65, 96–97
Automaton motif, 44, 81
Avant-garde, 33
Awful Truth, The, 63
Axelrod, George: career of, 17, 20; and
    Frankenheimer, 16–19, 49, 100, 170,
    174; and the making of The Man-
    churian Candidate, xi, 1, 16–19, 20,
    22, 23, 52; and opinion of The
    Manchurian Candidate, 49, 76, 99,
    114, 124
Axis powers, 33

Baby boom, 37
Barney Miller, 22
Baron, John, 53, 67, 68–71
Bates, Norman, 52
Bay of Pigs, 83
Beat poets, 44
Beatty, Warren, 22
Beirut, 179
Bel Geddes, Barbara, 58
Bentley, Eric, 85
Berlin Wall, 50, 57, 176, 192, 193
Bernstein, Walter, 84, 85

Big Heat, The, 66
Bill of Rights, 35
bin Laden, Osama, 192
Biskind, Peter, 79
Bissell, Whit, 80–81
Black death, 54
Blacklisting. See Hollywood: and
    blacklisting
Black Power, 124
Blue Hawaii, 21
Bob and Ray, 85
Bogart, Humphrey, 7, 67
Bomb and bombing. See Atomic
    bomb(s)
Borgnine, Ernest, 3
Boys, 37, 59, 60, 133, 144. See also
    Mother-son dynamic
Brainwashing, ix, 13, 14, 15, 17, 20, 79,
    151, 193; and assassination plots,
    14–15, 24, 26–28, 30, 81; and
    deprogramming, 77, 165; as Man-
    churian, 47, 119; as "Oriental," 119–
    20, 176; racialization of, 46, 119–21,
    123; scenes of, 48, 78, 112, 122, 127,
    130; of Shaw's platoon, 24–27, 75.
    See also Ladies' garden club scene
Brain-washing in Red China: The Calcu-
    lated Destruction of Men's Minds, 47
Breadwinning: anxieties surrounding,
    58–60
Breakfast at Tiffany's, 17, 22, 124
British, the: culture of, 102, 105
British House of Commons, 175–76
Broadway, 16–17
Brothel scene, 19, 69, 110, 112–15,
    116–17. See also Miss Gertrude's
Browder, Earl, 137
Brown v. Board of Education, 124
Buck, Pearl S., 106
Bull, Sitting, 46
Bush, George W., 189–91, 192, 193
Bush, George H. W., 189
Bush, Jeb, 191
Butterfield 8, 21
Byrnes, Secretary of State James, 95

Caine Mutiny, The, 40
California, 19, 67, 78, 99, 190

Capitalism, 35, 47. *See also* United
States: economy of
Capitol Records, 2, 11
Capote, Truman, 17
Captivity narratives, 116, 134
Cars, 36, 37, 39, 61, 152
Casablanca, 176
"Case of Milo Radulovich, A0589839,
The," 89
Casting: of Asian actors, 125; of *The
Manchurian Candidate*, 76, 154. *See
also* Hollywood
Catholicism and Catholics, 5, 62, 63
CBS, 88, 174
Censorship. *See* Film(s): censorship of;
Press, the
Cheney, Dick, 189, 190, 191, 192, 193
Cheyney, Eugénie Rose (Rosie), xiii–xiv,
20, 21, 25, 87, 157–62, 187; and
communism, 150–51, 158, 163; as
Eleanor's doppelganger, 164; and
Marco, 20, 52, 130, 150, 158–60,
164, 165–66; as mother-figure, 164;
scenes of appearance, 164–66; as
sexually aggressive, 157, 162–64,
165, 167
Chin, Frank, 124
China, 31, 83, 124
Chinatown, xiii, 107, 124
Chinese, 6, 13, 17, 19; as communist
agents, 23, 24, 46, 47, 77, 110, 125,
150–51; and Hollywood, 100; immigration of, 104; as inscrutable, 105;
and material culture imported to the
United States, 101, 105; as sexually
deviant, 59; and Soviets, 116, 117,
122, 120, 165, 179, 184; and the
West, 112. *See also* Orientalism
Chinese Exclusion, 105; Act, 106
Chomsky, Noam, 112
Christianity, 37, 40, 60, 182. *See also*
Catholicism and Catholics
Chunjin, xii, 23, 25, 28, 101, 116, 117,
121, 123, 124, 128, 145; casting of,
125; as communist agent, 119;
duplicity of, 117–18; as feminized
houseboy, 117–19
Churchill, Winston, 31

CIA, 42, 83, 111, 154, 156, 187
Ciro's nightclub, 9
Citizen Kane, 2, 52
"Citizen soldier," 133–37
Citizenship, xiv, xv, 37; court cases
regarding, 106–7; and domesticity,
131–32; and gender, 133–37
Civil rights, 123
Civil War (American), 2
Clift, Montgomery, 4
Clinton, Hillary, 191
Cold War: anticommunism of, 133;
cinematic construction of, xi, 16, 41,
44, 48, 53, 55, 60, 64, 65, 70, 81, 96,
97, 99, 125, 128, 131, 149, 154, 167,
176, 177, 184; and the culture of
consensus, 31; and the domestic
sphere, 66, 71, 145, 148, 137; and
gender arrangements, xiv, 140–41,
151, 161; racial politics of, 123–24;
"second," xiv; sexual politics of, 131,
153–54; and state power, 57; strategy
of, 123; and un-Americanness, 98;
U.S. culture and ideology of, xii, ix–
x, xii, xiii, 12, 30–31, 33, 35–40, 42–
48, 55, 96, 102, 128, 177; and the
"war on terror," 192–93. *See also*
Culture of contradiction;
Technology
Colonialism, 103, 104
Committee for the First Amendment, 7
Communicable disease metaphor, 54–57
Communism, ix; agents of, 13, 15, 23,
81, 121; anti-, 30, 31, 39, 40–42, 45,
48, 60, 65, 70, 79, 83, 84, 86, 88, 98,
99, 148, 167; and brainwashing, 24–
25, 27, 80; brutality of, 178, 193; and
communist plots, 27, 30, 70; containment of, 31, 55, 123, 140; as a
"crime," 70; "disease" of, 55, 207n.5;
and domesticity, 37, 62, 65, 69, 137,
141, 144, 147; and the Hollywood
Ten, 4; ideology of, 34, 63; infiltration of, 57, 99; and gender, 131–32,
137; and momism, 132–33, 146–
47; and Nazism, 176; and patriot
dichotomy, 70; and pod people,
79; political party of, 139–40;

Communism (*continued*), and postwar
    witch hunts, 7, 45; as a result of bad
    parenting, 132–33, 137, 139; and
    sexuality, 133, 138–39; and Frank
    Sinatra, 7, 9–11; threat of, xii, xiii,
    39, 40, 58, 60, 64, 71, 83. *See also*
    Cold War, the; McCarthy, Joseph;
    McCarthyism
"Communists and queers," 137, 138
Condon, Richard, x, xi, 13–15, 17, 18,
    19, 44–45, 47, 48, 52, 53, 65, 69,
    85, 95, 108, 141, 153, 160, 172–73,
    176, 187
Conformity, xi, 34–35, 40–42, 45, 79;
    non-, 44
Congress, 4
Congressional Medal of Honor, 13,
    14, 15, 23, 24, 25, 28, 30, 48, 143,
    166, 175
Congressional rights, 40
Conspiracy motif, xii, 13, 15, 19, 70,
    75, 83, 95, 98, 180, 187
Consumerism, 39, 43; and manipulation
    of consumer, 48
Containment, 31, 55, 123, 140
Contamination, 54–59
Coolidge, Calvin, 67
Coontz, Stephanie, 137
Corber, Robert, 153, 156, 164
Costume party scene, 66, 146
Counterculture, 127–28
Countertorture, 192
Cracker Jacks, 22
Crichton, Michael, 107
Crisis of masculinity. *See* Masculinity:
    crisis of
Cromer, Evelyn Baring, 102
Cromer, Lord, xiii, 103, 104
Crosby, Bing, 63, 183
Crowther, Bosley, 168, 170, 171
Crucible, The, 41, 85
Cuba, 39, 83, 171–72
Cuban Missile Crisis, 171–72
Cukor, George, 21
Culture of contradiction, xi, xii, 30–32;
    affluence of, 36, 38–39, 43–44, 128;
    authority and, 41, 45, 47; commu-
    nism and, 33, 37, 34; conformity

and, 34–35, 40–42, 45; individualism
    and, 34, 35, 40; industrialism and,
    36, 50, 51; liberty and, 34, 35, 39,
    40; materialism and, 36, 39; race
    and, 46–47; technology and, 3, 6, 37.
    See also Normativity; Public/private
    collapse; Surveillance
Cumings, Bruce, 116
Curtis, Tony, 21
Czech crisis of 1948, 31

Days of Wine and Roses, 16
D-Day, 174
Defense Department, 65, 93, 144, 181
Defiant Ones, The, 4
Demme, Jonathan, xiv, 185–93
Democracy, 36, 40, 41, 47, 50, 123,
    187, 191
Democratic National Convention, 9, 11
Democratic Party, 5, 9, 12, 19, 182,
    183, 191
Depression era, 42
Desperate Hours, The, 66
Destructors, The, 125
Detective films. *See* Film(s): detective
Detroit, 2
Dhiegh, Khigh (Kenneth Dickerson),
    101, 121, 125, 126, 127–28; roles
    taken by, 128, 129; and Taoism,
    127–28
Dictatorship, 47, 50, 69
Dies, Martin, 33
Disney, Walt, 13
Dmytryk, Edward, 40
Domesticity, 37, 68, 113, 116, 131, 139–
    40; and citizenship, 131–32
Domino theory, 55–56, 59, 83
Donovan, King, 78
Dorsey, Tommy, 5
Douglas, Kirk, 4
Douglas, Nathan E., 4
Douglas, Paul, 54
Dream sequences, 13, 24–28, 75, 193;
    See also Marco, Bennett; Melvin, Al;
    Shaw, Raymond
Dr. Strangelove, 99
Duck Soup, 63
Dulles, John Foster, 123

Dumbo, 13
Dunne, Irene, 63
Durkheim, Emile, 50
Dylan, Bob, 44

Earth vs. Flying Saucers, 45
East, the: comparison to the West, 102–5; "Far," 104–6, 115 sexual politics of, 114–15. *See also* Orientalism
Eastern European immigrants, 54. *See also* White ethnics
Eastwood, Clint, 191
Ebert, Roger, 151, 173, 184
Economics. *See* United States: economy of
Edwards, Blake, 16
Egypt, 104
Eisenhower, Dwight, 37, 55, 82, 101, 139, 189
Eliot, T. S., 50
Elise, Kimberly, 187
Employment of Homosexuals and Other Sex Perverts in Government, 138
Engelhardt, Tom, 48, 49, 56, 148
England, Lynndie, 134
Enloe, Cynthia, 134, 140, 143
Enron, 190, 191
Ernst, Morris, 97, 137
Esquire, 140
Eternal Fight, The, 55
Europe, 3
Eve, Lady, 154–56, 162, 163
Even Cowgirls Get the Blues, 125
"Evil empire" speech, 175–76
Examiner, 11
Execution of Private Slovik, The (novel, 1954), xi, 2–4, 9–10, 12
Exoticism, 125, 128
Expert: culture of the, 56, 65

Fahrenheit 9/11, 91
Fantasia, 13
Fascism, 7, 34, 69, 111
Fatherhood, 37, 58, 59, 60, 133
FBI, 34, 41, 61, 62, 63, 67, 79, 97, 187
Federal Employee Loyalty Program, 84
"Federation of Evil Oriental Supervillains, The," 127

Feminine Mystique, The, 44
Femininity, 59, 65; normative, 131, 134, 140–41; and Orientalism, 103, 114–15. *See also* Gender
Film(s): black and white, 175; censorship of, 19–20; detective, 53, 73, 74; industry of, 4, 7, 13, 33, 39; noir, 53, 72–73; prisoner of war rescue adventures, 178–79; and race, 49, 122–28; and special effects, 23; and surveillance, 62, 65, 73; violence of, 173. *See also* Cold War, the; Hollywood
Fleming, Ian, 19
Fontainebleau Hotel, 9, 18, 20
Forbidden Area, 16
Ford, Glenn, 66
Ford, John, 116
Foreign Affairs, 55
Foreign policy. *See* United States: foreign policy of
For Whom the Bell Tolls, 16
France, 3
Frankenheimer, John: and Axelrod, 16–19, 49, 100, 170, 174; career of, 16, 22; and casting, 76, 143; cinematic influences of, xii, 21, 72, 79, 151, 157, 161, 168, 207n.2; editing choices of, 27, 65, 66, 69; ideology of, 116; and the making of *The Manchurian Candidate*, xi, 17, 20, 23, 52, 53, 81, 95, 100, 102, 108, 114, 117, 121, 162, 166, 170, 176, 186–87, 188, 189, 193; and opinion on *The Manchurian Candidate*, 28, 99, 116; and television, 173–74
Frankfort School, 36
Franklin, H. Bruce, 178, 179, 187
Freedom, 34, 39, 176; of expression, 42; individual, 97; institutional, 31–32; of will, 50. *See also* American-style "liberty"
Freedom from Fear and *Freedom from Want*, 137
Freedom of Information Act, 84
Free market, 47, 193
French culture, 102
French Indochina. *See* Vietnam War
French New Wave, 21

Fried, Richard, 89
Friedan, Betty, 44
Friendly, Fred, 89
From Here to Eternity, 3, 21
Fu Manchu, xii, 46, 100, 105, 117, 125, 127; as Chinese communist, 120; and Marco, 100; productions featuring, 124; as stereotypical Asian villain, 124, 126, 170; and yellow face, 107–8

Gaddis, John Lewis, 31–32
Gaines, Holborne, 120, 144
Galbraith, John Kenneth, 36–37, 38, 39
Gangsters. *See* Mafia
Garavente (Sinatra), Natalia, 4–5
Gaslight, 21
Geisha, 101, 115. *See also* harem
Gender, xiii–xiv; and citizenship, 133–37; and communism, 131–32, 137; and nationalism, 131, 133; and normativity, xiii, 59, 131; and war, 134. *See also* Femininity; Masculinity; Orientalism; Sexuality
Generation of Vipers, 37, 45, 132–33, 137, 154
Genocide, 112
German-Americans, 102
Germany and Germans, 31, 121, 142
Gershwin, Ira, 9
Ginsburg, Allen, 36, 44, 45, 127
Godfather films, 2
Going My Way, 63
Golden Oracle, The, 127
Goldfinger, 124
Goldwyn Studios, 28
Good Earth, The, 106
Goodman, Paul, 44
Governance, 50; blind dependence on, 55; and the "culture of the expert," 56, 65; ineffectiveness of, 179–80; and state authority, 55, 56, 64–65
Grable, Betty, 135, 137
Gramsci, Antonio, x
Granger, Farley, 151, 152
Grant, Cary, 63, 155
Greece, 33
Green Mansions, 128

Gregory, James, 22, 95
Griswold v. Connecticut, 96
Growing Up Absurd, 44
Guatemala, 39
Gulf Wars, 50, 134, 189

Hague, Frank, 4
Hale and Dorr, 91–92
Hall, Stuart, x
Halliburton, xiv, 189–90, 193
Hamill, Pete, 4
Hammer, Mike, 73–74, 77
Hampton, Lionel, 5
Happy Days, 125
Harem, 101, 114, 115
Harvey, Laurence, 2, 21, 22, 28, 76, 143, 151, 170
Hawaii, 3
Hawaii Five-O, 125, 126
Hayden, Sterling, 6! 8
Hayes, Helen, 60
Hearst writers and press, 7, 10, 11, 17, 133
Heflin, Van, 61
Hemingway, Ernest, 16
Henderson, Douglas, 52
Hepburn, Audrey, 22
Heroin, 21
Hidden Persuaders, The, 47
High art, 42, 44
"High Hopes," 12
Highsmith, Patricia, 153
Higonnet, Margaret, 134
Hirohito, Emperor, 117
Hitchcock, Alfred, xiv, 21, 52, 61, 151, 152, 53, 154, 160, 161, 162, 168, 171, 207n.2; and *The Manchurian Candidate*, 151, 157
Hitler, Adolf, 132–33
Hoberman, J., 172
Hoboken, 5
Holliday, Judy, 17
Hollywood, xii, 16, 19, 59, 100; and blacklisting, xi, 4, 11, 12, 4! 0, 84, 85; B movies of, ix, 41, 71, 182; classical narrative of, 73, 77, 162; conservatives of, 11; golden age of, 13; and hiring practices, 101, 129;

and Orientalism, 100–101; politics
of, 98; and race, 122–23, 128;
stereotypes of, 100; studios of, 28;
and wartime propaganda, 136. *See
also* Casting; Cold War: cinematic
construction of; Film(s)
Hollywood Independent Citizens
Committee of Arts, Sciences, and
Professions (HICCASP), 7
Hollywood Ten, 4, 40, 84
Holmes, Sherlock, 74
Homefront/front dichotomy, 134–37
Home invasion motif, 66–67, 72, 77
Homeland security. *See* National
security
Homoeroticism, 151–54
Homosexuality, 59, 61, 131; and *The
Manchurian Candidate*, 141, 142;
politicization of, 138–39, 153. *See
also* Momism; Sexuality
Hoover, J. Edgar, xiii, 34, 37, 97, 133,
137, 139–40, 144, 147, 149
Hooverism, 84, 99
Hopper, Hedda, 11
House I Live In, The, 4, 7
House Un-American Activities
Committee (HUAC), 4, 7, 10, 33,
39, 40, 84, 98
Housewives, 49, 68
Howl, 44, 45, 127
Hudson, Rock, 188
Huie, William Bradford, xi, 2
Humphrey, Hubert, 182
Hungary, 31
Hussein, Saddam, 192
Hyannis Port, 19

"I Can't Get Started," 9
ICBM, 49, 192
I Ching, 127
Immigration laws, 107
Immigration and Naturalization Services
(INS), 85
Incest motif, xiii, 22, 27, 141, 142–43,
147, 148, 150, 164. *See also* Sexuality
Individualism, xi, 34, 35, 40, 42, 43–
44, 50
Industrialism, 36, 50, 51

In Every War But One, 17
Inherit the Wind, 4
Insanity, 74, 80–81, 91
Insidious Dr. Fu Manchu, The, 107–8
Invaders from Mars, 40
Invasion of the Body Snatchers, xii, 40, 43,
44, 52, 53, 77–81, 97, 208n.27; and
The Manchurian Candidate, 79, 96
Iran, 104, 192
Iraq, 101, 134, 190
Iron Curtain, 31, 56
Isaacs, Harold, 104, 107, 109, 119–
20, 124
Iselin, Eleanor, xiii, 13, 14, 15, 23, 24,
49, 76; assassination of, 77, 148; and
Chunjin, 101, 117–18; as communist
agent, 6, 47, 65, 66, 130–31, 145,
146, 164, 181; eleven scenes of, 143–
48; false patriotism of, 74, 180; and
Jocie, 26, 145–46; and Johnny, 86,
87, 93–94, 131, 145–46, 181; and
McCarthyism, 93; and politics, 30;
and presidential assassination plot,
48, 164, 180; as a senator, 186,
191; and Senator Jordan, 145, 146;
sexuality of, 142–43, 147, 148, 150,
164; and Shaw, 27, 145–46, 131,
145–47, 150, 186
Iselin, John Yerkes (Johnny), xii, xiii,
13, 15, 22, 23; appearances of, 85–
86; assassination of, 77, 86, 180; and
communism, 24, 30, 47, 65–66, 82,
93, 98, 144; and Eleanor, 86, 87, 93–
94, 131, 141, 145–46; impotence of,
141; likeness to McCarthy, 93, 94,
95, 99; and Marco's dream, 25; and
presidential assassination plot, 27,
48; and presidential election, 26,
146, 164; and Senator Jordan, 26,
45, 86, 94, 146; sexuality of, 141–
42; and television, 87–88, 94,
144, 146
Iselin/Shaw family, xiv, 18, 57, 85;
as dangerously matriarchal, 45,
133, 148
Islam, 50, 101, 104
Islamic fundamentalists, 192, 193
Italian-Americans, 102

Italian immigrants, 4. *See also* White
　ethnics
Italy, 18
I Was a Communist, 70

Jagger, Dean, 60
Japan, 3, 38, 104, 105, 110; and atomic
　bombings, 110
Japanese: Anti-Japanese sentiment, 106;
　racist portrayals of, 102, 111, 115,
　123, 137
Japanese-American Internment, 102, 107
Jazz, 112, 115
Jefferson, Thomas, xi, xii; memorial of, 61
Jews and Jewishness, 7. *See also* White
　ethnics
John Birch Society, 45
Johnson, Lyndon B., 83
Jones, Carolyn, 78
Jones, James, 3
Jordan, Jocelyn (Jocie), 18; assassination
　of, 26–27, 49, 98, 150, 166; romance
　with Shaw, 26, 45
Jordan, Senator Thomas, 22, 192; accu-
　sations against, 94, 180; assassina-
　tion of, 26–27, 49, 86, 146, 150, 166;
　and politics, 26, 30, 45, 98; and
　Shaw, 65, 130, 145, 150, 166

Kamikazi pilots, 118
Karate Kid, The, 125, 127
Karloff, Boris, 107–8, 125
Kauffman, Stanley, 170–71
Kazan, Elia, 53, 54
Kelly, Grace, 160
Kelly, Walt, 187
Kennan, George, 31, 55
Kennedy, John F.: assassination of, 167,
　173, 193; election campaigns of, 9,
　12, 18, 21; presidency of, 83, 148,
　171; and *The Manchurian Candidate*,
　172, 173, 174, 183; and Sinatra, 2, 9,
　10, 11–12, 19, 20, 171, 172, 174, 183
Kent, Frank R., 6
Khrushchev, Nikita, 38, 39
Kijich'on, 114
King, Larry, 191
King, Martin Luther, Jr., 112, 123

King Lear, 132
Kinsey Reports, 153
Kipling, Rudyard, 102
Kiss between Eleanor Iselin and Ray-
　mond Shaw, 27, 143, 147, 148, 164
Kiss Me Deadly, xii, 53, 72–73, 97,
　208n.22; and *The Manchurian
　Candidate*, 77
"Kitchen debate," 38, 39, 44
Klein, Christina, 123
Koch, Howard, 19–20
Korean War: and brainwashing, 47, 48,
　120, 176; casualties of, 111, 113–14;
　as a "Civil War," 116, 117; and the
　Cold War, 110; cinematic represen-
　tations of, 19, 60, 62, 67, 75, 112;
　integration of U.S. troops during,
　122; and *The Manchurian Candidate*,
　12, 13, 23, 24, 25, 80, 81, 166; and
　McCarthy, 83, 86; and North Korea,
　46, 111, 116, 176; Orientalist con-
　struction of, 114, 115; and postwar
　conditions, 113–14; and prisoners
　of war, 17; racist portrayals of, 105,
　111; and South Korea, 114; and U.S.
　interests in Asia, xiii, xiv, 32, 39,
　101, 109
Knute Rockne, All-American, 64, 175, 178
Kramer, Stanley, 4
Kremlin, the, 31, 98
Krim, Arthur, 19
Kung Fu, 125
Kuwait, 185

Ladies' garden club scene, 23, 75, 119,
　121, 122, 127, 162
Ladies' Home Journal, 134
Lady Vanishes, The, 160
Lancaster, Burt, 16
Lane, Edward William, 102
Lang, Fritz, 66
Lansbury, Angela, 2, 21–22, 28, 30, 49,
　76, 143, 208n.25
Lardner, Ring, Jr., 4, 98
Laurie, Piper, 16
Lawford, Peter, 10, 183
Lawyers' Guild, 91–92
Lay, Kenneth, 190

Lazar, Irving, 16

Leahy, Patrick, 190

Lee, Wen Ho, 125

Left, the, xii, 6, 11, 39, 123; and totalitarianism, 15, 34, 39

Leigh, Janet, xiii, 2, 21, 28, 150, 151, 157, 160–61

Leit, Jack, 133

LeMay, Major General Curtis, 110, 111

Lembeck, Bobby, 20, 24, 120, 150, 203–4n.47

Lemmon, Jack, 17

LeRoy, Mervyn, 7

Liberalism, 9, 22, 43, 64, 83, 122, 148, 182

Life, 13, 47, 137

Lincoln, Abraham, 65–66, 86

Lincoln Day, 84, 86, 87, 93

Lincoln Memorial, the, 63

Lindon, Lionel, 2

Lonely Crowd, The, 36, 43, 69

"Long Telegram," 123

Los Angeles Examiner, 10

Los Angeles Times, The, 11

Lovecraft, H. P., 72

Loyalty, 34, 40, 131, 183, 187

Luce, Henry, 32

Luciano, Lucky, 9

Luger, Frank, 22

Lynch, Private Jessica, 134

Macdonald, Dwight, 39, 42

MacLeish, Archibald, 40

Madison Avenue, 47

Madison Square Garden, 26, 27, 53

Mafia, 8–9, 63, 70, 129, 183

Maltz, Albert, 4, 7, 9–11, 17

"Mama's boy," 154, 156. *See also* Momism; Mother-son dynamic

Manchuria, xii, 13, 46, 100–101, 102

Manchurian Candidate, The (film, 1962), ix–xiv, 1–2; advertising of, 168, 69; casting of, 76, 143; and the Cold War, 99, 101–6, 175, 167, 177; and communism, 98–99, 149; cultural influences of, 31, 44–45, 49, 50, 52, 67, 81; cultural impact of, 29, 48–49, 81; and gender, 130–31, 151; and the

Kennedy assassination, 173, 174; making of, 12–20, 22–23, 28–29, 53–54, 74; matriarchy of, 45, 133, 148; and McCarthy, 85–88, 92, 93, 95, 96; and McCarthyism, 83, 93, 96; and Orientalism, 46, 100–103, 105, 108–9, 112, 115; paradoxes within, 45–46, 98; plot of, 24–27, 30, 70, 75–77, 204n.49; and politics, 45, 47, 71, 72, 79, 99, 112, 148–49, 185–89; and privacy, 97; and the Reagan era, 174–75, 178; re-release of, xiv, 184; reviews of, 170–71, 184; and sexuality, 69; and television, 173–75

Manchurian Candidate, The (film, 2004), xiv, 185–93

Manchurian Candidate, The (novel, 1959), x–xi, 44–45, 47, 53, 153, 176; adaptation of, 13–19, 23, 53, 65, 69, 72, 160, 172, 177, 189; Orientalism of, 108; racial politics of, 47, 108; sexual politics of, 141–43

Manchurian Global, 185–86, 187, 190, 193

Man in the Grey Flannel Suit, The, 34–35, 45, 48

Manoff, Arnold, 85

Man with the Golden Arm, The, 21

Mao Zedong, 24, 47, 121

Marco, Bennett, ix, x, xi, xiii–xiv, 1, 13, 20, 23, 48, 51, 52, 157–58; brainwashing of, 46, 75; and brothel scene, 112–13; and Chunjin, 118, 164; and communism, 124, 144, 151; dreams of, 13, 24–27, 80, 118, 119, 122, 162, 168, 179; as insane, 74; nervousness of, 157–58, 162; as an organization man, 187; and presidential assassination plot, 27–28, 53, 77; and Reagan, 177; and Rosie, xiv, 20, 52, 130, 150, 158–60, 164, 165–66; and service in the army, 83, 159, 179–80; sexuality of, 162; and Shaw, 76, 130, 185, 186, 187; weakness of, 157, 162–64, 165, 167. *See also* Train scene(s): of *The Manchurian Candidate*

Marco-Melvin pairing scenes, 123, 124

Marcus, Greil, 1, 52, 72, 75–76, 150,
    161, 173, 174

Marcuse, Herbert, 36

Mardell, 19–20

Martial arts, 118

Martial law, 27, 41

Marx, Karl, 38

Marx Brothers, 63

Marxism, 133

Mary Backstayge, Noble Wife, 85

Masculinity: crisis of, 80, 131, 162–63,
    167; and midlife crisis, 17; and nor-
    mativity, xiv, 59, 60, 62, 134, 157,
    161; and Orientalism, 103, 114–15;
    and the softening of American
    manhood, 132–33

M*A*S*H, 116

Mass media, xv, 14, 16, 17, 18, 27, 53,
    87, 96, 100, 176

Mass production, 35

Materialism, 36

Matricide, 77

Mavole, Ed, 14, 19–20, 24, 74, 120, 150

May, Elaine Tyler, 37, 131, 140, 143

McCarey, Leo, 53, 63–64, 65

McCarthy, Joseph, x, xiii, 22, 39, 83–85,
    98; communist allegations of, 82, 84,
    85, 86, 93, 95, 89–90, 92, 93, 94–95,
    137; as insane, 91; and *The Man-
    churian Candidate*, 28, 47, 48, 75, 82,
    85–86, 94, 96, 97, 98, 149; parodies
    of, xii, 47, 82, 85; on sexual deviance,
    137, 138; and television, 88–91, 95.
    See also Iselin, John Yerkes

McCarthy, Kevin, 77, 80

McCarthy hearings, 33, 39, 87, 91,
    92, 96

McCarthyism, xi, xii, 64; anti-, xii, 41,
    44, 45, 83–86, 89, 98; and *The
    Manchurian Candidate*, 79, 93, 94;
    and momism, 132

McDonald's, 193

McGiver, John, 22, 30

McPhee, John, 36

Media, 14. *See also* Mass media; Press, the

Meeker, Ralph, 73

Meighan, Winona, 141

Melodrama, 67

Melvin, Al, 24, 187; dreams of, 24–26,
    75, 119, 121; and Marco, 123, 124;
    racial significance of, 123, 124; and
    Yen Lo, 124

Memory, ix, 47; collective, 91, 95; as
    manipulation, 164

Menand, Louis, 13, 15

Menopause, 65

Miami, 20

Middle Ages, 54, 55

Middle class, 58, 68

Middle East, 104, 105; U.S. sentiment
    toward, 102

Midlife crisis, 17. *See also* Nervous
    breakdown

Midway, 125

Militarism, 112

Military intelligence. *See* U.S. Army

Miller, Arthur, 41, 85, 91, 92

Miller, J. P., 16

Mills, C. Wright, 35, 44, 48

Milt, Colonel, 52

Mind control, 77, 79. *See also*
    Brainwashing

Minnelli, Vincent, 21

Miss Gertrude's, 19–20, 23, 112–13,
    203n.47

Missing in Action trilogy, 178–80

Missouri, 31

Mob. *See* Mafia

Model minority, 106

Modernity, 50

Momism, 65, 69, 132–33, 143–44, 147,
    154, 156; and homosexuality, 153

Mongolian race, 106

Montgomery Bus Boycott, 124

Moon, Katherine, 113

Moore, Michael, 91

Morality, 37, 140. *See also* Motherhood:
    as an American duty; Normativity

Morgan, Ted, 84

Morita, Pat, 125, 127

Morocco, 104

Morone, James, 37

Mortimer, Lee, 7–9, 133

Moscow, 44

Moss, Annie Lee, 89

Mother figure, xii, 21–22, 49, 52, 60–62, 64, 65, 68, 69, 72, 76, 81, 134. *See also* Momism; Motherhood
Motherhood, 37; as an American duty, 131, 132, 137, 139, 140
Mother-son dynamic, 64, 69, 81, 153, 154, 156
Movie industry. *See* Film(s): industry of
Mulan, 125
Mulvey, Laura, 162
Mundt, Karl, 10
Murrow, Edward R., 38, 88, 89–91, 93, 95
Museum of Modern Art, 42
Mutually Assured Destruction, 38
My Lai, 111
My Son John, xii, 40, 41, 45, 53, 60–65, 99, 133, 153; and *The Manchurian Candidate*, 65–66, 96; and *Suddenly*, 69, 70, 71, 81
Mysterious Dr. Fu Manchu, 109

Naked Society, The, 97
Naropa Institute, 127, 128
Nation, 172
National anthem, 27
Nationalism, 42, 131; and gender, 131, 133; and sexuality, 131, 133, 143
National security, xii, xv; and the Cold War, 31–32, 34, 37, 41, 131; "homeland security," xv. *See also* "War on terror"
National security state, 64–65, 71
NATO, 31
Naturalism, 42
Nazis, 142, 176
NBC Saturday Night at the Movies, 174
Nelson, Deborah, 96, 97, 131, 138
Nelson, Michael, 183
Nervous breakdown, 25, 62, 65, 157, 162
New Age, 127–28
New Deal, 5, 9, 182
New Jersey, 23, 84, 119, 121
New Orleans, 53, 54, 58
New Republic, 170
New York, xiii, 5, 19, 25, 26, 28, 76, 101, 107, 117, 118–19, 144, 153, 154, 157, 160, 168, 170, 185, 186
New York Film Festival, 184

New York Times, 9, 11, 28, 92, 174
New Yorker, 47, 171
Nightmares. *See* Dream sequences
Nile Queen, The, 59
1984, 42
Nixon, Richard, 38, 39, 84, 148, 149, 182
Normativity, 37, 47, 68, 131. *See also* Nuclear family; Sexuality; Subversion
Norris, Chuck, 178
North by Northwest, 151, 154–56, 160–64
"Nose art," 136
Novak, Kim, 160
NSC-68, 31–32, 117
Nuclear family, xii, xiii, 36–37, 57–58, 60, 64, 131, 136, 137, 139; as a defense against communism, 68, 71, 137, 140; deviant forms of, 138, 144; threats to, 66–67
Nuclear warfare. *See* Atomic bomb(s)

Ocean's Eleven (1960), 12
Oland, Warner, 109
One-Dimensional Man, 36
Open Door Notes, 104
Operation Desert Storm, 185
Organization man, xi, xiv, 35–36, 39, 43, 45, 48, 53, 69, 100, 186, 187, 188, 189, 127
Orient, the, xiii, 101, 102–6; sexual politics of, 113–15
"Oriental," the, 103–5, 110; barbarity ascribed to, 103, 107–12, 114, 120, 124, 178; duplicity ascribed to, 117–19, 123; and gender, 117–18; homogeneity of, 116; inscrutability ascribed to, 102, 103, 106, 112, 117
Orientalism, xiii, 46, 49, 99, 100–109, 123; commercialization of, 105–6; and the East/West dichotomy, 102–5, 114–15, 127; gaze of, 102; historicity of, 128; imagery of, 107–8, 119; industry of, 125; political, 106; positive, 127–28, 129; sexual politics of, 59, 112–14
Orientalists, 102–6
Origins of Totalitarianism, The, 97
Orphan of China, The, 105

Orwell, George, 47
Oscars. *See* Academy Awards
Ostherr, Kristen, 55
Oswald, Lee Harvey, 173
Ottoman Empire, 104

Pacific Stars and Stripes, 115
Packard, Vance, 34, 36, 48, 79, 97
Palance, Jack, 54
Palm Springs, 11
Panic in the Streets, xii, 53, 54–59, 64–
    65, 66; and *The Manchurian Candi-
    date*, 56–58, 60
Patriot Act, 192
Patriotism, 11, 28, 37, 67, 70, 131; Cold
    War imagery of, 65–66; and religion,
    60, 62, 63
Pavlovian conditioning, 193
Pavlov Institute, 24, 47, 119
Pearl Harbor, 3, 110
Pedophilia, 59
Pegler, Westbrook, 6, 18
People's World, 99
Peppard, George, 22
Pentagon, 77
Perversion, xiii, 59, 131, 133, 138, 153.
    See also Subversion: sexual
Phfft!, 17
Philippine-American War, 104, 110,
    111, 112
Photography, 62, 65; and journalism,
    14, 15
Pierce, Hawkeye, 116
Pink Panther films, 118
Pin-ups, 135–36
Plague, the, 53–58, 59
Playboy, 182
Playhouse 90, 16
Pod people, 43, 53, 78–80
Police, 25, 47, 54, 59, 66, 74, 118, 154,
    164–65
Polonsky, Abraham, 85
Popular Front, 4, 42, 123
Possession motif, 75, 77.
Postindustrialism, 43–44
Postwar period: and the state of the
    world, 31–32; and U.S. culture, 32,
    33, 35, 39, 42–44, 56, 58, 68, 176

Potsdam, 31
Preminger, Otto, 4
Presidency: elections, 13, 26; politics of,
    18, 70, 67
Presidential assassination plot, 21, 27–
    28, 53, 71, 77, 81, 164
Presidential conventions of 1956 and
    1960, 26, 27
Presidential Medal of Freedom, 184
Presley, Elvis, 21
Press, the, 15, 104, 153; censorship of,
    17, 56; and conservatism, 7. *See also*
    Photography
Prisoner of War, 176–78, 181
Prisoners of War (POWs), 13, 17, 46,
    175, 176–79, 184; rescue adventures
    (film genre), 178–79
Privacy, 96–98, 131. *See also* Public/
    private collapse
Privacy and Freedom, 97
Privacy Invaders, The, 97
Privacy: The Right to be Let Alone, 97
Private citizen: civic duties of, 136–
    37, 145
Private property, 35
Private sphere. *See* Domesticity; Public/
    private collapse
Production Code Administration
    (PCA), 19–20
Prohibition films, 129
Prostitution, 19–20, 23, 112–15
Psychiatry, 13, 47, 119, 124; doctors of,
    78, 79, 80, 170; medications used
    within, 62; and U.S. Army, 75,
    76, 81
Psycho, 21, 52, 161
Psychoanalysis, 96
Psychology, 85
Psychopath: figure of, 69
Psychosocial dynamics, 44, 50
Public health, 55
Public/private collapse, xiii, xv, 37,
    45, 62, 64, 66–67, 71, 96–99, 131,
    147–48
Pulp novels, 100

Quarantine, 55, 57. *See also*
    Containment

Race, 6–7, 46–47, 49, 54, 100–6, 123–28; and sexuality, 19, 112–14, 141

Racial imagination, 101

Racial and religious tolerance, 6–7

Racism, 101–2, 106, 111–12, 124, 182; anti-, 123; and communism, 123; and militarism, 112

Radio, 32, 85, 172, 176; censorship of, 33; and the "Hit Parade," 6

Rambo films, 179–80

Rat Pack, 10, 183

Reagan, Nancy, 180–82, 183, 191

Reagan, Ronald, 148, 174–83; and communism, 176, 177; era of, xiv, 174, 193; and Hollywood, 176, 179, 180 manipulation of, 180–82; and Sinatra, 182–84; and television, 180–81

Rebel without a Cause, 133

Recurring dreams. *See* Dream sequences

Red-baiting, 13

Red fascism, 96

Red queen, 25, 27, 75, 130, 146, 165

Red scare, the, 64

Regionalism, 42

Religion, 6–7, 37, 40, 50, 60, 62, 63, 140, 182

"Report on Senator Joseph R. McCarthy, A," 89, 91

Reprise Records, 2, 11

Republican Party, 10, 34, 182, 189

Return of Mr. Moto, The, 128

Riesman, David, 35–36, 43, 44, 48, 69, 156

Right, the, xii, 17, 64, 79; radical faction of, 15

Riis, Jacob, xiii

Rising Sun, 107

Robards, Jason, 16

Robertson, Cliff, 16

Robinson, Earl, 7

Rock and roll, 44

Rockwell, Norman, 137

Rodgers, Gabby, 53

Rogin, Michael, 64, 70, 83, 97, 137, 167, 174–75, 177, 180, 182

Rohmer, Sax, xii, 107

Room at the Top, 21

Rooney, Mickey, 124

Roosevelt, Eleanor, 5

Roosevelt, Franklin D., 5–6; and the Soviet Union, 31

Rosenberg, Ethel, 137, 144

Rosenberg, Julius, 137

Rosie. *See* Cheyney, Eugénie Rose

Rosie the Riveter, 140

Rothman, William, 161

Rovere, Richard, 82

Said, Edward, x, 102–5, 114, 128

Saint, Eva Marie, 154, 155

Sakata, Harold, 124

Salem witch trials, 41, 85

Sanford and Son, 125

Saturday Evening Post, 13, 47

Saturday Review, 170

Sayre, Nora, 60, 63

Schlesinger, Arthur, Jr., 35, 36, 39, 40, 43, 45, 48, 49, 50, 51

Schrecker, Ellen, 84

Schreiber, Liev, 185, 186

Science fiction, 41, 45, 53, 81

Scott, Joan, x

Sears, Fred, 45

Sears, John, 180

Seconds, 188–89

Secrecy, 60; culture of, 56, 57, 65; and Orientalism, 123; and state power, 53

Secret service, 68, 71, 187

Sedition, 34

See It Now, 89, 90–91

September 11, 50, 101, 190, 192, 193

Sevareid, Eric, 110

Seven Year Itch, The, 17

Sexuality, xiii; hetero-, xiii, 37, 131; and normativity, xiii, 37, 113; and perversion/deviance, xiii, 59, 131, 133, 138, 153; and race, 19, 112–14, 141; and subversion, xiii, 19. *See also* Homosexuality; Orientalism

Shaheen, Jack, 128

Shakespeare, 89–90, 107, 132

Shaw, George Bernard, 32

Shaw, Raymond, ix, 13, 14, 15, 18, 19–
    20, 23, 51; and the army, 25, 83,
    187; and assassination of Mavole, 24,
    120, 150; and brainwashing, 47, 48,
    53, 80, 146, 188; and brothel scene,
    112–13; casting of, 21, 22; and
    Chunjin, 117; and communism, 97,
    119, 144; and Eleanor, 27, 65, 77,
    142–43, 147, 148, 150, 164, 166; and
    Jocie, 26, 45, 49, 65, 86, 96, 130,
    141, 150; and Johnny, 85–86; and
    Lembeck, 150; likeness to Eleanor's
    father, 142–43; and Marco, 24–27,
    76, 130, 145; platoon of, 74, 75; and
    presidential assassination plot, 28,
    71, 164; and Reagan, 177; and
    Senator Jordan, 49, 65, 130, 145,
    150, 166; sexuality of, 69–70, 113,
    141, 203n.47; suicide of, 77, 148,
    166; and television, 143. See also
    Kiss between Eleanor Iselin and
    Raymond Shaw
Shor, Toots, 6
Shurlock, Geoffrey M., 19, 20
Siegel, Don, 53, 77, 79, 80
Silva, Henry, 28, 101, 125, 128; as the
    "dark villain," 128, 129
Sinatra, Frank, xi, xiii, 1–6, 21; and
    blacklist, 12; and communism, 7–11;
    and Democratic Party, 9; and Ken-
    nedy, 2, 9, 10, 11–12, 19, 20, 171,
    172, 174, 183; and leftism, 6–7; and
    liberalism, 9; and the Mafia, 7–9;
    and The Manchurian Candidate, 17–
    20, 28–29, 150, 151, 157, 166, 170,
    171, 175, 180; and politics, 6–7, 11–
    12, 18, 133, 182–84; and Suddenly,
    53, 70, 67, 71
Sinatra, Frank, Jr., 6
Sinatra, Tina, 191
Slavery motif, 50, 137. See also
    Conformity
Sloan, Web, 176–77
Smith, Al, 5
Smith, David, 44
Smith, Gerald L. K., 7
Smith, Jake, 111
Soap operas, 21

Social science, 39
Sokolniki Park, Moscow, 38
Sokolsky, George, 7, 18
Solitaire, 25, 26, 48, 80, 146
Some Came Running, 21
Soviets and the Soviet Union, 13; and
    anti-Soviet sentiment, 49; and
    brainwashing, 120; and China, 116,
    117, 122, 120, 165, 179, 184; col-
    lapse of, 192–93; and communist
    agents, 23, 24, 30, 45, 46, 47, 48,
    63, 77, 97; conspiracy of, 98; and
    Cuba, 171–72; and Korea, 32; and
    nuclear warfare, 16, 31; and the
    United States, 31, 33, 39, 40, 50,
    99; and technology, 37–38. See also
    Containment; United States: foreign
    policy of
Spartacus, 4
Speakes, Larry, 180
Spillane, Mickey, 72, 74
Sputnik, 31
Spy stories, 13, 14
Stagecoach, 113, 116
Stalin, Joseph, 24, 47, 121; and World
    War II, 31
Stalinism, 44
Stapleton, Maureen, 16
State Department, 39, 84, 94, 96,
    137, 138
Steinbeck, John, 44
St. Louis, 14, 20
Strangers on a Train, 61, 151–54, 157,
    160, 161
Streep, Meryl, 186, 191
Suburbia, 36–37, 43, 44, 58, 96, 127, 188
Subversion: artistic, 42; conflation of
    political and sexual subversion, 142,
    143, 154; political, 34, 64, 65, 97,
    131, 141, 142, 154; sexual, xiii, 19,
    131, 133, 138–39, 141, 142, 154
Suddenly, xii, 53, 67–71; and The
    Manchurian Candidate, 69, 70–71
Sung, Kim Il, 32
Supreme Court, the, 96
Surveillance, xv, 34, 41, 96–97, 99, 187;
    and sexuality, 138–39
Sylbert, Richard, 2

Taiwan, 123
Tall T, The, 128
Taoism, 127, 128
Taylor, Elizabeth, 21
Tchen, John Kuo Wei, 105
Technicolor, 21
Technology, 36, 37, 38, 43, 44; and
    information technology, 43
Television, xv, 15, 16, 17, 22, 24, 26, 27,
    37, 38, 41, 70, 96, 116; and *The
    Manchurian Candidate*, 86–88, 186;
    and McCarthyism, 84, 85, 86, 87–
    88; and violence, 173
Telotte, J. P., 72–73, 74
Temporary Commission on Employee
    Loyalty, 34
Terror, 33, 38, 132, 190. *See also* "War
    on terror"
Texas, 190
Them!, 41–42, 46, 96
Theocracy, 50
Third World, 123
Thirteen Frightened Girls, 125
Thomas, J. Parnell, 33, 84, 98
Thoroughly Modern Millie, 124, 125
Thurber, James, 47
Time, 32, 170
"Times They are A-Changing, The," 44
Totalitarianism, xv, 15, 34, 39, 43, 47,
    48, 55, 96–97, 176
Train scene(s), 160; of *The Manchurian
    Candidate*, xiii–xiv, 151, 157–64,
    165; of *North by Northwest*, 151,
    154–56, 161, 163, 164; of *Strangers
    on a Train*, 151–53
Traitor motif, 64, 88
Truman, Harry, ix, 32, 33, 34, 82, 94, 98,
    101, 116
Truman Doctrine, 33, 39
Trumbo, Dalton, 4
Turkey, 33
Tyranny, 43, 132

Uncommon Valor, 178
Underclass, the, 54
Unguarded Moment, The, 67
United Artists (UA), 19, 20
United Nations, 55

United States, 15; cultural violence
    of, 173; domestic policies of, 40;
    economy of, 33, 36, 39, 43–44, 47;
    foreign policy of, x, xiii, 31–32, 34,
    51, 55, 101, 129, 192; and the Soviet
    Union, 31, 33, 39, 40, 50
U.S. Army, 3, 13, 24, 190; integration
    of, 122; and McCarthy hearings, 87,
    91, 92, 96; and military intelligence,
    23, 77, 186; and the "military-sexual
    complex," 114; psychiatrists of, 75,
    76, 81, 170
U.S. Information Agency, 42
U.S.–Islamic conflict, 50
U.S. Navy, 55
U.S. Public Health Service, 53, 54
Urban life, 107, 129
USA Confidential, 133

Variety, 18, 21, 191
V-E Day, 3
Vietnam War, xiii, 39, 101, 175, 178–
    9, 193, and the Cold War, 31, 32;
    era of, xiv, 34, 112, 123, 124, 127;
    racist portrayals of, 111–12, 129;
    and U.S. interests in Asia, 56, 83,
    109, 110
View from the Bridge, A, 85
Vital Center, The, 43, 45
Viva Zapata!, 128
Voight, Jon, 192
Voyeurism, 65

Walker, Robert, 53, 60, 61, 151, 152
Wallach, Eli, 16
Wal-Mart, 193
Wanniski, Jude, 148–49
War Advertising Council, 136
"War against racism," 111
Warfare, 70, 129; gendering of, 133–34;
    as private duty, 136–37. *See also*
    Atomic bomb(s): and nuclear
    warfare
"War on terror," xiv, 49, 192–93
Warren, Earl, 102
Warren Commission, 173
Washington, D.C., 23, 61, 65, 85, 98,
    143, 153, 160

Washington, Denzel, 185
Washington, George, 101, 105, 165
Washington Post, 33
Wayne, John, 11, 17, 21
Weapons: industry of, 39; of "mass
    destruction," 190
Welch, Joseph, 87, 92, 95
Welles, Orson, 52, 161
West, the, 15, 102, 103, 104–5, 114–15;
    compared to the East, 102–3, 120;
    consciousness of, 120; sexual politics
    of, 114–15
Westbrook, Robert, 135, 137
Western films, 21, 116, 118
Westin, Allen, 97
Wheeling speech, 84, 87, 92, 94, 96
Wherry, Kenneth, 6
"White collar" man, 35. *See also*
    Organization man
White ethnics, 3, 5, 183
White House, 6, 15, 27, 83, 172,
    183, 185
White slavery, 107, 117, 124
Whyte, William H., Jr., 35, 39, 43, 44,
    45, 48, 69, 79
"Why we fight," 136, 137
Widmark, Richard, 53
Wiener, Jon, 7
Wilder, Billy, 17, 76
Williams, Esther, 67
Will Success Spoil Rock Hunter?, 17
Wilson, Sloan, 34, 45, 48
Wing and a Prayer, A, 175
Wisconsin, 33, 84
Witch hunts. *See* Communism
Wo Fat, 125, 126, 127

Women: as characters in *The Man-
    churian Candidate*, 48; as overly
    masculine, 133; postwar demobiliza-
    tion of, 140–41; and submissiveness,
    xiv, 49; as sexually aggressive, 157,
    162–64; and undue influence on
    men, xii, xiii, 14, 21, 53, 64, 93, 121,
    130, 131–33, 144, 147. *See also*
    Femininity; Gender; Sexuality
World War I, 134
World War II, 2, 33, 34, 43; era of, 102,
    121, 160; gendering of, 135–36; and
    the U.S.–Soviet alliance, 31
World Youth Rally, 6
Wyler, William, 66
Wylie, Philip, 37, 132–33, 137, 140,
    143, 147, 154
Wynter, Dana, 78

Yale, 18
Yalta, 31
Yellow face, 107–8, 124
Yellow Peril, 46, 101, 105, 108
Yen Lo, Dr., xii, 23, 47, 48, 127, 130;
    and brainwashing, 24, 25, 26, 112,
    170; casting of, 125; as Fu Manchu,
    100, 108, 119, 170; laughter of, 120–
    21; as stereotypical Asian villain,
    108–9, 120, 123, 124, 128; treachery
    of, 101, 112
Young Americans for Roosevelt, 6
Young, Nedrick, 4
Young Savages, The, 16
Young Stranger, The, 16
You are There, 85

Zilkov, 120

Matthew Frye Jacobson is professor of American studies and history at Yale University. His books include *Roots Too: White Ethnic Revival in Post–Civil Rights America*.

Gaspar González is an independent scholar and journalist in Miami. He has taught American studies at Yale University and film studies at the University of Miami.